# VANISHING BORDERS: THE NEW INTERNATIONAL ORDER OF THE 21ST CENTURY

# Vanishing Borders: The New International Order of the 21st Century

*Edited by*
LEE BOON-THONG AND TENGKU SHAMSUL BAHRIN
*Department of Geography*
*University of Malaya*
*Kuala Lumpur*

# Ashgate

Aldershot • Brookfield USA • Singapore • Sydney

Published by
Ashgate Publishing Limited
Gower House
Croft Road
Aldershot
Hants GU11 3HR
England

Ashgate Publishing Company
Old Post Road
Brookfield
Vermont 05036
USA


**British Library Cataloguing in Publication Data**
Vanishing borders : the new international order of the 21st
    century
    1.Boundaries 2.Boundaries - Economic aspects 3.Territory,
    National 4. Geopolitics 5. World politics -1989-
    I.Boon-Thong, Lee II.Bahrin, Tengku Shamsul
    320.1'2


**Library of Congress Catalog Card Number:** 98-071963

ISBN 1 84014 363 0


Printed in Great Britain by
Antony Rowe Ltd, Chippenham, Wiltshire

# Contents

## PART V: CONCLUSION

# List of Figures

# List of Tables

# List of Contributors

Abdul Rahim MOHD NOR, Department of Geography, National University of Malaysia, 43600 Bangi, Selangor, Malaysia.

AGOT Kawango, Department of Geography, Moi University, P.O. Box 3900, Eldoret, Kenya.

Andrew CHURCH, Department of Geography, Birkbeck College, University of London, 7-15 Gresse Street, London WIP 2LL, United Kingdom.

Chandra Pal SINGH, Professor, Department of Geography, Delhi School of Economics, University of Delhi, Delhi 110007, India.

Christian M. ROGERSON, Professor and Head, Department of Geography and Environment Studies, University of Witwatersrand, Private Bag 3, P.O. Wits, 2050 Johanesburg, South Africa.

Daniel BUOR, Senior Lecturer, Department of General and African Studies, Faculty of Social Sciences, University of Science and Technology, Kumasi, Ghana.

George CHO, Associate Professor, Faculty of Applied Science, University of Canberra, P.O. Box 1, Belconnen ACT 2616, Australia.

Gerald H. BLAKE, Professor and Director, International Boundaries Research Unit, University of Durham, Durham DH1 3VR, United Kingdom.

Gerard CHEONG, Department of Geography, University of Sydney, Sydney, New South Wales 2006, Australia.

Jacqueline LIDGARD, Research Fellow, Department of Geography, University of Waikato, Private Bag 3105, Hamilton, New Zealand.

John OVERTON, Professor and Director, Institute of Development Studies, Massey University, Private Bag 11222, Palmerston North, New Zealand.

LEE Boon-Thong, Professor and Head, Department of Geography, University of Malaya, 50603 Kuala Lumpur, Malaysia.

Michael ROCHE, Associate Professor, Department of Geography, Massey University, Private Bag 11222, Palmerston North, New Zealand.

NOMURA Shigeharu, Associate Professor, Division of International Relations, Osaka University of Foreign Studies, Aomadanihigashi 8-1-1, Minoo-shi, Osaka 562, Japan.

Peter John REID, Department of Geography, Birkbeck College, University of London, 7-15, Gresse Street, London WIP 2LL, United Kingdom

Richard BEDFORD, Professor, Department of Geography, University of Waikato, Private Bag 3105, Hamilton, New Zealand.

TAKAYAMA Masaki, Associate Professor, Division of Development and Environment, Osaka University of Foreign Studies, Anomadanihigashi 8-1-1, Minoo-shi, Osaka 562, Japan.

Tengku Shamsul BAHRIN, Professor, Department of Geography, University of Malaya, 50603 Kuala Lumpur, Malaysia.

Ziaush Shams HAQ, Professor and Chairman, Department of Geography, Science Amex Building, University of Dhaka, Dhaka 1000, Bangladesh.

# Foreword

In August of 1996, the Department of Geography, University of Malaya, Kuala Lumpur, organised an International Conference on "The Vanishing Borders: The New International Order of the 21st Century" on behalf of the Commonwealth Geographical Bureau. It attracted more than 35 participants from around the world including participants from non-Commonwealth countries like Japan, Finland and Germany. This volume except for Chapter 1 is a selection of papers that were presented at that highly successful Conference.

# Acknowledgement

One of the rewards associated with the publication of this volume is the steady stream of correspondence with the contributors from different parts of the world. We would like to express our thanks to all of them for responding speedily to our requests and queries. Our appreciation goes also to the Organising Committee of the Commonwealth Geographical Bureau Conference on 'Vanishing Borders: the New International Order of the 21st Century' especially to Tan Wan Hin, Richard Dorall, Abdullah Naib and other members of the Department of Geography, University of Malaya. We would like to mention the financial support to the Conference from the Commonwealth Foundation. In addition, we would also like to express our appreciation to Professor Yue-man Yeung (Chinese University of Hong Kong), Professor Denis Dwyer (Keele University) and Professor John Overton (Massey University) for their encouragement and support. We also like to mention Hasimah Hamidun for the careful and meticulous word processing; Lim Teik Leong for the time spent on vetting every page of this book; and V. Palani for the cartographic presentations. We are responsible for any shortcomings and errors.

The Editors

# PART I

# INTRODUCTION

# 1 Wither the Borders? Towards a New Dimension of Geographical Differentiation

*LEE Boon-Thong and Tengku Shamsul BAHRIN*

## Introduction

The world is moving towards greater interdependence and globalisation - two terms which are often vague and could mean different things to different people. Despite the vagueness of these terms, they, nevertheless, reflect on how the world is moving along or ought to move along in the present century. The most evident form of interdependence and globalisation is the greater interconnectedness among nations in cross-border movements of commodities, assets, goods, people, labour, financial flows, services and communications. Even a simple atomistic discussion of the contemporary flows of economic and non-economic indicators is sufficient to indicate that national political borders are no longer sufficient to describe such activities. A vivid illustration of this new dimension is the institutional primacy of the transnational corporations (TNCs) in many countries of the world. Clearly, greater interdependence and globalisation imply that borders are increasingly 'vanishing' or that the economic landscape is becoming 'borderless' (Ohmae 1990) although this may not literally mean the absence of such boundary impediments. Whether this is judged to be desirable or undesirable can be polemically argued. It is, nonetheless, pertinent and important to address the issue through a practical diagnosis of the global situation in the light of empirical realities. In this context, the basic formative processes and conditions, impacts and implications of the 'vanishing borders' from the late 1980s through the mid-1990s deserve greater attention.

## The Basis for Global Interconnectedness

In the 1970s, it was easier to talk about the economic dependence of the North upon the South where the major resources needed by the industrialised world lay within the less developed world of the South. Even in this respect, some would argue that it is necessary to diagnose specific import dependence. For instance, in the case of minerals, the European Union was 100 per cent dependent on imports for cobalt in 1986 but mercury imports amounted to only 15 per cent (Jones 1995). A reverse dependence of the South upon the North also existed. While the Less Developed Countries (LDCs) produced and exported agricultural commodities, they were dependent upon the Newly Industrialised Countries (NICs) for a range of basic foodstuffs to a variety of high value-added goods. The interdependence between the North and South was a mutual need that led to growth and development.

The global economic history of the late 20th Century is certainly about greater and more complex economic integration and globalisation - a trend that is benefitting both developing and industrial countries. The strong growth of international trade can be seen in Figure 1.1 where, except for Latin America and the Caribbean, all the regions of the world had registered at least a 12 percentile

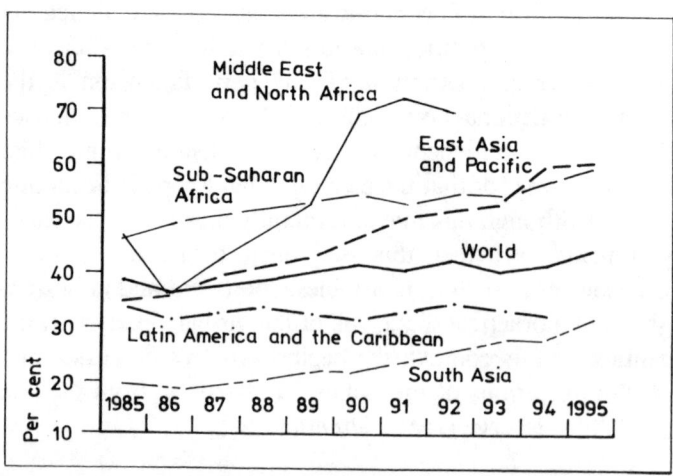

**Figure 1.1    Ratio of trade to GDP, 1985-1995**
*Source:*        *Finance and Development* (1997:46)

increase in the last decade. In terms of FDI into developing countries, the 1995 figure of US$91.8 billion is almost four times that of 1990. A notable development that has taken place is generally referred to as the 'Pacific Century'[1] - a somewhat loosely formulated concept to refer to the rise of Asia as an economic powerhouse that will result in a greater cross-Pacific trade volume than the cross-Atlantic trade volume. Between 1990 and 1995, the average annual growth rate was 10.3 per cent in East Asia and only 2.3 per cent in the high-income countries (*Finance and Development 1997*). Indeed, the International Monetary Fund predicts that half of the world's gross products will come from East Asia alone. The world is, indeed, seeing a higher level of globalisation and interdependence which is the result of several factors, chief among which are the increasing liberalisation of markets worldwide, the achievement of the Uruguay Round and other multilateral agreements throughout the world, falling tariffs, the dismantling of nontariff barriers, greater financial integration, and technological change that has facilitated information transmission. This growing order of global interdependence which is marked largely by the dynamics of industrial capitalism is very often more complex and profound than expected (McGrew and Lewis 1992). Consequently, the practices and principles of embedded statism are stretched and challenged by the growing global interdependence.

Much of the substance and distinctiveness of interdependence arise from a politically fragmented world that jealously guards its sovereignty, competence and independence (Jones 1995). Nation states may be defined as sets of spatial units that have the power and legitimacy to organise people and institutions within a specific boundary within which all subsets of population enjoy similar propensities or constraints for action and interactions. Consequently, globalisation and interdependence arise partly from the spatial strategies of TNCs to exploit the national differences in labour force, market conditions, and regulatory environments, etc. (Knox and Agnew 1994:125). It is obvious that nation states, just like individuals, cannot live in isolation from other nations; and other nations, in turn, are affected by the actions of some nations. Thus, there is a need for regional and global integration and cooperation. An essential question that needs to be answered is how a group of countries, each with its own agenda, manages to get along in such a manner that each is willing (or reluctantly agree) to 'dismantle' some aspects of border impediments? In some instances, the furtherance of common welfare far outweighs the myopic considerations of state independence. For example, where rampant transborder smuggling leads to loss of state revenues, the need for countries with such common borders to cooperate is clear. Leaking borders necessitate leaping borders. Patchell (1996) suggests five reasons for the need for regional cooperation:

- The need to cooperate in order to realise their own potential and economic vitality in the region locked in a state of interdependence
- The need to cooperate in order to achieve the effective functioning of the unique regional organisational structure
- The need to cooperate to achieve intra-regional competition that generates technological change and maintains economic vitality
- The need to cooperate in order to create an external governance system (largely through firms) to achieve a synergistic economic force
- The need to cooperate in order to mediate control and competition to the mutual satisfaction of all parties which will, then, determine the nature of their relationship and interdependence.

Working on the basis of international interactions and interdependencies that are immediately observable, spatial scientists, international economists, and geographers have been fascinated by the fact that borders that traditionally describe the geography of countries may be no longer relevant to explain geographical phenomena. That borders can be excised from spatial analysis, usher in a new dimension of geographical perspective that is both challenging and new. Certainly, this is a major paradigm shift in the *modus operandi* in the geographers' analytical horizon. It is obvious that globalisation and inter-connectedness are more than fashionable semantics, for they hint at the increasing significance of the external context for many issues that were formerly deemed to be national issues or deemed to be amenable to local or national resolution. Now, it appears that a single nation state no longer exerts an influence on the many activities that are external or international in origin. The presence of transnational corporations is one good example.

### The World Sans Nation States?

Ohmae's (1990) seminal work on the borderless world highlights the market mechanism that propels TNCs across nation states. Four global trends facilitated the borderless world:

- the spatial fluidity of investment patterns of private individuals or firms
- the globalised nature of industries and the increasing placelessness of TNCs who do not necessary owe allegiance to their country of origin
- the information technology revolution which enables corporations to operate anywhere in the world
- a globalised consumer behaviour that cuts across nation states.

What takes the place of nation states are 'region states', which are geographical units playing their role as natural growth units because of their interconnectedness with the global economy. It is possible to imagine these region states as 'globs' of territoriality within a country or straddling several adjoining countries that reduce the nation states to a condition of powerlessness in controlling these globalised activities, so to speak. 'Power over economic activities will inevitably migrate from the central governments of nation states to the borderless network of countless individual, market-based decisions' (Ohmae 1995:39). That the institutional primacy of the TNCs implies the notion of the powerlessness of nation states in the borderless world has been argued (Yeung 1996; Dicken 1995; Dunning 1995). It is not the intention of this introductory chapter to argue for or against the world sans nation states. While the world is not exactly borderless, in that central governments still have a prevailing influence, its role seems to be diminished in some instances. It does not necessarily imply the loss of power to control. States will have to restrain the use of overt power because of the unpredictable social, economic and political consequences of the synergised global activities to such globs themselves or onto the globs' peripheries which have hinged their existence upon these globs. Sometimes, these consequences may be just perceived apprehensions but they, nonetheless, are pervasive enough to immobilise actions and reactions. Less endowed countries are also unable to deal with the whole web of complex interdependencies because of their limited resources and constrained opportunities to redress any negative externalities that may result.

While the loss of power of nation states may be true in the arena of economic globalisation, the increasing global interdependence and integration addressed to in this volume is extrapolated beyond the economic realm to include integrated regions or blocs of nations that have voluntarily come together for various reasons or other: countries that share common borders, history, geography, politics and ideology, religion, forms of economic development, and other forms of common identity. These regional integrations may range from formal associations between states to establish new economic and/or political entities (APEC, ASEAN, EU, Growth Triangles anf Growth Polygons, etc. ) to informal arrangements (like the Trans-Asia Railway Project, the Indo-Bangladesh power deal, etc.). When the Asia-Pacific Economic Cooperation (APEC) forum was started in 1989, it simply began as an informal grouping for the trading partners in the world's fastest growing trade region of the Pacific Rim. Its aims, then, were to encourage economic cooperation throughout the region and to counter potentially protectionist trade blocs that were developing in Europe and North America. However, by 1994, APEC leaders have formally made a commitment to achieve 'free and open trade' by the year 2010 for the industrialised nations and 2020 for the less-developed countries. Thus, this objective has become the consolidating factor behind APEC. It is obvious that within the more formal regional organisations, regulated constraints weaken. Although borders appear not to be the restraining barriers in working together to bring about a greater convergence of economic, political or environmental conditions, nation states can still effectively utilise them to bargain and to achieve their national and economic objectives. In fact, Jones (1995:15) has argued for such a central role of political purposes and processes in the generation of contemporary international interdependence and globalisation:

> 'Far from being automatic and self-generating conditions, most instances of interdependence and globalisation have arisen as a result of the patterning of the modern world into sovereign states and the uneven manner in which these states have then acted and interacted. Interdependence and globalisation are, it will be argued, always changeable, as well as manipulable, conditions; and it is in the realms of the 'politic' that the immediate sources of such change or manipulation are to be found' (Jones 1990:15).

## Case Studies from Around the World

This chapter is not meant to be an exposition of global interdependency and globalisation but serves as an introduction to the rest of the chapters that follow. The contributors to this book deal with the issue of vanishing borders from various perspectives, some emphasising the economic, others the political or social impacts of global interdependence and integration. Considering the enormous changes that have taken place in the last decade with the end of the Cold War, the collapse of the Soviet Union, and increasing globalisation, the chapters that follow present a fairly holistic and exciting discussion of the new world order of the 21st Century.

Chapter 2 suggests that the geographical manifestation of the borderless world is actually complex as seen through an analysis of international trade and its recent reforms. Focussing on the spatial implications arising from GATT and GATS, George Cho concludes that the resulting global imbalance where one-fifth of the world's population in the developed countries produce four-fifths of the world's output and accounts for four-fifths of the world trade, may prove to be intractable to any solution. In spite of this, George predicts the pattern for the future, that is, countries are leaning towards greater international cooperation in order to enhance their own opportunities for development. The trend is that globalisation have induced the growth of regional trading blocs which may prove to be a turbulent future especially for the developing economies.

Part 2 comprises 5 case studies on the impact of this 21st Century vanishing border phenomenon. Takayama Masaki and Nomura Shigeharu look at the impact of globalisation on the economic and demographic structure in Japan and how Japan is adapting herself to the changing global conditions. An aging population is characterised by a greater concentration in the major metropolises and a more mobile transborder movement of both Japanese and foreigners. A structural change of the economy in favour of the tertiary sector is accompanied by a hollowing out of industries, as the Japanese economy becomes more internationalised. This chapter clearly reveals that increasing economic globalisation has pertinent social/demographic consequences - a theme argued also by other contributors to this volume.

While globalisation may bring about benefits accruing to the dismantling of trade barriers and the world-wide integration of production and distribution systems, John Overton, in Chapter 4, argues otherwise for the case of the small islands in the South Pacific. The economies of the Pacific Islands have well adjusted to the Old World Order characterised by the Cold War, superpower rivalry, economic nationalism and protectionism, and neo-colonial relationships. The New International Order may seriously undermine these relationships especially for existing trade and aid arrangements. On the other hand, Overton balances this viewpoint with the social and cultural contention that the Pacific Islanders are 'proto-global citizens' with their history of 'trans-national corporations of kin' and the impact of globalisatiom may need to incorporate the social and cultural dimension as well.

As New Zealand becomes more integrated into the world economy, Michael Roche looks at how this Pacific Century is affecting the prevailing notions of national identity among the New Zealanders especially those of a European-settler descent. In this respect, Roche shows how globalisation can also heighten the indigenous people's awareness to reassert their identities and rights over natural resources which would destabilise prevailing notions of identities. Thus, he lends further support to Overton's thesis that economic globalisation cannot be separated from its socio-cultural dimensions.

In Chapter 6, Richard Bedford and Jacqueline Lidgard examine how New Zealand attempts to posit herself in the Asia-Pacific region through the visa-waiver mechanism. Bilateral visa-waiver agreements between New Zealand and other countries serve not only to facilitate access by New Zealanders to other countries but also to achieve specific foreign policy objectives such as the encouragement of tourism, investment and trade. In particular, they investigated the role of visa-waiver in the explosion of Asian arrivals (both visitors and migrants) in the last one-and-half decades that generated heated debates and eventual policy change. In essence, they argue that while borders can be made more porous to accommodate the trend of world-wide globalisation, the role of the state remains sovereign where necessary.

Christian Rogerson examines how the dramatic transformations within South Africa are reshaping the geo-political and economic landscape of South Africa and a wider Southern Africa. In the first instance, he analyses the spatial developmental changes occurring within post-apartheid South Africa as a consequence of the dismantling of the Homelands and their reintegration into a non-racial democracy. The death of apartheid within South Africa has reper-cussions beyond her borders as she competes for international investment opportunities. It also permits renewed prospects for cross-border international development projects and opens doors for more active South African parti-cipation in regional economic integration and associations. Clearly, Rogerson shows that intra-national changes have extra-national repercussions.

Part 3 surveys some aspects of the political dimension involved in regional economic groupings. Chandra Pal Singh in Chapter 8 looks at the role of India and ASEAN within the context of the new geopolitical order. Although Singh agrees that economic considerations were given primacy over security considera-tions in the conduct of international relations since the end of the Cold War, he contends that maintaining sovereign control has not diminished in an era of multipolarity. Tracing the historical linkages with Southeast Asian countries and the common colonial heritage, Singh analyses the interconnectedness between India and ASEAN and the possible role India can play to ensure the stability and security of the Indian Ocean region upon which much of the world's trade and fuel movements will occur.

Ziaush Shams Haq, in Chapter 9, takes a broader view of regional inter-dependency between two contiguous regions, ASEAN and SAARC. As these individual groupings strive for intra-regional benefits, he appraises the possibility of promoting inter-regional cooperation between the two groupings. Arguing that although typologies for both regions may differ, the lessons in the process of development in the realtively more advanced ASEAN states may be valuable to SAARC itself. Understanding the possibility of promoting a dynamic interdependence between ASEAN and SAARC, is certainly an exciting preview towards achieving the dream of a world millennium.

Agot Kawango takes the reader to the Sub-Saharan African states in Chapter 10 where she contends that the strong individuality of countries, traced to the colonial legacy of economic exploitation, has become a stumbling block towards achieving integration in this continent. Despite this setback, the author traces the efforts of the Sub-Saharan states to achieve African unity, be it in the areas of politics, economic, environment, transport and communications, religion and language, academic and professional or socio-cultural. The plethora of organisations that exist in this continent, however, are not indicative of African unity as Agot points out the intractable political and economic counterforces at work to achieve that dream.

In Chapter 11, Peter Reid and Andrew Church examine a case of transfrontier cooperation in the European Union between local authorities of the United Kingdom and France. Highlighting the problems and advantages of such a horizontal relationship to complement the vertical relationship between national member states, they analysed the implications of increasing transfrontier cooperation on the national borders of the European Union. It is a possible likelihood that borders would be viewed as less important and, over time, be eroded with a consequent new power rearrangement.

Part 4 addresses some economic and environment issues of cross-border cooperation. It is obvious that many projects, environmental problems, and resource management cut across nation states and cannot be undertaken or resolved by any single nation alone. As these problems transcend political boundaries, they represent unique challenges of collaboration and cooperation for the plurality of states that share the common issue, fate or exposure. Abdul Rahim Mohd Nor begins by looking at the much-discussed Trans-Asia Railway that will snake its way from Singapore to China. Abdul Rahim contends that if the geopolitical hindrances are satisfactorily put aside by the participating countries, there is much to be gained economically by all countries, in particular, the development of the Mekong Basin region, the tourism potential, and the track-based freight transportation of off-shore oil and gas. However, it is apparent that before such a mega-project can be realised, regional cooperation among the countries has to be reached to deal with the myriad of obstacles such as conflicting country interests, border disputes, right of way, and the funding mechanism.

Gerard Cheong zooms in on the Mekong Basin, which is a good example of shared consequences and interrelated ecological implications that can result from the unilateral action of a neighbouring country (Jones 1995:76). Such instances, where the actions of those further upstream directly affect those downstream, warrant the joint cooperation of the plural states surrounding the Mekong in the management of a common resource. It is, however, easier said than done. National sovereignty is still a powerful and assertive force in the Basin. Nonetheless, Cheong is able to show that economic and environmental issues are no respecter of political boundaries. To circumvent such boundary impediments, regional and local actors rather than the nation states become more relevant in tackling problems of resource management. He argues that, a multi-perspective approach involving country perspectives, sectoral perspectives as well as the perspectives of key players such as the government, business, local and international community, is the key to unlocking the natural wealth of the Basin.

In Chapter 14, Daniel Buor focusses on the need for a regional economic integration to urgently overcome underdevelopment in West African countries which are still at an early stage of restructuring their economy. Diagnosing the pre-ECOWAS and post-ECOWAS trade patterns in West Afrca, Buor highlights the massive problems in attempts to 'make borders vanish', to create an interdependency within the sub-region, and a holistic economic union to achieve a more competitive position in the global scene.

Lest the increasing global interconnectedness and interdependence convey the notion that boundaries do not matter anymore or that there is now a unified system or a concretised new order of world cosmopolitanism, Gerald Blake reminds the reader that the separate existence of the political entities that are the basis for interdependence are still very evident and important. While acknowledging that globalisation will lead to changes in the form and function in the present system of nation states, Blake argues for the resilience of nation states as exemplified by the emergence of new states and the behaviour of existing states. There could be as many as 25 to 100 new states by the middle of the 21st Century. He argues that, in certain respects, nation states have become more entrenched for reasons of security, protection, nationalism and territoriality. He concludes that the world political map in the 21st Century will superficially appear much as it is today, with boundaries and state territories the dominant features although regional groupings will be extremely important.

## Conclusion

The new challenges along the path of globalisation in the 21st Century will have significant implications for the world citizen. Contemporary international interdependence and globalisation are indeed varied and complex and the future, perhaps, unpredictable. It appears, nonetheless, that the world would be getting more integrated and complex. The contributors to this volume have, in their own ways, thrown light on the various perspectives of the 21st Century phenomenon of the vanishing borders.

## Note

1  The term 'Pacific Century' is a generally more recognised term than 'Asian Century' as the former would include the United States as an inseparable part. For the 21st Century, some have argued for a 'world' or 'global' millennium - 'a single commonwealth of common wealth and co-prosperity' (Mahathir 1997; Lingle 1997).

# References

Dicken, P. (1995), 'How the World Works?', *Review of International Political Economy*, Vol. 2, pp. 197-204.

Dunning, J.H. (1995), 'The Global Economy and Regimes of National and Supranational Governance', *Business and the Contemporary World*, Vol. 7, No. 1, pp. 126-136.

*Finance and Development* (1997), 'Economic Trends in the Developing World', March, pp. 46-48.

Jones, R.J.B. (1995), *Globalisation and Interdependence in the International Political Economy*, Pinter Publishers: London and New York.

Knox, P. And Agnew, J. (1994), *The Geography of the World Economy: An Introduction to Economic Geography*, Edward Arnold: London.

Lingle, C. (1997), 'Asian Century about to Lose out to the Global Millennium', *Asia Times*, 22nd April 1997.

Mahathir Mohamad (1997), 'Working Towards a World Century in the New Millennium', *Asia Times*, 10th January 1997.

McGrew, A.G. and Lewis, P.G. (eds.) (1992), *Global Politics: Globalization and the nation-state*, Polity Press: Cambridge.

Ohmae, K. (1990), *The Borderless World: Power and Strategy in the Interlinked Economy*, Collins: London.

_____ (1995), *The End of the Nation State: The Rise of Regional Economics*, Collins: London.

Patchell, J. (1996), 'Kaleidoscope Economies: The Processes of Cooperation, Competition, and Control in Regional Economic Development', *Annals of the Association of Geographers*, Vol. 86, No.3, pp.481-506.

Yeung Wai-Chung, Henry (1996), 'Is the World Really Borderless? A Geographical Perspective on Nation States and Transnational Corporations', Paper presented at the CGB International Conference on Vanishing Borders: The New International Order of the 21st Century (August).

World Bank (1997), *World Development Indicators 1997*, World Bank: Washington, D.C.

# 2 Global Interdependence and the Developing Economies

*George CHO*

## Introduction

In a 'borderless' world the old distinctions between 'North' and 'South' as well as between 'East' and 'West' are becoming blurred. On a global scale societal issues can no longer be divided into 'domestic' and 'international'. In such a society a country can neither afford to risk social disintegration nor choose social or economic isolation. Rather, all countries look towards benefiting from participation in a growing global and international economic system. Notions of security are being redefined while greater attention is being placed on the needs and concerns of human beings and the quality of their environments. However, even within such a borderless world the responses to and grasping of opportunities are geographically uneven, and these patterns are manifest on the human and economic landscape.

A borderless world is also one in which there is a 'convergence' of time and of space no less ushered in and led by the convergence of technology. The almost instantaneous transmission of messages means that neither space nor time are barriers. Such a usage presents one example of the 'time-space' convergence defined by Brunn and Williams (1983:468) as 'the rate at which places are moving closer together measured by travel time and communication time'. At a local level the convergence of technology (CCG 1994:3) now means that it does not matter that a rival bank's automatic teller machine (ATM) is used to draw money from one's bank account managed by a different bank; that the facsimile machine is linked directly to the personal computer and to the photocopier or

15

printer; or that the mobile phone with a 'roaming' facility may be used overseas and yet be billed in the home country.[1]

The borderless world is thought to be seamless; but it is not so simple. It is a central theme of this chapter that the geographical manifestation of this globalisation is very uneven. This unevenness may be demonstrated through a study of international trade and its recent reforms. Such reforms have spatial implications which produce unique patterns. This chapter begins with a discussion of the term 'globalisation' in the light of the 'internationalisation' of the world economy and the interest of the geographer. More specifically, these have implications with regards to trade in commodities and trade in services arising from the General Agreement on Tariffs and Trade (GATT) and General Agreement in Trade in Services (GATS). The spatial implications arising from both GATT and GATS are discussed prior to a consideration of the spatial patterns that international trade induces. Then general observations of spatial unevenness are made and how trans-border bases of the product cycle match with empirical observations with a suggestion that globalisation may have been responsible for inducing the growth rather than the decline of regional trading blocs. A conclusion to this chapter is that the emergent triad of trading blocs may suggest a turbulent future in world trade which, unfortunately, may impact heavily on all developing economies.

## Globalisation

Dicken (1993:27) observed that while one measure of the changing global map of production and trade is through the lens of national aggregate performance, much is left hidden. The aggregate figures hide the massive changes in the organisation of business enterprises especially their increasing internationalisation and in some cases globalisation. Some trends are clear-cut while others show substantial differences between sectors and geographical locations. This is where the geographers' interest is excited because the differences become manifest on the landscape. Also it may be noted that Dicken (1993) makes a subtle distinction between globalisation and internationalisation of production. The term globalisation describes the conduct of business across national boundaries and the taking of a world-wide perspective. The term is both a buzz word and a trend in international trade and production. The underlying motivation seems to be the need for continuing market access and the circumvention of all kinds of barriers - fiscal, physical and cultural.

The term transnational corporation (TNC) or multinational corporation (MNC) have been used to describe a particular mode of operation. According to Cowling and Sugden (1987:60) a TNC is 'the means of coordinating production from one centre of strategic decision-making when this coordination takes a firm across national boundaries'. A feature of such an operation is the coordination of activities irrespective of whether or not the ownership is across national boundaries. TNCs may have its head offices in one country but branch offices in developed and developing countries. Common examples include Amatil-Coca Cola, Mitsubishi Corporation, Philips, IBM, British Petroleum and Exxon Corporation.

TNCs are enormous in size and influence. Through various means of corporate mergers and company takeovers, TNCs have grown to a point where many now control large research and development (R&D) budgets and their boardrooms negotiate with as much power as some small developing country. In many cases, they control or influence whole industrial processes from extraction of raw materials to manufacturing, transport, finance and end use. According to a report by the UN Commission on Transnational Corporation (UNCTC) in 1991, the top 500 companies of the world controlled about 70 per cent of the world trade, 80 per cent of foreign investments and about 30 per cent of the world GDP. It is probable that these relative proportions will remain unchanged through till the end of the decade (UNCTC 1991).

TNCs are able to control the way the developing countries can and do develop while taking advantage of cheap labour. Together, TNCs control the economic and social performance of many countries and also determine consumer tastes and patterns of consumption. Thus, any discussion of TNCs must include its role in fostering interdependence. A fragmentation of production processes follows the establishment of TNC links so that there is now a global division of specialities, one country focussing on the extraction of raw materials, another on primary processing and fabrication, and a third on the assembly of components and final manufacture. Implicit in all these activities is the division of labour, the so-called new international division of labour (NIDL) (Frobel *et al.* 1980).

This international division of labour has been observed to have occurred in three recognised phases each following colonisation, then independence and through to developed status. The first NIDL occurred when colonies produced raw materials for export to metropolitan powers in exchange for manufactured and industrial goods. In the second NIDL, newly independent developing countries launched into import substitution industries (ISI). Such programmes were funded by both domestic and international capital. The third NIDL witnessed the true fragmentation of the production process and large capital flows from within the core (the developed country) and from the core to the periphery (the developing country).

The geographical impact of all three periods is quite evident. All three types of NIDL described above can be seen to operate in various forms throughout the world. The impact of the NIDL on each host nation varies according to circumstances. For example, huge capital investments are flowing into resource extraction projects such as Japanese investments in Indonesian timber resources. In contrast, in Latin America, ISI has spawned a local automotive industry which has gone beyond mere assembly to sole producers of vehicles that are no longer produced any where else in the world. The Brazilian and Mexican Volkswagen is produced solely for the South American market. A similar phenomenon is taking place in India in respect of motor vehicles and motor cycles.

The NIDL may be viewed as one of a progression of trade, growth and development for different countries. The changing metropolitan core-periphery relationship is hinged on wages, costs, occupational health and safety, and pollution concerns. The reduced capacity to generate profits within the metropolitan core as a result of a rising wage bill, rising fuel costs and attendant costs to ensure occupational health and safety issues together with pollution concerns has encouraged the quest for new markets. At the periphery, aided by an eager government bent on achieving development at any cost, cheap labour costs act as a strong magnet. As capital investments penetrate the countryside in the periphery, a large army of displaced labour has found its way into urban areas swelling the ranks of the available labour (including the unskilled and the unemployed) and sustaining an ever growing informal sector. In addition, in some countries TNCs are offered special incentives to take up segregated economic zones such as free trade zones (FTZs) and economic processing zones (EPZs) with added 'tax holidays' for a generous period of time. TNCs have been known to take advantage of such lucrative investment opportunities and often move on to other countries when the special incentives expire. Figure 2.1 shows how global interdependence links with the various ideas related to the global trading system.

The descriptions above demonstrate the impact on the geography of any developing country. Physical development of the country can be very uneven under such circumstances, often concentrating on the major urbanised areas with a large undeveloped hinterland. As investments move inland, there is a concomitant movement of displaced labour towards the urbanised areas, exacerbating even further the 'development disparity' in terms of physical infra-structure, population density, demographics, economic patterns of production and consumption and employment. The convergence of technology now means that financial services become internationalised because of ready access to funds through electronic transfers. Accumulations of capital are thus put to best use at all times with surpluses recycled many times over because the financial market is now a 'virtual' 24-hour operation world-wide.

A critique of the NIDL is that the world can be divided into two or three self-contained camps: core, semi-periphery, and periphery. This may be misleading given that it may be difficult to place any country in one or the other of the categories but also that within one country along the tripartite division may exist with a relatively rich city as against the 'impoverished' countryside and all other districts in between. The NIDL, moreover, is geographically selective with core capital being invested in a very narrow range of countries for various reasons. The availability of resources, labour skills, existing infrastructure and government in power may determine the uneven pattern of investments. As discussed previously whether through deliberate policy or strategy, the spatial impact of such investments may be confined to the urban centres of developing countries.

The link between NIDL and global recession and/or expansion cannot be established conclusively. Yet, it may be postulated that a causal relationship exists, for example, the recession in core areas being transmitted to the periphery

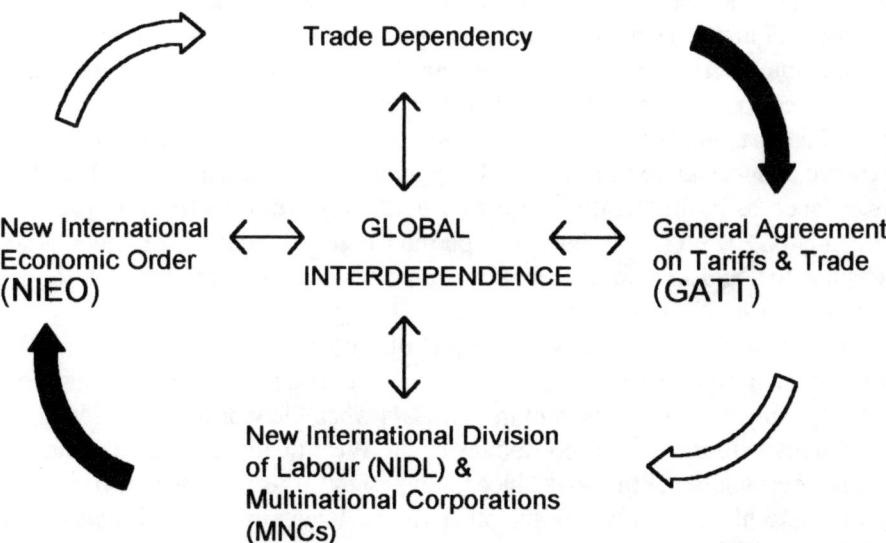

**Figure 2.1   Spatial perspectives of the international trading system and global interdependence**

with a built-in time-lag for the effects to be felt at the periphery. While the apparent causation may seem to be clear, it is arguable if these are unrelated processes. There are obviously complex processes taking place which may be more than simply the result of the NIDL phenomenon. Other more convincing arguments must be sought.

## Implications on Trade in Commodities and Trade in Services

The NIDL phenomenon underlies the importance of both economic and non-economic variables in this era of global interdependence. One nation's welfare is to some extent dependent on the decisions and policies made in another country. The reverse also occurs. Sometimes a supra-national body supplants these relationships and new rules are forged.

A dominant theme of the 1990s is the GATT. This international body was set up in 1947 to examine ways and means of reducing tariffs on internationally traded goods and services. To achieve these ends several conferences or 'rounds' of talks were held to decide on the level of tariffs for primary commodities around the world. The GATT multilateral trading system is founded on rules of equality of opportunity in terms of access to markets and equality of treatment inside national bodies. Membership of the GATT pledges a country to the general expansion of trade on a multilateral and non-discriminatory basis. The basic rules include non-discrimination among members (except by members of free trade areas and customs unions) and that protection should be by means of tariffs only, rather than quantitative restrictions and similar devices. Taxes and regulation of domestic and foreign producers should apply equally. These rules spell out key issues such as multilateralism and free trade and avoid confronting regional agreements. The GATT, however, permits regional trade agreements as an exception to non-discrimination. Figure 2.2 portrays a graphical depiction of the various models of economic integration.

The GATT may be seen as the engine of globalisation. It is based on the premise of a rigorous, profitable and peaceful commerce between nations. Paradoxically, the GATT was in its elements when the world was divided into two halves with the market economies of the West taking up one side and the command economies of the Soviet bloc taking up the other. Trade was promoted precisely to blunt the might of the other camp. However, in the climate of the 1990s, the distinctions have become blurred with the break-up of the Soviet Union, the economic and political integration of Europe through the European Union (EU) and the spawning of various regional trade blocs such as the North American Free Trade Agreement (NAFTA), Asian Pacific Economic Commission

(APEC) and ASEAN Free Trade Agreement (AFTA). The growth of these regional blocs could over time supplant and undermine global cohesion. Whether such developments are good or bad remains to be seen, but it is certain that failure of the GATT will push the world economy towards greater regionalism (GATT 1988).

## The GATT and GATS Spatial Implications

*The GATT*

The basic objective of the GATT is to liberalise world trade and to contribute to economic growth and development. The GATT is both a code of rules and a negotiating body. Such rules (principles) are set in place through a series of multilateral trade negotiations. Since 1947 there have been eight rounds of trade negotiations. Figure 2.3 shows the GATT and the various trade negotiation rounds.

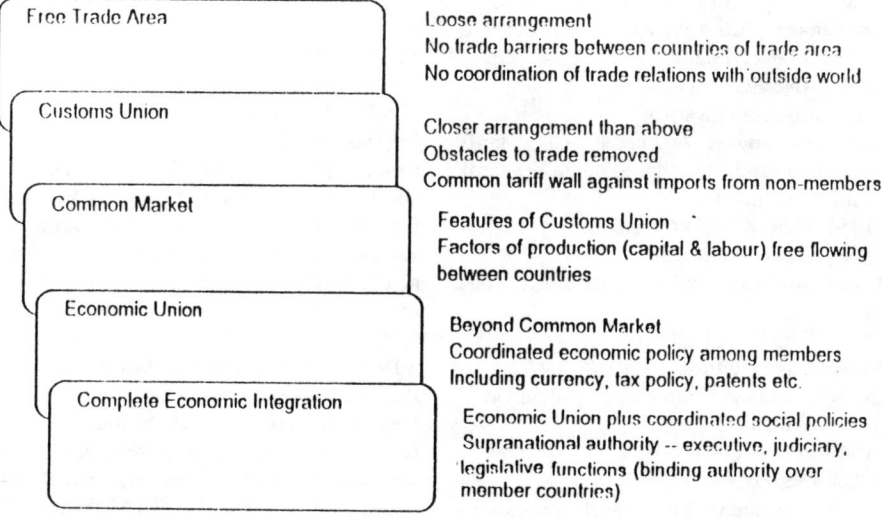

Figure 2.2   **Models of economic integration**

1947 GENEVA ROUND
Participating countries: 23
**Result Summary**: Agreement on 20 schedules covering 45,000 tariff concessions. Manufacturing tariff in industrialized countries started dropping from average of 40 per cent to 25 per cent over decade.

1948 ANNECY ROUND
Participating countries: 13
**Result Summary**: Additional 5,000 tariff concessions exchanged to continue the tariff cutting momentum.

1950 TORQUAY ROUND
Participating countries: 38
**Result Summary**: 8,700 tariff concessions exchanged.

1956 GENEVA ROUND
Participating countries: 26
**Result Summary**: About US$2.5 billion worth of tariff reductions.

1960-61 DILLON ROUND
Participating countries: 26
**Result Summary**: 4,400 tariff concessions covering US$4.9 billion worth of trade.

1964-67 KENNEDY ROUND
Participating countries: 62
**Result Summary**: Introduced across-the-board rather than product-by-product approach to cutting tariffs. Concessions covering US$40 billion worth of trade. Anti-dumping rules introduced. By end of decade, industrial tariffs averaging about 17 per cent.

1973-79 TOKYO ROUND
Participating countries: 99
**Result Summary**: Tariffs reductions covering US$300 billion of trade. Preferential treatment for developing countries. codes agreed on subsidies, countervailing measures and other non-tariff-barriers. Led to progressive lowering of industrial tariffs to current level of 4.7 per cent.

1986-93 URUGUAY ROUND
Participating countries: 116
**Result Summary**: If successful, will bring range of important trading areas: agriculture, services, intellectual property rights and investment — under the GATT, which will become the Multilateral Trade Organization with revamped rules and dispute-setting machinery.

**Figure 2.3   The GATT and trade negotiation rounds**

The most recent Uruguay Round is by far the most ambitious and comprehensive and has established a new order in world trade through the Multilateral Trade Organisation (MTO). During the negotiations, developing countries succeeded in gaining the inclusion of temperate and tropical agriculture, textiles and clothing in the GATT agenda and improved rules pertaining to safeguards such as anti-dumping and countervailing duties, dispute settlement and the functioning of the GATT rules. The developed industrial countries introduced trade in services, trade related investment measures and intellectual property rights and protection. In these negotiations the responses of developing countries have depended upon relative economic strength and relative development. The dynamic newly industrialising countries (NICs) were interested in market access for their exports, whereas the largest group of developing countries, represented by the small, vulnerable economies experiencing serious debt problems, and with fragile distorted economic structures, were simply eager to be included in international trade activities.

Trade related investment measures refer to government regulations and policies that has the potential to distort and restrict investment flows and patterns of trade. For example, the requirements of local employees and local content rules have been widely used in Southeast Asian, the Caribbean and South American countries. While agreement has been reached on tariff reductions and the strengthening of GATT rules, as well as for trade-related investment measures and market access in natural resource-based products, that of agricultural products has led to delays in agreement. Disagreements in substantive reforms to agricultural policies led also to the breakdown in negotiations in mid-December 1990 in Brussels. The US, EU, Japan and South Korea were unable to agree on agricultural policies such as the reform of world farm trade, liberalisation of services and market access. For example, reductions in export subsidies, internal price supports and market access in the EU were contentious issues that were resolved only after prolonged negotiations.

The threat of regional trade blocs has underlined the importance of a rules-based multilateral trading system. Whereas previously developing countries were satisfied with a 'separate and different' treatment, there are signs suggesting a jettisoning of such ideas. Some Latin American countries and India, which have in-built anti-trade biases in their development policies were keen to retain their separate but different status while others were negotiating new trade agreements. On the other hand, the poorest developing countries like those in Sahel Africa have no interest in the GATT negotiations and have tended to rely on aid and preferential access for exports. Not surprisingly, East Asian countries have the strongest interests in the trade system since they depend on export growth for their development. Hence, a liberal multilateral trade system suits their interests best.  The US seems keen on pursuing its free trade policies without imposing new barriers on its trade partners.  The EU in pursuit of its single market, has attempted to reduce its support for agriculture by re-examining its Common Agricultural Policy (CAP).  The above description alone suggests the unevenness in response and in impact of the newly negotiated WTO.  How and to what extent these measures will become evident may require empirical investigations of the patterns of trade in terms of the partners, commodities, volumes and direction.  A world trading system that leads to strong global economic growth may be one manifestation of the success of the WTO.

## GATS

The GATS, an offshoot from the Uruguay Round (1986-1993) of the GATT is given separate treatment because it has the potential to determine the outcomes of bilateral trade negotiations internationally and because it deals with an important emergent trade activity.  The intention under GATS is to create a GATT-style regime for services.  In 1993 the world services trade accounted for US$850 billion, which is about 20 per cent of the total world trade.  Services are a key value-adder in many economies and there is a trend towards the internationalisation of services.  The services sector are also the fastest growing single component of world trade, increasing by about 66 per cent in the period between 1985 and 1990 (World Bank 1992).  This sector generically includes financial services, telecommunications, aviation and consultancy services among others.

There are three components to the negotiation in services.  The first is the establishment of a GATS framework that lays down rules governing trade in services.  The second component comprises a package of agreements on market access in the services sector between all GATT signatories.  The final component is that the members make guarantees on market access and national treatment in specific sectors.  As a result GATS will encourage foreign access to particular services leading to an internationalisation of this sector.  Access to the services market will thus be open and non-discriminatory.

The geographical impact of GATS is again borderless.  There are vast opportunities for trade in services given the growth of the world economy and the relative affluence of industrial and NICs.  In the case of Japan, tourism is a strong performer given a relatively affluent ageing Japanese population combined with new attitudes to work and leisure.  The two-week overseas holiday for most *salarymen* is now *de rigueur* as is the packaged tour and whistle-stop photo shoot.  Other East Asian countries exhibit growing opportunities in different sectors. Hong Kong appears to be a lucrative market for high value-added services notably, engineering services, infrastructural development and building and construction. On the other hand, in Taiwan the growing service sectors are tourism and education services, whereas in southern China the growth service sectors are in telecommunications and education. For most of Southeast Asia generally the stronger service sectors appear to be in telecommunications, education and training, transport, building and construction and in health and medical services. Again the geographical impact arises from the observation that different countries will require different types of services. This may simply be a reflection of the variety and relativity of different stages of development, growth and relative needs.

**Spatial Patterns**

This section begins with the general observation that the actual geographical extent of the internationalisation of both production and trade during the last four decades of the century is highly uneven (Dicken 1993:24). In addition, although industrialisation has increased in the developing world, both its breadth and its depth are very limited. The Asian NICs are becoming significant exporters of manufactured goods and are exceptions rather than the rule. To further underline the disparity 'a mere twenty-five countries produced 93 per cent of the world output; as few as seven countries produced three-quarters of the world trade' (Dicken 1993:24). The geography of international trade is also extremely uneven at a global scale. While only 20 per cent of the world's population live in the developed world, their share of global output is more than 80 per cent and of world trade even more (83 per cent) (Cho 1995:151). Thus, as a group, developing economies are far from being fully integrated into the global economy despite the rhetoric to the contrary. A statistical summary of international trade is given in Tables 2.1 to 2.4.

*Transborder Strategies*

A closer examination of the performance of the more successful NICs especially those in Asia suggests that there is a certain 'method' to the scheme of things. Successful transborder production and trade strategies deserve closer study. This may be achieved firstly by describing the so-called 'relationship enterprises' so common in Asian countries. The discussion on the rise of such strategic collaborations is followed by an examination of the building of human bridges across continents.

*Relationship enterprises*. Relationship enterprises may be seen as an alternative model to the MNC but put within the context of trade and development (Cho 1995:115-116). One of the most visible forms of the relationship enterprise is that of the role of overseas Chinese business networks. In Asia, twenty to thirty very large business groups, mostly owned by ethnic Chinese dominate the commerce and industry of the region. For example, the Lippo Group in Indonesia and Hong Kong, the Salim Group in Indonesia, the Sophonpanich Group in

**Table 2.1    Growth of merchandise trade, 1980-1990**

|  | Exports 1990 US$ (mil.) | Imports 1990 US$ (mil.) | Average annual growth rate (%) Exports 1980-90 | Average annual growth rate (%) Imports 1980-90 | Terms of Trade (1987 = 100) 1990 |
|---|---|---|---|---|---|
| Low income economies | 141,176 | 144,431 | 5.1 | 2.8 | 100 |
| [China & India | 80,059 | 77,037 | 9.8 | 8.0 | 103] |
| Middle-income economies | 491,128 | 485,897 | 3.8 | 0.9 | 102 |
| Lower-middle income | 184,340 | 195,680 | 7.2 | 2.1 | 99 |
| Upper-middle-income | 306,789 | 290,217 | 1.9 | 0.1 | 105 |
| Sub-Saharan Africa | 34,056 | 32,377 | 0.2 | -4.3 | 100 |
| East Asia & Pacific | 217,030 | 224,021 | 9.8 | 8.0 | 103 |
| South Asia | 27,699 | 38,217 | 6.8 | 4.1 | 95 |
| Europe | 94,082 | 126,493 | .. | .. | 103 |
| Middle East & North Africa | 112,644 | 89,842 | -1.1 | -4.7 | 96 |
| Latin America & Caribbean | 123,181 | 101,119 | 3.0 | -2.1 | 110 |
| Severely indebted | 135,856 | 99,721 | 3.4 | -2.1 | 101 |
| High-income economies | 2,555,661 | 2,725,419 | 4.3 | 5.3 | 100 |
| [OECD members | 2,379,089 | 2,501,753 | 4.1 | 5.2 | 100] |
| **World** | **3,187,955** | **3,355,746** | **4.3** | **4.5** | **100** |

*Source*:    World Bank (1992), Table 14 pp. 244-245

Thailand and the Kuok Group in Malaysia are prominent players within their respective countries as well as in their offshore establishments.

Overseas Chinese networks are so named because they are dominated by expatriate native-born Chinese or their offsprings living outside China. The aggregate wealth of the 40 million or so overseas Chinese has been estimated conservatively to be about US$2,500 billion. The networks are held together by

**Table 2.2   Structure of merchandise imports, 1990 (percentage share of merchandise imports - weighted averages)**

|  | Food | Fuels | Other primary commodities | Machinery & transport equipment | Other manufactures |
|---|---|---|---|---|---|
| Low income economies | 12 | 9 | 8 | 33 | 38 |
| [China & India | 8 | 7 | 10 | 34 | 41] |
| Middle-income economies | 11 | 12 | 8 | 34 | 35 |
| Lower-middle-income | 11 | 10 | 8 | 34 | 37 |
| Upper-middle-income | 10 | 13 | 9 | 33 | 34 |
| Sub-Saharan Africa | 16 | 4 | 3 | 40 | 37 |
| East Asia & Pacific | 7 | 9 | 10 | 38 | 35 |
| South Asia | 13 | 16 | 10 | 20 | 41 |
| Europe | 11 | 17 | 9 | 34 | 34 |
| Middle East & North Africa | 17 | 6 | 6 | 33 | 37 |
| Latin America & Carribbean | 12 | 13 | 7 | 31 | 35 |
| Severely indebted | 15 | 11 | 9 | 31 | 35 |
| High-income economies | 9 | 9 | 7 | 34 | 39 |
| [OECD members | 9 | 11 | 8 | 34 | 39] |
| **World** | **9** | **11** | **8** | **34** | **39** |

*Source*:   World Bank (1992), Table 15 pp. 246-247

## Table 2.3  Structure of merchandise exports, 1990

*(Percentage share of merchandise exports - weighted averages)*

|  | Fuels, minerals & metals | Other primary commodities | Machinery & transport equipment | Other manufactures | Textiles & clothing |
|---|---|---|---|---|---|
| Low income economies | 27 | 20 | 9 | 45 | 21 |
| [China & India | 10 | 17 | 15 | 58 | 26] |
| Middle income economies | 32 | 20 | 17 | 33 | 9 |
| Lower-middle income | 32 | 30 | 11 | 27 | 9 |
| Upper middle-income | 32 | 13 | 20 | 37 | 9 |
| Sub-Saharan Africa | 63 | 29 | 1 | 7 | 1 |
| East Asia & Pacific | 13 | 18 | 22 | 47 | 19 |
| South Asia | 6 | 24 | 5 | 65 | 33 |
| Europe | 9 | 16 | 27 | 47 | 16 |
| Middle East & North Africa | 75 | 12 | 1 | 15 | 4 |
| Latin America & Caribbean | 38 | 29 | 11 | 21 | 3 |
| Severely indebted | 42 | 22 | 14 | 22 | 4 |
| High-income economies | 8 | 11 | 42 | 40 | 5 |
| [OECD members | 7 | 12 | 42 | 39 | 4] |
| **World** | **12** | **13** | **36** | **39** | **6** |

*Source*:    World Bank (1992), Table 16 pp. 248-249

**Table 2.4  Origin of exports classified by country groupings\* and destination of exports, 1989 (US$ mil.)**

|  | Destination of Exports | | | | | | | | | | |
| Origin of Export | Australia | NAFTA | EU | EFTA | East 3 | Japan | ASEAN | NICs | NZ | Other | Total |
| --- | --- | --- | --- | --- | --- | --- | --- | --- | --- | --- | --- |
| Australia | .. | 4,470 | 5,088 | 654 | 180 | 9,761 | 3,549 | 3,103 | 1,890 | 8,342 | **37,037** |
| NAFTA | 9,302 | 205,342 | 100,312 | 12,946 | 683 | 53,765 | 17,365 | 36,518 | 1,269 | 71,730 | **509,232** |
| EU | 8,795 | 100,753 | 677,824 | 118,185 | 10,220 | 23,216 | 14,807 | 18,725 | 1,419 | 159,708 | **1,133,652** |
| EFTA | 1,622 | 17,113 | 105,878 | 25,870 | 2,897 | 4,485 | 2,641 | 3,731 | 211 | 22,319 | **186,767** |
| East 3 | 82 | 922 | 9,081 | 3,023 | 2,999 | 362 | 242 | 66 | 7 | 13,466 | **30,250** |
| Japan | 7,773 | 102,629 | 47,986 | 7,982 | 362 | .. | 25,858 | 43,312 | 1,340 | 37,355 | **274,597** |
| ASEAN | 2,771 | 27,131 | 17,625 | 1,413 | 223 | 22,970 | 21,611 | 11,976 | 314 | 15,435 | **121,469** |
| NICs | 3,947 | 71,176 | 28,965 | 4,647 | 141 | 26,927 | 15,101 | 17,291 | 631 | 34,671 | **203,497** |
| NZ | 1,675 | 1,444 | 1,523 | 48 | 20 | 1,538 | 488 | 614 | .. | 1,499 | **8,849** |
| Other | 2,856 | 74,946 | 129,959 | 14,952 | 11,044 | 54,911 | 13,716 | 32,847 | 2,387 | .. | **337,618** |
| **Total** | **38,823** | **605,926** | **1,124,241** | **189,720** | **28,769** | **197,935** | **115,378** | **168,183** | **9,468** | **364,525** | **2,842,968** |

*Source:*  IMF (1989)

\*Country Groupings: **NAFTA**: Canada, Mexico, US; **EU:** Twelve current member countries; **EFTA:** Iceland, Finland, Norway, Sweden; **East 3:** Czech Republic, Hungary, Poland; **ASEAN**: Brunei, Indonesia, Malaysia, Philippines, Singapore, Thailand; **NICs**: Hong Kong, Republic of Korea, Taiwan

capital flows and joint ventures as well as by marriage and by commonalities in cultural and business ethics. Such networks have been formed in trade, finance, real estate, processing and assembly and have grown in sophistication from the informal one person patriarch decision-maker to the more formal board of directors using western-trained business administration executives applying modern Harvard-style management techniques. Such networks produce linkages with international capital although there still remain vestiges of family relationships and filial obligations among relatives.

The growth of such relationship enterprises in Asia is seen as the result of a need to service Chinese clients in Asia. In Hong Kong and Singapore, for instance, relationship enterprises in the form of Asian MNCs are present in banking (Hong Kong and Shanghai Bank, Standard Chartered Bank, which have extensive operations in Asia); and in telecommunications (Singapore Telecom, for example, has expanded aggressively into Asia). Strategic alliances are being formed such as the Mitsui Group's joint venture with overseas Chinese in Thailand. The Lippo group in Indonesia has moved out of its traditional financial business into cognate industries such as investment banking, securities, property and information technology. In insurance, the Australian Colonial Mutual Group has entered into a tripartite joint venture with Jardine CMG Life Group (Hong Kong) and PT Astra — an association which reflects the attitude and favourable perception Western firms now have of Asian-style MNCs. Rather than a debilitating competitive model, the trend appears to be one involving joint ventures and strategic alliances between Western and Asian MNCs. No longer are such firms seen as adversaries and competitors but rather as partners in cooperation and facilitation.

There are other relationship enterprises that are based on alliances other than along ethnic lines. Such mergers of production functions derive scale advantages especially with large projects where it may be beyond the resources and capabilities of a single corporation. These transnational conglomerates may be less subject to national commercial trade practice laws and as a force may have greater access to both national and global markets. There are many such examples, such as, Boeing-Airbus, McDonnell Douglas-Misubishi-Kawasaki, Intel-Microsoft, Mazda-Ford and General Motors-Toyota.

*Strategic collaborations.* Strategic collaborations are becoming the norm and may suggest the way forward although much work still needs to be done to avoid misunderstanding.[2] Business International (1987) (cited in Dicken 1993:33) has identified seven factors for the upsurge in strategic collaborations:

- advances in communication technology and in the world's communication infrastructure which have led to the globalisation of the market place in information, finance, manufacturing and technology
- rising costs of R&D, product development, manufacturing facilities and equipment
- quickening of technological innovations and shortening of product lead times and life cycles
- convergence of technologies of previously separate market segments
- rise of protectionist measures in many countries
- creation of vast new markets through government initiatives in deregulating financial, telecommunications and other markets
- for Western countries, the rise and global competitive threat of Japan.[3]

It may be seen that each factor, either singly or in combination, produces geographical biases that determine the different spatial patterns and impacts that are evident today. With the possible exception of the rise and global competitive threat of Japan, all of the above points have a spatial element in its reach. Where data is readily available maps could be constructed showing the isocosts, the diffusion of technological innovation, convergence of technology, varying degrees of trade protection and the creation of new market segments. These maps may demonstrate the unevenness and differential impacts of globalisation and internationalisation. Indeed these may re-draw the familiar political boundaries with new borders based on commonalities in relative success and achievement.

*Human bridges.* The phenomenon of establishing 'satellite families' among the Chinese of Hong Kong has been an on-going one, given the uncertain status of the colony after July 1997. This global commuting of the male spouse between Hong Kong and countries such as Canada and Australia where the satellite families eventually grow up has emerged because of changes to immigration laws, improved communication and the easy mobility of capital. Extensive Vietnamese emigration and resettlement in Australia and North America are gradually building up community networks in these countries but which remain largely isolated from Vietnam. The impacts of these communities have yet to be analysed. However, Naisbitt and Aburdene (1990:185) have suggested that the human bridge to Hong Kong has not only stimulated investments in Canada but also that the connections that Hong Kong maintains with China are potentially of great benefit. The authors have no doubt in the belief that Hong Kong immigration is the key to long-term economic growth in several provinces of Canada.

**Theory and Practice**

One theory of international trade has been described as the product cycle (Vernon 1973). In this theory, labour is deemed to be *the* most important factor of production by comparison to land, capital and skill. Here, three stages of demand for any one commodity, in which labour plays an important role, may be identified. In the first stage, demand for the product is small and large scale production may not be feasible. The inputs of skilled labour are large when compared to inputs of capital and unskilled labour. In stage two, as demand increases, more capital is used as an input together with managerial and engineering skills which are necessary for moving towards large scale production. Then, in the third stage of extensive demand, product standardisation takes place where large amounts of capital and unskilled labour are combined with smaller amounts of skilled labour. R&D may take place in one country while production takes place in another. Such product cycle goods are highly sensitive to cost differences and tend to be produced where labour costs are relatively cheap. Examples of such products include the advent of the pocket calculator, that costs hundreds of dollars when first put on sale, to virtual give-aways when the product reached maturity. A further example is the digital watch, the instamatic camera and the ubiquitous personal computer. The third stage in the product cycle may contribute to the industrialisation of developing countries because the mature product is manufactured using simple technology and very low production costs. The NIDL and the more general phenomenon of the globalisation of production is seen here at its peak because the technology is now more appropriate and more amenable to widespread use and adoption. However, it is at this stage also that developing countries become exposed and vulnerable to corporate decisions. As the product cycle reaches maturity the goods produced become less profitable because higher wages push up the cost of production, rural labour is no longer available and labour is becoming organised. The MNC may decide to move elsewhere in search of cheaper labour and cheaper overall costs.

Analogous to the concept of the product cycle, the growth of some Asian economies has been described as a 'flying geese' pattern. This pattern refers to the tendency for Asian economies to move up the manufacturing services chain sequentially from labour-intensive to capital-intensive manufacturing and then into technology-intensive manufacturing and finally into services-related activities. In the case of South Korea and Taiwan the emphasis has been on R&D with the government taking a greater role in Taiwan. In South Korea, greater reliance has been put on the larger conglomerates or *chaebols*. In the high-wage economies of Hong Kong and Singapore, there has been the development of niché markets such as computer component manufacturing and financial services, especially offshore banking and insurance. There is increasing specialisation in manufacturing with each of the Asian nations concentrating on their comparative advantages so that Hong Kong and Singapore are seen as having advantages in banking and insurance, electronics and pharmaceuticals, whereas South Korea and Taiwan may have advantages in steel, paper and textiles. Similarly, Thailand, Malaysia, Indonesia and the Philippines may have comparative advantages in textiles, fertilisers and cement but have disadvantages in banking, transport and precision equipment.

## Economic Integration

The examination of financial flows (Alvstam 1993:64) and the volume of trade patterns suggests several geographical patterns. The export of manufactured goods from toys to textiles right through to sophisticated products like cars from South Korea and Malaysia suggests a change in the nature and direction of trade. Finance and producer services emanating from Hong Kong and Singapore are no longer regionally oriented. The global impact of the yen is readily acknowledged as is the massive investment surge in land, property and production. Other Asian NICs have also partaken in the impressive global investment portfolios (Dixon and Drakakis-Smith 1993). The flows are also not merely the inanimate objects of things and finance but also the inflow of people entering the international labour market. The flow of workers internationally are distinguished both by their relative numbers and their professional skills. The flow of professional and skilled labour to Australia and North America on a semi-permanent basis further emphasises the internationalisation of an integrated world economy. Pacific Asia, for example, is now emerging as a region that is more economically integrated into the world economy than ever before. Yet, the region is no more homogenous because of the in-built social, cultural, political and economic contrasts and conflicts within and between individual countries in a region that is considered to be one of the potentially most volatile in the world (Forbes 1993).

By any measure the trends suggest that economies in Asia are becoming more interdependent. The study of the indices of inward and outward trade as a proportion of overall trade linkages suggests that, both imports and exports between Pacific Basin countries is growing more quickly than trade with countries outside the region. Perhaps one exception is Japan as it concentrates on dominating the global economy through to the new millennium as a global powerhouse (Wong 1993).

## Conclusion

Towards the close of the 1990s, developing countries have to contend with and adjust to a global financial and trading system which is in a state of flux. Other uncertainties that confront these countries include security, political unrest, technological advances, the energy outlook and environmental damage. These are daunting challenges. In 1992, Ekins (1992) suggested that a new world order may develop in one of three ways. First a neo-liberal order in a world made up of a global market where an increasing number of people and resources are engaged in exchange relationships. In such a market property owners and consumers stand to be better off under this regime. The main protagonists in this scheme of things would be the World Bank, the International Monetary Fund and the GATT.

Second, the social democratic new world order will be a state based on the new international economic order where markets and nation states are accepted and valued with broad social and democratic principles. Here the UN and political units such as the EU and ASEAN are integral parts of the order.

Third, a grass roots new world order will emerge in which there is a 'bottom-up' ethic initiated by local groups. Such an order is aimed at combating the four holocausts of war and militarisation, human oppression, economic destitution and environmental degradation. Such a new world order works hand in glove with peace, green development and the human rights movement. The main objectives of this movement are to increase creativity and cultural diversity, to promote holistic development and a world order that is committed to social development, non-violence and the environment. This is in stark contrast to the previous two models which are characterised by being Western oriented and with the rest of the world entertaining a vision of becoming like the US. Human progress is defined in economic terms of GNP and all planning is centralised and 'top-down' managed in part by government, TNCs and international bureaucracies.

Whichever model is to succeed and to dominate the world scene, there appears to be no magic cure for economic underdevelopment. While there may be more than one route to success, the evaluation of success must be made according to the various dimensions of development and not merely hinged on income growth. The interaction between domestic markets and the global economy are crucial for a new world order to come about. Effective domestic markets have a tendency to attract foreign investments which in turn boost productivity. International trade links also allow countries to make use of comparative advantage to help domestic economies make more efficient use of their resources.

The global imbalance equation is simple to state but may be intractable and insoluble. Developed countries, making up only one-fifth of the world's population produce four-fifths of the world output and account for more than four-fifths of world trade. All exports of capital and technology originate from the developed world. Ironically, with the establishment of the WTO following the Uruguay Round of the GATT, the way towards an integrated global market is via the development of regional trading blocs. The development of the regional markets in the guise of NAFTA, EU and the Pacific Rim forum discussed elsewhere suggests a triad of sorts. But three is an awkward number because it may encourage two to gang up on the third; or one to play the other two off against each other. It reminds one of George Orwell's *1984* where the superstates of Eurasia, Eastasia and Oceania are engaged in global rivalry. The global trend is that despite the uncertainties, more countries are adopting market friendly approaches leaning towards strong international cooperation in order to enhance their own opportunities and, collectively, global trade and development.

## Notes

1   See Ward's (1995) fascinating study of a measure of relative distance between Pacific Island countries using international phone charges as a measure of distance and interaction.
2   Mann (1989) describes the joint venture between American Motors and Beijing Automotive Works set up in 1972 following the euphoria of President Nixon's visit which turned sour and unprofitable.
3   The internationalisation of the *sogo shosha* network has given Japanese companies more flexibility. This is because such conglomerates can draw upon the necessary finances from many sources both domestic and foreign. The rise of the Korean *chaebols* add further variations to the pattern of strategic collaborations.

## References

Alvstam, C. (1993), 'The Impact of Foreign Direct Investments on the Geographical Pattern of Foreign Trade Flows in Pacific Asia with Special Reference to Taiwan', in Dixon, C. and Drakakis-Smith, D. (eds.), *Economic and Social Development in Pacific Asia*, Routledge: London and New York, pp. 63-84.

Brunn, D.D. and Williams, J. (1983), *Cities of the World: World Regional Urban Development*, Harper and Row: New York.

Business International (1987), *Competitive Alliances: How to Succeed at Cross Regional Collaboration*, Business International: New York.

Cho, G. (1995), *Trade, Aid and Global Interdependence*, Routledge: London and New York.

Copyright Convergence Group (CCG) Australia (1994), *Highways to Change. Copyright in the New Communications Environment*, AGs Legal Practice: Canberra.

Cowling, K. and Sugden, R. (1987), 'Market Exchange and the Concept of a Transnational Corporation', *British Review of Economic Issues*, Vol. 9, pp. 57-68.

Dicken, P. (1993), 'The Growth Economies of Pacific Asia in Their Changing Global Context', in Dixon, C. and Drakakis-Smith, D. (eds.), *Economic and Social Development in Pacific Asia*, Routledge: London and New York, pp. 22-42.

Dixon, C. and Drakakis-Smith, D. (eds.) (1993), *Economic and Social Development in Pacific Asia*, Routledge: London and New York.

Ekins, P. (1992), 'A New World Order — for Whom?', *Development Bulletin*, pp. 23:35.

Forbes, D. (1993), 'What's in it for Us? Images of Pacific Asian Development', in Dixon, C. and Drakakis-Smith, D. (eds.), *Economic and Social Development in Pacific Asia*, Routledge: London and New York, pp. 43-62.

Frobel, F., Heinrich, J. and Kreye, O. (1980), *The New International Division of Labour*, Cambridge University Press: Cambridge.

GATT (1988), *Review of Developments in the Trading System*, GATT: Geneva.

International Monetary Fund (IMF) (1989), *Direction of Trade Statistics Yearbook, 1977-83, 1983-89.*

Mann, J. (1989), *Beijing Jeep: The Short and Unhappy Romance of American Business in China*, Simon and Schuster: New York.

Naisbitt, J. and Aburdene, P. (1990), *Megatrends 2000: Ten New Directions for the 1990s*, William Morrow and Coy: New York.

Orwell, G. (1949), *1984*, Secker and Warburg: London.

UN Commission on Transnational Corporations (1991), *Report on Transnational Corporations*, UNCTC: New York.

Vernon, R. (1973), *Multinational Enterprises*, Colmann-Crug: Paris.

Ward, R.G. (1995), 'The Shape of Tele-costs Worlds: The Pacific Island Case', in Cliff, A.D., Gould, P.R., Hoare, A.G., and Thrift, N.J. (eds.), *Diffusing Geography: Essays for Peter Haggett*, IBG Special Publications, Series No. 31, Blackwell: Oxford and Cambridge, pp. 222-240.

Wong, J. (1993), 'ASEAN Economies: Continuing Dynamic Growth in the 1990s', in Dixon, C. and Drakakis-Smith, D. (eds.), *Economic and Social Development in Pacific Asia*, Routledge: London and New York, pp. 115-127.

World Bank (1992), *World Development Report 1992*, Oxford University Press: New York.

# PART II

# CASE STUDIES:  IMPACT OF VANISHING BORDERS

# 3 Japanese Adaptation to the Globalisation of the World Economy

*TAKAYAMA Masaki and NOMURA Shigeharu*

## Introduction

The Japanese society and economy have begun to change rapidly now with the advent of the 21st Century. This chapter's objective is to analyse the structural change in terms of human capital, goods and services, and capital. There are three key words to decribe and explain this recent change in the Japanese economy. They are 'internationalisation', 'the aged society', and 'structural adjustment'. First of all, it is essential to consider them in the framework of the historical development of the Japanese economy in the postwar era. The period from 1945 to 1950 is called the 'reconstruction period'. The major problem in this period was to secure a self-reliant economic foundation through an industrial recovery. To this end, the limited resources (raw materials and foreign exchanges) were channelled into key industries such as coal and steel. This practice is called the 'priority production system' whereby the government hastened economic growth by drawing up a series of medium-range plans and mobilising the scarce resources.

Active government intervention played an important role in the economic development of Japan. For instance, the government's role could be seen in the setting up of sectoral priorities; the allocation of subsidies and the facilitation of financial flows to priority sectors; infant industry protection; and the regulation of excessive competition. Consequently, during the period of high economic growth in the 1960s, the development of heavy industries such as automobiles, petroleum products, machinery and electrical appliances were encouraged. In

39

order to enhance the industrial development in these sectors special measures were implemented. For example, essential technology was introduced from abroad and advances in plant and equipment were actively encouraged. With regards to financing, the Japan Development Bank made available priority financing to heavy and chemical industries. Various tax measures, such as special depreciation allowances were introduced. On the other hand, as the Japanese economy strengthened its international competitiveness, the government attempted to abolish import restrictions and to reduce the tariff rates on some commodities.

The Japanese economy was greatly affected by the Gulf Oil Crisis in 1973 which brought along a stable but low rate of growth. From then on, assembly manufacturers such as the automobile and household appliances industries became the leading sectors in the national economy. Furthermore, the Oil Crisis also brought a structural change in the industrial structure from heavy and chemical industries to knowledge-intensive industries in order to enhance the value-added production. Examples of the research-and-development intensive industries were high-level construction industries, fashion industries, and information management industries. In addition, the share of the service sector in GDP had also increased steadily. The trade surplus in 1986 exceeded US$100 billion. The appreciation of the yen (the Japanese currency) was recognised by the Plaza Accord in September of 1985. Subsequently, the shift of the production base to foreign countries had increased steadily. From 1987 to 1991, the Japanese economy experienced an economic boom which has been labelled as the 'bubble economy'. The bubble burst in May 1991 and the recession has since continued. Consequently, some structural adjustments in the framework of the economy and the society were required in order to attain a stable economy.

At the same time, the Japanese society is also becoming an aged one, largely because of the decrease in the birth rate. The total fertility rate declined from 2.14 in 1971 to 1.43 in 1995 (Figure 3.1). The decline in the birth rate has attracted the attention of the nation's planners in view of the social and economic implications of such a trend. In addition, the concentration of population in big cities such as Tokyo and Osaka has also resulted in many intractable problems notably the unbalanced regional development between the highly industrialised metropolitan regions and the rest of the country. This chapter reviews the changes in the Japanese economy from the viewpoint of population change and movements, the change of the industrial and trade structure; and firms' activities in foreign countries over the last ten years when 'internationalisation', the 'aged society' and 'the structural adjustment' are becoming key issues.

**Population Change and Movements**

*The Decrease of the Birth Rate and the Aged Society*

The population of Japan is 125,569,000 according to the 1995 population census. The last five years have recorded the pos twar's minimum population growth rate of 1.6 per cent. Total fertility rate dropped to 1.43 in 1995. This is the reason why the Japanese society is becoming an aged society. About 14.4 per cent of the Japanese population were over 65 years old in 1995 (Table 3.1) which is almost the same level as in Western countries. Not only is the Japanese society becoming an aged one, it is also quickly becoming so because of the recent sudden reduction in the birth rate. The estimate by the Ministry of Health and Welfare in 1992 indicated that 28.2 per cent of the Japanese population would be over 65 years old in 2050. This would be double the present figure of 14.4 per cent (Table 3.1).

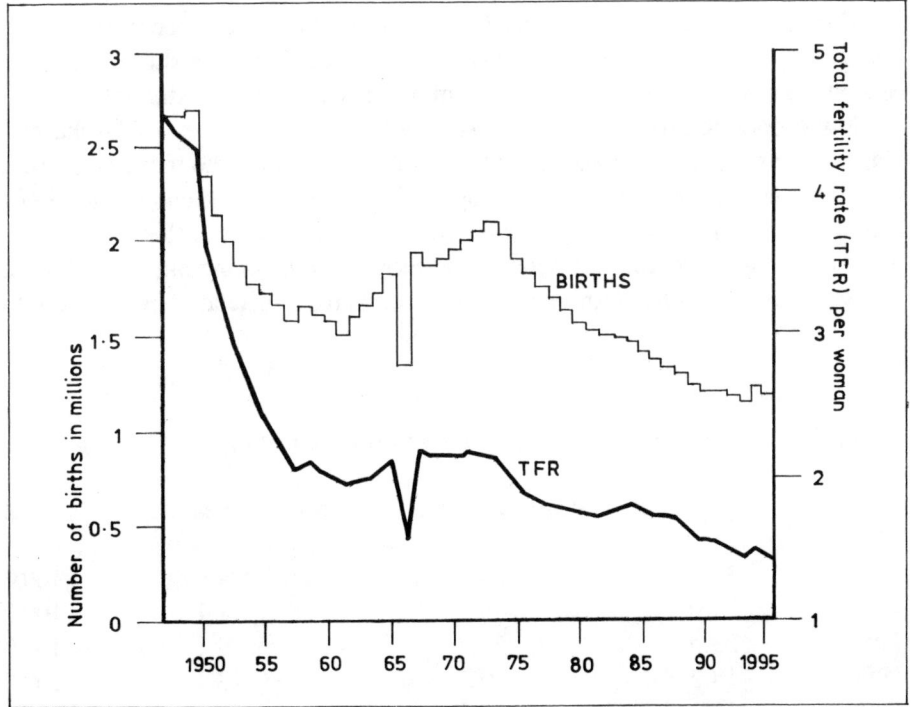

**Figure 3.1  Number of births and total fertility rate, 1950-1995**
*Source*:        Ministry of Welfare (1996)

Given this trend, it is essential to build a societal system that gives due recognition to social insurance and welfare services suited to the aged society. The implications on the social and economic structure need to be understood. At present, the ratio of senior citizens is higher in local provincial areas and relatively lower in the urban areas. A sharp increase in the number of senior citizens in the future would increase the administrative demand for welfare services all over Japan. The Japanese corporations would have to share half the cost of the pension funds in the present system. As the number of senior citizens increases, the social insurance fees would also increase. Consequently, the Japanese corporations' financial burden would also increase and they would lose the competitive strength in the world markets.

*Shift of Population*

The movement of population from provincial areas into the big cities has continued unabated. As a result, overpopulation in the big cities on the one hand, and depopulation in the rural districts on the other hand, have occurred. While many people moved from the rural districts into the big cities during the high economic growth period, the number of migrants decreased substantially during the low economic growth period. This may be seen in the case of Osaka and Nagoya metropolitan regions where the number of people who moved out from the cities has been in excess of the people who moved into the cities since 1974 (Figure 3.2). This trend is also true in the Tokyo Metropolitan Region in 1994. It is interesting to note that the people who moved out from the big cities did not always return to their hometowns in the provincial areas. Instead, they moved into

**Table 3.1   Age composition of population (percentage)**

|      | 0-14 years old | 15-64 years old | Above 65 years old | Total |
|------|----------------|-----------------|--------------------|-------|
| 1950 | 35.4           | 59.7            | 4.9                | 100.0 |
| 1970 | 24.0           | 68.9            | 7.1                | 100.0 |
| 1980 | 23.5           | 67.4            | 9.1                | 100.0 |
| 1990 | 18.2           | 69.7            | 12.1               | 100.0 |
| 1995 | 16.1           | 69.5            | 14.4               | 100.0 |

*Source*:   Census of Population (1995)

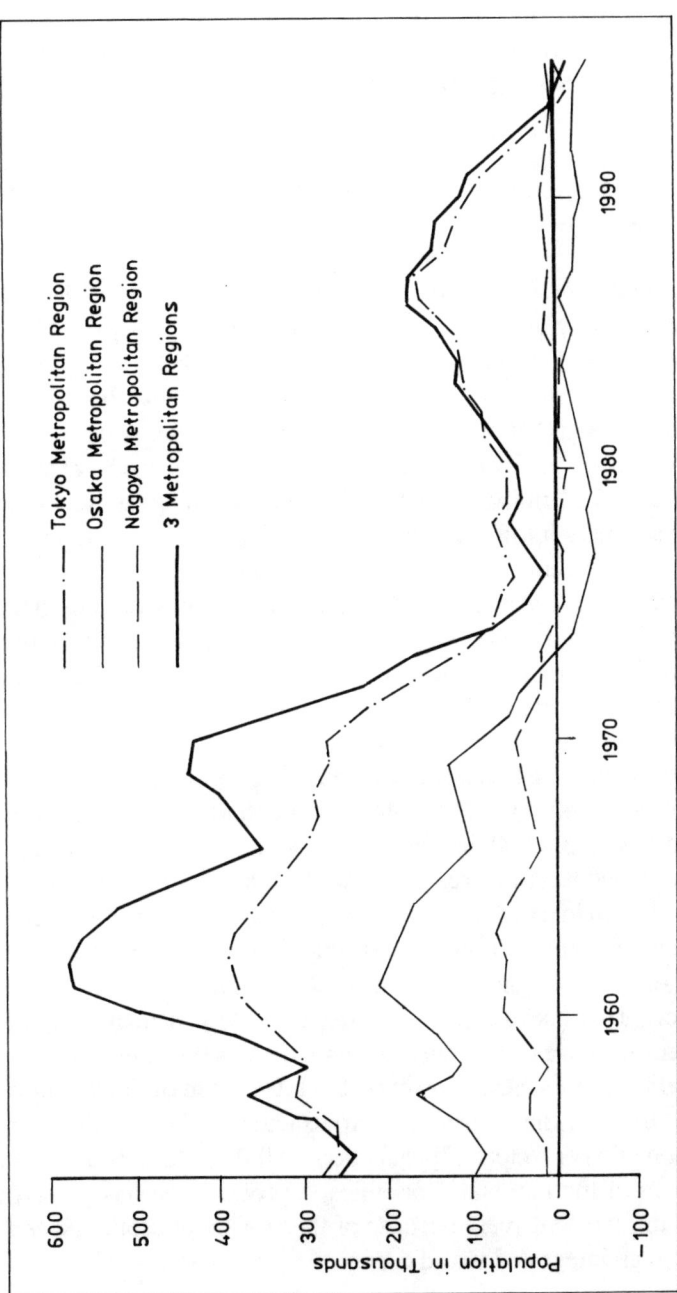

**Figure 3.2  Net population increase in metropolitan regions, 1960-1990**

*Source:*  Economic Planning Agency of Japan (1992)

the fringe areas of the big cities. In this sense, the Metropolitan Regions have actually expanded further. On the other hand, the decline in the movement of people from the principal cities to the big cities may be indicative of a more matured society, or it may simply mean that the pool of young people in the provincial areas has been depleted.

*The Trend of Japanese Who Stay in Foreign Countries and Foreigners Who Stay in Japan*

With the internationalisation of business activities in the 1980s, the number of Japanese who stay in foreign countries has increased very rapidly. According to the Ministry of Foreign Affairs, the actual numbers were 241,102 in 1970; 480,739 in 1985; and 687,579 in 1993. It is obvious that the increase since 1985 (which is doubled that of 1970) has been remarkable. The number of passports issued in Japan has been in excess of 4 million every year since 1990. It amounted to 5.21 million in 1994. The number of Japanese who stay in North America accounts for 40 per cent of all the Japanese citizens abroad in 1993, in Europe 19 per cent, and South America 17.5 per cent. The relatively high percentage in South America is due to the huge number of emigrants into South America. However, Asia (16 per cent in 1993) is likely to take the second rank after North America in future because of the increasing trade and investment opportunities in Asia.

On the other hand, the number of foreigners who stay in Japan has also increased sharply of late. They amounted to 1.35 million in 1994. The population census of 1st October 1995 indicated that the share of foreigners staying in Japan exceeded 1 per cent of all the Japanese. About 50 per cent of the foreigners came from South and North Korea and have been living in Japan since prewar times.

Most of them live in the major of cities Tokyo, Osaka and the Aichi Prefecture. Newcomers to Japan largely live around Tokyo where jobs are more abundant. Some of them stay legally and others, illegally; the latter is estimated to be over 0.3 million. They take the '3D' jobs which are 'dirty, demanding, and dangerous'. The recent increase of foreign workers indicates the high mobility in the labour market among countries. However, the integration of the labour market occurs not only through the international transaction of labour, but also through the transaction of other factors of production. All these factors are influenced by the integration of the national economies, a process that has gained considerable momentum in recent years because of the erosion of economic and institutional barriers in an integrated world economy.

**Industrial and Trade Structures**

*The Industrial Structure*

As Japanese industries developed, the proportion of the labour force in the various industrial sectors also changed. The share of population working in the primary sector decreased sharply, while the number employed in the tertiary sector has increased substantially (Table 3.2). The proportion of the population working in the secondary sector, however, has been quite stable since 1970 in sharp contrast to the proportion of workers employed in the tertiary sector which has increased from 46.6 per cent in 1970 to 60.8 per cent in 1994. Thus, the tertiarisation or the expansion of the service sector in the Japanese economy is obvious - a phenomenon difficult to grasp in the framework of the traditional concept and classification of the Japanese economy. The component share in the manufacturing industry has also changed over the last twenty years reflecting the progressing internationalisation of the Japanese economy. The focus of the postwar manufacturing industry changed from light industries to heavy-chemical industries. The latter invested heavily in plants and equipment during the period of high economic growth and were mainly located in the coastal zones. In particular, the raw-material industries such as steel, petrochemicals, machines and other industries achieved remarkable growth. These are the so-called 'heavy and large-scale industries or the 'foot-tight' industries. On the other hand, during the period of low economic growth, the electronic industries such as computer and semi-conductor industries were major areas of growth. They produced high-technology and knowledge-intensive goods to enhance value-added productivity. They are called 'frivolous and small-sized industries' in contrast to the 'the heavy and large-scale industries'.

*The Trade Structure*

Lacking natural resources, Japan has no choice but to import raw materials and export manufactured goods to earn foreign currencies. However, the imports of manufactured goods have been increasing recently. This is especially true with the import of input goods such as machines and production equipment (Table 3.3). America is the biggest partner in both the export and import trade, and the share of trade with the East Asian region has also been increasing recently (Table 3.4). Japan's balance of trade showed a surplus even in the 1960s. Trade surplus has continued since the 1960s in spite of the Oil Crisis in the 1970s. The value of the trade surplus increased substantially to exceed US$100 billion in 1986. This resulted in the appreciation of the yen and the Japanese firms were forced to 'internationalise'. A striking feature of the Japanese trade structure was that, until recently, Japan had an unusually low amount of intra-industry trade (Table 3.5). This was because Japan had been exporting capital and technology-intensive goods, and importing labour and resource-intensive goods. It might also be due to Japan's policy of restricting foreign products to Japanese consumers. However, of late, Japan has come to import more manufactured goods. As Japan's foreign direct investment (FDI) increases, the rate of production abroad and the export of foreign affiliates of Japanese firms has also increased. Trade with Asian countries tends to be more balanced. For example, the trade balance in terms of textile products, general machines and electronic machines tends towards an equilibrium. Thus, the Japanese trade structure is changing from the vertical division of labour to the horizontal division of labour. The latter is divided into two categories. The first is made up of products differentiated by quality and prices. For example, Japan exports more sophisticated and high-quality products, on the one hand, and imports cheaper, lower-quality products from Asian countries, on the other hand. The other category consists of products at different production stages.

## Shift of Production Base Abroad and the Hollowing Out of Industries

*The Exchange Rate Factor*

The postwar's exchange rate was fixed at 360 yen per U.S. dollar. However, the Bretton Woods system collapsed in August 1971 by suspending the exchange of gold for dollars. After that, although the Smithsonian Agreement was reached,

**Table 3.2  Share of workers by industrial sectors (percentage)**

|                   | 1950  | 1960  | 1970  | 1980  | 1990  | 1994  |
|-------------------|-------|-------|-------|-------|-------|-------|
| Primary sector    | 48.3  | 32.6  | 19.4  | 10.9  | 7.1   | 5.8   |
| Secondary sector  | 21.9  | 29.2  | 34.0  | 33.5  | 33.3  | 33.4  |
| Tertiary sector   | 29.8  | 38.2  | 46.6  | 55.6  | 59.6  | 60.8  |
| Total             | 100.0 | 100.0 | 100.0 | 100.0 | 100.0 | 100.0 |

*Source*:  Nihon Kokusei Zue (A Charted Survey of Japan) (1996:94)

the fixed rate of exchange also finally failed. A flexible exchange rate system was adopted in 1973. Since then, the yen had greatly appreciated by the end of the 1970s. By the first half of the 1980s, the exchange rate per U.S. dollar fluctuated between 200 and 250 yen.[1] By the Plaza Accord in 1985, where the ministers of the Group of Five (G5) - the U.S., Japan, U.K., France, and Germany - gathered at the Plaza Hotel in New York to devise a plan to push down the value

**Table 3.3  Japanese exports and imports by commodity (percentage)**

| Exports | 1970 | 1985 | 1995 |
|---|---|---|---|
| Machinery | 23.9 | 39.0 | 49.7 |
| Iron and steel | 14.7 | 7.8 | 4.3 |
| Textile products | 12.5 | 3.6 | 2.0 |
| Ships | 7.0 | 3.4 | 2.5 |
| Precision machines | 3.3 | 4.9 | 4.7 |
| Motor vehicles | 9.6 | 19.5 | 12.0 |
| Plastic | 2.2 | 1.3 | 1.9 |
| Others | 26.8 | 20.5 | 22.9 |
| Total | 100.0 | 100.0 | 100.0 |

| Imports | 1970 | 1985 | 1995 |
|---|---|---|---|
| Oil | 14.4 | 31.3 | 10.6 |
| Machinery | 11.0 | 6.6 | 18.6 |
| Timber | 8.3 | 2.9 | 3.0 |
| Coal | 5.3 | 4.0 | 2.0 |
| Raw materials of textile | 5.1 | 1.3 | 0.4 |
| Copper ore | 2.6 | 0.5 | 0.4 |
| Natural gas | 0.6 | 7.7 | 3.3 |
| Clothes | 0.5 | 1.5 | 5.6 |
| Fish food | 1.4 | 3.5 | 5.2 |
| Iron ore | 6.4 | 2.4 | 1.1 |
| Motor vehicles | 0.3 | 0.4 | 3.0 |
| Others | 44.1 | 37.9 | 46.8 |
| Total | 100.0 | 100.0 | 100.0 |

*Source*:  Nihon Kokusei Zue (1972:159; 1987:362; 1996:350)

of the U.S. dollar, the value of yen began to appreciate again. The exchange rate rose to 145 yen in 1987 (Table 3.6). The exchange rate achieved a record 79.95 yen on 19th April 1995. After that, it has been depreciating and it is now about 100 yen. The high appreciation of the yen strongly influenced direct investments and local production abroad by Japanese firms. This hollowing out of industries is indeed worrying to the domestic economy.

**Table 3.4   Exports and imports by regions (percentage)**

| Exports to | 1970 | 1985 | 1995 |
|---|---|---|---|
| Asia | 31.2 | 32.7 | 45.7 |
| (China) | (2.9) | (7.1) | (5.0) |
| North America | 33.7 | 39.7 | 28.6 |
| (U.S.A). | (30.7) | (37.1) | (27.3) |
| Latin America | 6.1 | 4.8 | 4.4 |
| Europe | 17.4 | 16.1 | 17.2 |
| Africa | 7.4 | 2.7 | 1.7 |
| Oceania | 4.2 | 4.0 | 2.4 |
| Total | 100.0 | 100.0 | 100.0 |
| Imports from | 1970 | 1985 | 1995 |
| Asia | 29.4 | 51.2 | 46.1 |
| (China) | (1.3) | (5.0) | (10.7) |
| North America | 34.4 | 23.7 | 25.7 |
| (U.S.A). | n.a. | (20.0) | (22.4) |
| Latin America | 7.3 | 4.8 | 3.5 |
| Europe | 13.5 | 10.8 | 17.8 |
| Africa | 5.8 | 2.7 | 1.4 |
| Oceania | 9.6 | 6.8 | 5.5 |
| Total | 100.0 | 100.0 | 100.0 |

*Source*:    Nihon Kokusei Zue (1972:161; 1987:369; 1996:358)

*Hollowing out of Industries*

The appreciation of the yen has led to an increase of Japanese firms of all industries to shift their production bases abroad with a consequent decrease of

**Table 3.5   Intra-industry trade index by countries, 1987**

|  | 21 sectors | 94 sectors |
|---|---|---|
| Australia | 0.41 | 0.22 |
| Belgium | 0.87 | 0.79 |
| Canada | 0.67 | 0.68 |
| Finland | 0.58 | 0.49 |
| France | 0.88 | 0.82 |
| Germany | 0.69 | 0.66 |
| Italy | 0.71 | 0.61 |
| Japan | 0.30 | 0.25 |
| Netherlands | 0.77 | 0.78 |
| Norway | 0.62 | 0.51 |
| Sweden | 0.66 | 0.68 |
| U.K. | 0.82 | 0.78 |
| U.S. | 0.67 | 0.60 |
| Korea | n.a. | 0.48 |
| Switzerland | n.a | 0.61 |

*Source*:   Lawrence (1987)

Note:   The index is calculated by obtaining the sum of exports and imports for the $i^{th}$ industry, EXi - IMi, and then substracting the absolute values of the difference of the two, [EXi - IMi]. The measure of the index of intra-industry trade (m) = $\sum i[(EXi - IMi) - (EXi - IMi)] [/\sum i[EXi + IMi]$. A higher m indicates a higher degree of intra-industry trade

**Table 3.6   The exchange rate of yen per U.S. dollar**

| Year | 1985 | 1986 | 1987 | 1988 | 1989 | 1990 | 1991 | 1992 | 1993 | 1994 | 1995 |
|---|---|---|---|---|---|---|---|---|---|---|---|
| Rate/US$ | 238 | 168 | 145 | 128 | 139 | 145 | 135 | 127 | 111 | 102 | 94 |

employment in the domestic economy. Such a hollowing out of industries is strongly motivated by the need to increase exports. The affiliates of Japanese firms are exporting to third countries, and are exporting from host countries to Japan. They produce labour-intensive products for exports by taking advantage of the abundant labour in the host countries. This is especially true for textile products. On the other hand, although electronic-machinery products are capital-intensive, the availability of local labour in particular areas was exploited through selective FDI. This may be seen in their strategy of breaking up the entire production process into several sub-processes and locating labour-intensive sub-processes in labour abundant parts of East Asia. In other words, a division of labour is pursued internationally within a firm, and such a production system leads to the emergence of inter-process, intra-firm, and intra-industry trade.

In the textile industry during the period between 1992-95, both production abroad and exports increased (Figure 3.3). In the raw-material industries such as the steel and ceramic industries changes have not been substantial. Nonetheless, as manufacturing goods outside of Japan increase, the level of employment in the domestic economy tends to decrease. In terms of the decrease of employment in different regions in Japan, the rate of decrease in the number of workers is particularly high in the big city areas. In the textile industry, for instance, it is high in every district but in the electric-machinery industry, it is relatively high in Tohoku, the Inner area of Kanto, and Hokuriku.

*Direct Investments*

Japan's outward FDI expanded rapidly and substantially in the 1980s. There are two factors which contributed to the expansion of Japan's FDI. One was the sharp appreciation of the Japanese yen after the Plaza Accord in 1985 as discussed above. The other was Japan's large trade surplus with the United States and the European Union. Japan's FDI in the 1980s was directed largely to North America and Europe and mainly in services and the manufacturing sectors. These two sectors accounted for two-thirds of Japan's FDI outflows. The share of Japan's FDI to East Asia was relatively small in the 1980s. However, it has increased since 1990 focussing on the manufacturing and services sectors. A distinct characteristic of Japanese FDI in Asia is the relatively large share in the manufacturing sector by comparison with other regions (Figure 3.4). Until the mid-1980s, Japanese FDI in electronic machineries in East Asia had been relatively small, compared to that in other sectors.

However, since the mid-1980s the electric machinery sector has become the

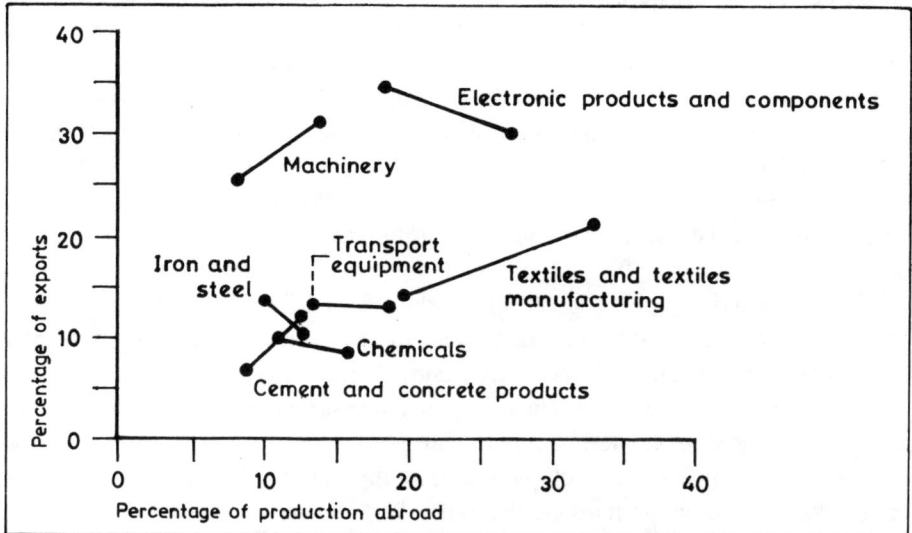

**Figure 3.3  Percentage of exports and production abroad, 1992-1995**
*Source*:          Ministry of Finance (1985-1996)

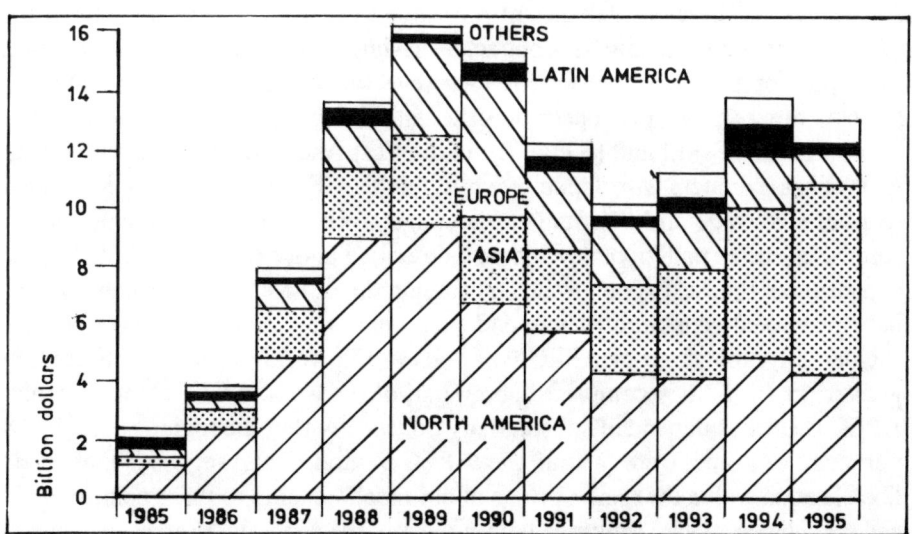

**Figure 3.4  Japanese direct investment to foreign countries in the manufacturing sector, 1985-1995**
*Source*:          Ministry of Finance (1985-1996)

most active in Japanese FDI. The number of Asian affiliates of Japanese manufacturing firms was 5,448 as of the end of 1995. Some 1,397 of them are included in the electronic machinery sector, 685 in chemical products, 539 in general machinery, 515 in textile products, and 377 in autoparts products. The number of affiliates in foreign countries of Japanese firms is 20,455 in 1995. It was 8,710 in 1986. Between 1987 and 1995, 11,745 firms had affiliates in foreign countries of which 64.1 per cent were located in Asia. About 38 per cent (7,739 firms) of the affiliates of Japanese firms were involved in manufacturing. Almost 23 per cent (4,709) went to Asia; 5.6 per cent (1,138) to China; 3 percent (651) to Thailand; 2.4 per cent (602) to Malaysia; and 2 per cent (422) to Korea. It is clear that Japanese FDI in manufacturing has shifted away geographically from the NIEs to ASEAN countries and China. This geographical shift is facilitated by host countries changing their economic policies from inward-oriented strategies to outward-oriented strategies and exercising the liberalisation of trade and FDI inflows actively and unilaterally. Of course, the earlier success of outward-oriented policies in the NIEs had prompted them to make such strategy changes.

A prominent feature of the foreign affliates of Japanese firms of the 1990s is that they have tried to not only export their products to Japan, but also import inputs from foreign suppliers in the Asian countries as much as possible. In other words, they have tried to make their business activities self-contained within the Asian regions. In short, Japanese firms have located their base operations for manufacturing, outsourcing, subcontracting, selling, and R&D in Asian countries. In the process, they have transferred Japanese technology and management know-how to other Asian producers as efficiently as possible. Subsequently, the accumulation of skill and technology in the East Asian countries have led them to be able to compete with Japan in world markets. Furthermore, they have tried to liberalise trade and the financial sector actively to avoid trade conflicts. It seems that such a pattern of development described above have contributed to the expansion of the East Asian trade and foreign direct investments which, in turn, have promoted economic growth and economic integration in Asian countries. Incidentally, the share of APEC countries in the world economy is becoming greater. In 1995, they comprised about half of the world's GDP. Not only that, APEC countries depended substantially on trade within the regions. About 68 per cent of trade were within the APEC region. This suggests that trade liberalisation within the region brings about much benefits to these countries. In addition, the developed countries within the regions generally protect the labour-intensive goods, while the developing countries within the regions generally protect the capital-intensive goods. Therefore, trade liberalisation tends to promote the complementarity within the regions. As a result, it is safe to say that the effect of exercising the trade liberalisation within the regions is positive and it is, therefore, important for Japan to join the free trade areas actively and promote the trade liberalisation multilaterally.

## *Affiliates of Foreign Firms in Japan*

Though direct investments within Japan have increased, it is considerably low compared with direct investments to foreign countries. This could be due to what might be called the 'non-market mechanism', that is, the 'keiretu' structures, the extensive pattern of intercorporate stockholding, the closed banking-business ties, subsidiary and sub-contracting networks, comprehensive trading companies, and industry associations. The net direct investments of foreign firms in Japan at the end of 1993 was US$19.2 billion. This constituted only about 4 per cent of the total in the United States; one-tenth of the total in the United Kingdom, and one-third of the total in Germany. In comparison, this was about 7 per cent of Japan's direct investments to the U.S. in 1993; 80 per cent to U.K.; and 40 per cent to Germany. Thus, Japan is prompted to promote more foreign direct investments in Japan. In terms of foreign companies in Japan, the developed countries accounted for about 70 per cent of all direct investments in Japan at the end of 1994. The U.S. accounted for about 40 per cent, Germany about 10 per cent and Switzerland about 6 per cent. The direct investments from Asia to Japan in terms of flow per year remained less than 5 per cent of the total, although it rose substantially to 15 per cent in 1993. The share of manufacturing and non-manufacturing industries in terms of accumulated investments was respectively 55 per cent and 45 per cent. The latter tends to increase recently. Machinery and chemicals in the manufacturing industry, and the trading service sector in non-manufacturing industries on the other hand, have also increased.

In terms of the performances of foreign firms in 1993 in Japan, the share of their total sales in the overall sales of all Japanese firms was 0.9 per cent, and that of the manufacturing industry was 2.3 per cent. It is quite clear that although foreign firms in Japan have a fair presence in the manufacturing sector, their presence in the non-manufacturing industry is negligible. The share of foreign firms in employment, R&D, exports and imports of all Japanese firms is respectively 0.4 per cent, 5.2 per cent, 4.0 per cent and 13.7 per cent. Thus, foreign firms are labour-saving, active in R&D, and have strong trade motives. In addition, the rate of return of the foreign firms tends to be higher than that of the Japanese firms - in terms of sales 3.0 per cent compared with 1.4 per cent with that of the Japanese firms. The trend is especially true in chemical and medical industries. Foreign firms are active in direct investments in Japan because of the potential growth of the Japanese market, Japan's position as the hub in the Asian region, and the opportunity to take advantage of the higher technology of Japan.

## Conclusion

This chapter has viewed the internationalisation of the Japanese economy from several perspectives. The international division of labour will be prompted to expand with the progress of freer trade. However, the Japanese economy has to deal with various problems such as the shifts in the industrial structure and adjustments in the labour market. Furthermore, it is necessary to resolve the problem of adjusting the social structure to suit the aged society domestically. In any case, it is beyond doubt that the economic relationship between Japan and East Asian as well as the Southeast Asian countries will become stronger. These future links will, however, be subjected to several unstable factors and differences among these countries particularly in the degree of economic performance, in the scale of the national economy, and in the type of political regime.

## Note

1   Many economists explained the overvaluation of the U.S. dollar during the first half of the 1980s as the result of the Federal Reserve Board adopting a tight monetary policy in order to counter inflation. In addition, tax cuts and an increase in military expenditure during the Reagan period caused high interest rate which, in turn resulted in the overvaluation of the dollar by attracting foreign capital. However, the Reagan Administration insisted that the strong dollar was a reflection of a strong U.S. economy and the trust of world investors.

## References

Daniel I. Okimato (1989), *Between MITI and the Market: Japanese Industrial Policy for High Technology*, Stanford University Press: Stanford.

Eaton, Jonathan and Akiko Tamura (1994), 'Bilateralism and Regionalism in Japanese and U.S. Trade and Direct Foreign Investment Patterns', *NBER Working Paper* No. 4758 (June).

Economic Planning Agency of Japan (1992), *The Economic White Paper*.

Economic Planning Agency of Japan (1996), *Regional Economic Report 1996*.

Lawrence, R.Z. (1987), 'Does Japan Import Too Little? Closed Minds Or Markets?', *Brookings Papers on Economic Acitivity,* Vol. 2, pp. 517-554.

Lawrence, R.Z. (1991), 'How Open is Japan?', in Krugman, P., *Trade with Japan,* University of Chicago Press: Chicago, pp. 9-49.

Ministry of Finance (1985-1996), *Zaisei Kin-yu Tokei Geppo* (Monthly Statistics on Government Finance Banking).

Ministry of Welfare (1996), *Jinko Tokei Shiryosyu* (Demographic Yearbook), Institute of Population.

Nihon Kokusei Zei (A Charted Survey of Japan) (1972; 1987; 1996).

Takatoshi Ito (1992), *The Japanese Economy,* The MIT Press.

Urata Shujiro (1993), 'Japanese Foreign Direct Investment and its Effect on Foreign Trade in Asia', in Takatoshi Ito and Krueger, Anne O. (eds.), *Trade and Protectionism,* University of Chicago: Chicago, pp. 273-299.

# 4 Global Markets and Global Citizens: Vanishing Borders in the Pacific Islands

*John OVERTON*

## Introduction

Much of the current interest in globalisation has been dominated by a discourse of economics, of the gains to be made from dismantling trade barriers and integrating production and distribution made systems world-wide through post-Fordist technologies. It is a clear vision for a world increasingly without economic borders but with shared prosperity. Within this vision, there is an assumption that the benefits of globalisation will be spread widely: all countries (especially their consumers and taxpayers) can benefit by dismantling costly protectionist policies, minimising the economic role of the state and by specialising in forms of production and trade in which they have a competitive advantage. Economic growth on a global scale is the central driving force, though it is recognised that widespread social change may follow as a result of increased prosperity and new divisions of labour.

Globalisation is not just a matter of trade and global economic integration. It is also closely linked to fundamental changes in the role of the state. Such change can take a number of forms. In many cases, they adhere to the Structural Adjustment Programme prescriptions of the International Monetary Fund and World Bank, involving free trade, export orientation, privatisation and deregulation. In other, but closely related, cases they can involve a shift from the public to the private sector and the minimisation of the economic role of the state. Thus globalisation as a development model should be seen as a universal process marked by homogeneity of policy prescriptions and market- and trade-oriented reform packages (Brohman 1995).

Yet, whilst much of the political rhetoric on globalisation adopts such a universal view, and one which is mostly positive and stresses mutual gains, one should question its application in different contexts. This chapter examines the small island states of the South Pacific, a group of countries where the discussion of globalisation should raise some alarm. All these countries (excluding the large and resource-rich state of Papua New Guinea) have populations of less than one million. There are limited natural resources (especially in the smaller states of Polynesia and Micronesia), and the fragmentation of the population over a vast ocean imposes major economic costs (Table 4.1). The chapter begins by discussing the implications for these states of an increasingly liberal trading environment and the moves to cut their public sectors. Although such an analysis leads to uniformly bleak conclusions at the national level, the second major section shifts the focus to the individual and household level, where the history of Pacific Island mobility is such as to suggest that many Pacific Islanders are well pre-adapted to a new open global order and could be regarded as 'proto-global citizens'.

## Global Markets and the Pacific Island

The Old World Order constructed a place for Pacific states that emphasised strategic importance, economic dependence and ambiguous political status. The countries, many characterised by relatively small resource and population bases, isolation from world markets, and limited economic integration across vast sea areas, were able to pursue economic development strategies which exploited, at the same time, their *de jure* status as independent nations and their *de facto* neo-colonial dependence (Bertram 1987; Connell 1986; 1988; Neemia 1992; Michal 1993). Preferential access to European and Australian markets for their agricultural and industrial products, coupled with some very high aid levels and remittance economies, allowed for the maintenance of high standards of living and increasingly Western consumption patterns.

One of the main features of Pacific Island countries in recent years has been their neo-colonial position. Some countries in the Pacific, such as Vanuatu, have pursued a strongly independent stance but others, notably the microstates of Polynesia and Micronesia, have maintained close relationships with their former (or in some cases, continuing) colonial masters. This latter group of countries have, as a result, received high levels of aid (Table 4.1) and, often, freer immigration and trade access to their respective metropolitan countries. Aid levels have been highest for countries which can be classified as having the most dependent external relations (Overton 1996). Bertram and Watters (1985; 1986),

**Table 4.1     Pacific Island States:  some basic data**

| | Population (000) 1991 | Land Area (km²) | Sea Area (000 km²) | GDP per capita 1989 ($A) | Aid per capita 1990 ($A) | Exports per capita 1991 ($A)[a] |
|---|---|---|---|---|---|---|
| *Melanesia* | | | | | | |
| Fiji | 742.0 | 18272 | 1290 | 2209[b] | 15 | 779 |
| New Caledonia | 173.3 | 19103 | 1740 | 16349 | 1901 | 3154 |
| Solomon Islands | 328.0 | 27556 | 1340 | 692 | 174 | 342 |
| Vanuatu | 151.9 | 11880 | 680 | 1282 | 337 | 120 |
| *Polynesia* | | | | | | |
| American Samoa | 49.0 | 197 | 390 | n.a. | 2117 | 8444 |
| Cook Islands | 17.4 | 240 | 1839 | 4703 | 912 | 407 |
| French Polynesia | 201.4 | 3265 | 5030 | 16559 | 1657 | 777 |
| Niue | 2.2 | 259 | 390 | n.a. | 4034 | 27 |
| Tokelau Islands | 1.6 | 10 | 290 | n.a. | 3750 | 179 |
| Tonga | 96.9 | 699 | 700 | 1267 | 389 | 222 |
| Tuvalu | 9.1 | 26 | 900 | 1130 | 694 | 34 |
| Wallis & Futuna | 13.9 | 255 | 300 | n.a. | n.a. | 5 |
| Western Samoa | 161.1 | 2935 | 120 | 839 | 160 | 62 |
| *Micronesia* | | | | | | |
| FSM | 111.6 | 701 | 2978 | 1717 | n.a. | 119 |
| Guam | 137.0 | 541 | 218 | n.a. | 878 | 781 |
| Kiribati | 73.5 | 690 | 3550 | 696 | 421 | 50 |
| Marshall Islands | 48.0 | 181 | 2131 | n.a. | n.a. | 76 |
| Nauru | 9.6 | 21 | 320 | 22418 | 27 | 3861 |
| Palau | 15.6 | 494 | 629 | n.a. | 907 | 382 |

*Sources*:    South Pacific Commission (1993); South Pacific Commission (1995)
[a] the largest returns under this heading (with the main commodities and share of export values in parentheses) include: New Caledonia (nickel 90%), American Samoa (tuna - to USA - 63%, 'special transactions' 34%); and Nauru (phosphate 99% - trade with Australia and New Zealand only).  Vanuatu excludes re-exports
[b] Fiji GDP data for 1990

Watters (1987) and Connell (1991) have described these as MIRAB states, with economies characterised by high levels of migration, remittances, aid, and (supported by aid) employment in the bureaucracy.

Given limited resources, isolation and the relatively high incomes supported by remittances and public sector employment, private sector development has been limited and exports per capita very low (Fairbairn 1985; 1987). Even the more independent countries have been able to cash in on aid, especially against the backdrop of the Cold War, when hints by some Pacific nations that the Soviet Union would be invited to give aid or set up embassies frequently brought a swift and lucrative response from Western donors (Campbell 1992; Connell 1986; Gibson 1991; Knapman 1986; Sevele 1987).

In countries without such strong neo-colonial ties, there have been other advantages in developing and maintaining close ties with former colonial and post-colonial regional powers. Aid donors have allocated relatively generous bilateral Official Development Assistance programmes to the Pacific but they have also used non-reciprocal preferential trade agreements as a hidden form of aid and as a means to promote economic development. Two of the most important of these are the Lomé Convention and SPARTECA. The Lomé Convention allows guaranteed access for the produce of former European colonies to the European market at stable prices usually well above world market rates. Access is governed by a number of commodity-specific protocols and, for the Pacific, arguably the most important is the Sugar Protocol which accounts for about half of Fiji's sugar exports (with another 10 per cent going to USA under preferential access terms). Grynberg (1993; 1995: 23), in a detailed analysis of Fiji's access to the European market for its sugar, calculated that benefits under the Lomé Convention amounted to over 3 per cent of Fiji's GDP since 1985 and they exceeded all other forms of cash and non-cash aid grants together.

SPARTECA is an agreement by which Australia and New Zealand have agreed to allow tariff-free imports of Pacific Island products (subject to rules of origin) (Grynberg and Powell 1995; Sutherland 1982). Again, perhaps the major example of benefit can be seen in Fiji, where a garment industry has grown rapidly in the past decade, generating substantial export revenues and employment (Chandra 1993; 1996). SPARTECA accounted for 87 per cent of garment exports from Fiji in 1989 but a growth in exports to USA lowered this to 54 per cent by 1994 (Chandra 1996:54). Neo-colonial trade concessions have proved an effective development strategy in many ways.[1]

Only the few resource-rich countries have been able to build relatively autonomous development strategies. These have involved the gold and copper mines of Papua New Guinea, the nickel industry of New Caledonia, the phosphate deposits of Nauru, and the forests of Papua New Guinea and the Solomon

Islands. Yet, these economies have faced a different set of constraints relating to the problems of commodity price fluctuations, resource depletion (especially in Nauru) or difficulties in negotiating compensation with traditional landowners. Furthermore, even these countries have not been blind to the opportunities to be gained from metropolitan aid donor beneficence or trade concessions.

For most, if not all, Pacific Island nations then, it can be concluded that their economies have become quite well adjusted to the Old World Order, characterised as it were by the Cold War and superpower rivalry, economic nationalism and protectionism, and neo-colonial relationships. Aid, remittances, preferential trade agreements and a subsidised public sector, in different degrees in different countries, have allowed for standards of living quite high compared to other developing countries. There has been a relative absence, with some exceptions, of poverty and hunger and many Pacific Islands have been able to combine the best of both worlds: some of the elements of a Western consumer society and many of the advantages of their established individual cultural and social hearths.

The economies and societies of Pacific Island nations, then, have been structured in such a way that allowed them a place in the Old World Order in the years from 1945 until about 1990. In this sense, the prospect of a New International Order and free trade may both seriously undermine what few gains that have been made in terms of production and trade in some of the larger economies, and substantially dismantle the aid-dependent employment structures in the smaller island nations. For many Pacific Island leaders, despite their rhetoric of independence, the prospect of a world economy without borders and a world polity without aid, is a bleak one indeed.

Perhaps the most immediate threat concerns trade. Globalisation and trade liberalisation is already advancing apace in the Pacific region. The SPARTECA agreement seemed to offer benefits for Pacific exporters to Australia and New Zealand. Such benefits are already being eroded as the two countries move closer to each other under the Closer Economic Relation (CER) agreement and both support the free trade outcomes of the APEC and GATT agreements (Robinson 1995; Chandra 1996). In the case of garments, the result has been a shrinking differential between Fiji and its low-cost, large-scale competitors in Asia. The prospects for Pacific industries (invariably small-scale and hampered by high transport costs) being able to compete internationally on more open markets are slim indeed. In addition, despite recent assurances that the Sugar Protocol of Lomé will remain in place, there can be little comfort for Fijian sugar producers in the long-term future for much of their industry if they have to compete in the open market, following an inevitable long-term weakening or dismantling of the Lomé Convention. Contraction of the sugar industry, hitherto the shinning example of successful commercial agriculture in the Pacific, cannot be averted and there are serious economic, social and ethnic[2] implications for the country. Trade as a development strategy for the Pacific, then, is either likely to become a lot less efficacious with globalisation, or there will have to be a great deal more attention given to the much-talked-about but rarely achieved strategy of niche production and marketing in a more integrated and open trading environment.

Aid is the second area of concern. With the ending of the Cold War and the restructuring of metropolitan economies, high aid levels to the Pacific are under threat. The strategic importance of the Pacific Ocean or the value of nationhood status (that allowed small Pacific countries a seat and a vote at international forums) have diminished considerably (Wartho 1995). Even in French Polynesia, the end of nuclear testing is likely to bring a substantial fall in aid revenues and support from metropolitan France. Similarly, the market-oriented restructuring of economies in New Zealand and Australia has created a political environment in which it is much more difficult to sustain a welfare-based aid programme, supporting large public sectors in the Pacific, at a time when welfare services and public sector employment at home have been cut severely (Scheyvens and Overton 1995). The implications of such changing aid policies are already being felt in the Pacific. Facing virtual bankruptcy and under pressure from New Zealand, the Cook Islands has slashed civil servants' salaries and there were plans to cut the public service from 3,200 employees to 1,200 in 1996 - this in a country of less than 18,000 people. Niue, the Marshall Islands, French Polynesia and, perhaps soon, Papua New Guinea are facing similar pressure as donor largesse ends.

Such consequences of the broad process of globalisation are serious, yet the likely outcomes are not well appreciated. Leaders, such as Cook Islands Premier Sir Geoffrey Henry suggest that out-migration, in this case to the dole queues of New Zealand and Australia, will be the inevitable consequence of public sector cuts. In addition, the hoped-for expansion of the private sector has to come at a time when the purchasing power within the local economy is falling rapidly through public sector retrenchment or decline in export receipts. It was noticeable, if worrying, that at a conference of Pacific Island leaders in Nadi in July 1996, there was much talk of public sector cuts but very little realisation of the other economic problems that will face Pacific Island countries in a globalised world economy. Only Prime Minister Kamuta Latasi from Tuvalu offered a plaintive plea for other Pacific nations to accept migrants from his country.[3] Ward's (1989; 1993) suggestions of an empty Pacific in the future or one characterised by pauperism may not be far-fetched.

## Pacific Islanders as Global Citizens?

Yet such pessimism must be tempered with an alternative view, one which stresses social and cultural relations instead of the economic and political, and individual and household levels of analysis rather than the national. The other side of neo-colonial dependence, for some countries at least, was free migration, with special status within metropolitan immigration laws. This is something many Polynesians, in particular, have been quick and adept at exploiting and the Pacific has been seen as an 'ocean of opportunity'.

It has been suggested that many thousands of households and kin groups have operated as 'trans-national corporations of kin', allocating their resources (labour and capital) in ways which exploit economic opportunities yet meet social and cultural objectives (Bertram and Watters 1985; 1986; Munro 1990; James 1991). It is common to find members of kin networks spread through the wider Pacific region. Some family members live in the home village, being fully involved in the village society. 'Home' is also the hub for many important social functions: for customary ceremonies, for raising young children in the ways of the village, for providing a retirement hearth for the elderly, and for maintaining rights to land. Periodic return to the village, for Christmas visits, or for indefinite periods, is common and acts to reinforce the social and cultural bonds of the group (Chapman 1991). Others live and work away, in Auckland, Wellington, Sydney, Los Angeles, Vancouver or Salt Lake City (McCall and Connell 1993; Larner 1990; Loomis 1990; Luke 1993; Stanwix and Connell 1995; Vete 1995). Here they engage in the work and lifestyles of the host country and culture, yet maintain many of their customary ways and affiliations. Money is remitted home, to contribute to the church, to village projects, to support relatives, or sometimes to invest in business (Brown and Connell 1993a; 1993b).

Furthermore, this whole pattern of geographical spread and interaction can be seen as a social and cultural network, with flows of people, ideas, produce and money being often carefully directed, sanctioned and controlled by kin group members. Within the network, people are engaged in a wide variety of activities: subsistence or commercial agriculture, public sector employment or entrepreneurship in the islands,[4] and wage employment, business, education, or access to welfare services in the host countries. Throughout, the wider family unit and other familiar institutions, notably the church, remain as anchors for such a widespread and mobile society. Such flexibility and mutual support allows Pacific Island kin groups to operate in ways which can react quickly to changing circumstances at home or in the host country, whether the demands to meet funeral expenses and obligations or to cover the cost of family support. Population mobility is thus a critical household and kin group development strategy, one which can seek and exploit income generating activities at home or abroad and yet maintain social bonds and traditional obligations.

One indication of the extent of Pacific Island 'transnational corporations of kin' is the way many groups have succeeded in exploiting immigration regulations and laws across the region. People from the Cook Islands, Niue and the Tokelau Islands can enter New Zealand as New Zealand citizens. Special concessions and a long history of family linkages have also allowed many thousands of Samoans and Tongans to migrate to New Zealand and gain residency or citizenship status (Bedford 1984; 1985; 1986). As such, they can then move to Australia and gain access to even wider opportunities. In Samoa, those in Western Samoa can often move freely to American Samoa because of traditional and kinship links. Many then gain the rights of American citizens. A history of movement between Tonga and Hawaii has also developed and the inhabitants of French Polynesia, Wallis and Futuna and New Caledonia are treated as French citizens. There are many routes out of the Pacific to the rest of the world.

A consequence of such movements has been the emergence of multiple identities. Whilst Pacific Islanders maintain a strong sense of their origins, they also seem to adopt their new national identities with some facility (Hau'ofa 1987). This is illustrated clearly in the case of sports people. Boxer Jimmy Thunder fought a match against an American opponent in Queensland two years ago. The prelude to the fight was interesting: the Australian crowd stood for the American national anthem played for the challenger but then had to stay on their feet for Thunder's three anthems - those of Western Samoa (the country of his birth), New Zealand (where he lived most of his life) and Australia (where he was then residing)! In another sport, rugby league, a recent article (Raganivatu 1996) discussed the history of Pacific Islanders who had played rugby leagues for top league clubs in Great Britain. This included many players who had also represented New Zealand at test level, for example Mark Elia and Va'aiga Tugamala from Samoa, the Iro brothers from the Cook Islands, Sam Panapa and Tea Ropati from the Tokelaus, and Kurt Sorensen and George Mann from Tonga. Increasingly, it is the face of Polynesian sports stars that reflect the widening prominence, identity and residence of Pacific Island peoples.

Hau'ofa (1993), in a seminal essay outlining this positive view of Pacific Island people and their development prospects, proposed the idea of an 'Oceanic peoples', not restricted to their small island states and limited resources but, in drawing on a long history of migration and enterprise, able to exploit wide horizons. Globalisation, then is not something new. Many Pacific Islanders are now 'proto-global citizens', skilled, experienced and highly mobile, organising their societies and household economies in flexible ways and ready to exploit new frontiers.

It might be argued that this phenomenon of movement may provide an important development strategy for the Pacific Island region. Instead of bolstering national economies and bureaucracies, 'aid' may be better seen not in monetary terms but as liberal immigration policies, promoting globalisation of labour. The small size of many Pacific Island populations and their propensity to maintain links with their home islands, mean that they could be accommodated in countries such as Australia, New Zealand, USA, France and Canada. More liberal immigration policies may facilitate freer movement and wider involvement in the wider Pacific regional economy. In this sense, globalisation for the Pacific Islands may be much more about the feer movement of people than freer trade.

Yet this view should be treated with some caution. Not all Pacific islanders are able to move freely. Those in countries which do not have a close relationship with metropolitan countries and special immigration treatment are not able to operate in this way. These include most of the countries of Melanesia (except New Caledonia) and a number of the smaller states (Kiribati and Tuvalu). In addition, the optimistic view of remittances and mobility has long generated debate. Critics point to the tendency for remittance incomes to be spent on consumer items rather than investment besides remittance incomes diminishing over time. It is also a dangerous dependence on the economic health and hospitality of the metropolitan countries.[5] There are also serious structural problems that can arise for the home economies, with the bulk of the productive labour force abroad, and few viable income-generating activities at home to meet the generally high income expectations. In addition, social problems may arise in the host countries, especially when the wider kin and social bonds are weakened. Migrants and their children who have become more permanent residents are increasingly divorced from their home ties but only exist at the margin of the new society. In this case, their livelihoods may be dependent upon uncertain and low-paid employment, diminishing social welfare services and a host society which is sometimes hostile to the immigrants (Larner 1990; Krishnan *et al.* 1994).

## Globalisation and the Pacific Islands in Prospect

Therefore, in the Pacific Islands context, globalisation is very much an ambiguous process. The dominant view of a universal, positive and trade-driven process adopts a macro and economic perspective, but for the Pacific Islands, this does not appear as a desirable vision for the future, involving as it does generally bleak trading prospects and a radically restructured balance between the public and private sectors.  The global economy may virtually by-pass the Pacific Islands, except for the exploitation of minerals in a few countries and as tourist destinations in others.

Yet such a pessimistic view of globalisation in the Pacific ignores other perspectives, notably those which stress micro-economic levels and social-cultural processes.  Here, it is suggested that globalisation is already a central element of the lives of many thousands of Pacific Islands people.  They have adapted quickly to the new opportunities in the wider Pacific region and have used their customary advantages of strong kin affiliations and mobility to exploit them.  The notion of flexible accumulation, usually seen in new production technologies, can thus be applied to social units, as in the Pacific, which are able to shift resources, chiefly labour, across wide areas in order to meet both economic and cultural objectives.  Therefore, this chapter suggests that the analysis of globalisation may need to be broadened.  Outcomes and impacts are likely to be variable, not universal, and they will differ markedly depending on the scale of analysis (global, national, regional or household) and whether  the discourse is economic and political or social and cultural.

## Notes

1   The disadvantages of such a model, however, have been noted by a number of commentators and these have included the insecurity of the agreements and the uneven spread of the benefits, notably in the low wages paid to garment and other workers.
2   The sugar industry mostly involves farmers of Indian descent and they are likely to be the first casualties.  Yet, much of the recent expansion of the sugar industry has involved indigenous Fijians, either as growers themselves or as landlords.  Such expansion has been on marginal land which is the most likely area for contraction.  Paradoxically, then, the decline of an 'Indian-dominated' industry may hit many rural Fijians harder than the established Indian farmers on good land.
3   Unlike in most of the smallest island states, Tuvalu citizens do not have easy immigration access to metropolitan countries.
4   Brown and Connell (1993a), in the case of Tonga, have noted examples of business operation tied to a wider kin network.
5   For the debate on remittances in the Pacific, see Ahlburg 1995; Brown 1992; Brown and Connell 1993a; Brown, Foster and Connell 1995; Connell 1980; 1981; Connell and Brown 1995; Crocombe 1992; Faeamani 1995; James 1991; Macpherson 1992; and Walker and Brown 1995.

# References

Ahlburg, D.A. (1995), 'Migration, Remittances, and the Distribution of Income: Evidence from the Pacific', *Asian and Pacific Migration Journal*, Vol. 4, No. 1, pp. 157-167.

Bedford, R.D. (1984), 'The Polynesian Connection: Migration and Social Change in New Zealand and the South Pacific', in Bedford, R.D. (ed.), *Essays on Urbanisation in Southeast Asia and the Pacific*, Department of Geography, University of Canterbury: Christchurch, pp. 113-141.

_____, (1985), 'Immigrant and Locally Born Pacific Island Polynesians: Two Populations?', *New Zealand Geography*, Vol. 41, No. 2, pp. 80-83.

_____, (1986), 'International Migration in the South Pacific: A New Zealand Perspective', *New Zealand Population Review*, Vol. 12, No. 1, pp. 32-48.

Bertram, I.G. (1987), 'The Political Economy of Decolonisation and Nationhood in Small Pacific Societies', in Hooper, A., Britton, S., Crocombe, R., Huntsman, J. and Macpherson, C. (eds.), *Class and Culture in the South Pacific*, Centre for Pacific Studies, University of Auckland, and Institute of Pacific Studies, University of the South Pacific: Auckland and Suva, pp. 16-29.

_____ and Watters, R.F. (1985), 'The MIRAB Economy in South Pacific Microstates', *Pacific Viewpoint*, Vol. 26, No. 3, pp. 497-519.

_____ and Watters, R.F. (1986), 'The Mirab Process: Earlier Analyses in Context', *Pacific Viewpoint*, Vol. 27, No. 1, pp. 47-59.

Brohman, J. (1995), 'Universalism, Eurocentrism, and Ideological Bias in Development Studies: From Modernisation to Neoliberalism', *Third World Quartely*, Vol.16, No. 1, pp. 121-140.

Brown, R.P.C. (1992), *Sustainability, Aid and Remittance-Dependent Pacific Island Economies: Lesson from Africa?*, Economics Division Working paper 92/2, Research School of Pacific Studies: Canberra.

_____ and Connell, J. (1993a), 'The Global Flea Market: Migration, Remittances and the Informal Economy in Tonga', *Development and Change*, Vol. 24, No. 4, pp. 611-647.

_____ and Connell, J. (1993b), *Entrepreneurs in the Emergent Economy: Migration, Remittances and Informal Markets in the Kingdom of Tonga*, Economics Division Working paper 93/3, Research School of Pacific Studies: Canberra.

_____, Foster, J. and Connell, J. (1995), 'Remittance, Savings, and Policy Formation in Pacific Island States', *Asian and Pacific Migration Journal*, Vol. 4, No. 1, pp. 169-185.

Campbell, I. (1992), 'A Historical Perspective on Aid and Dependency: The Example of Tonga', *Pacific Studies*, Vol. 15, No. 3, pp. 59-75.

Chandra, R. (1993), 'Contemporary Industrialization in Fiji', in Waddel, E. and Nunn, P.D. (eds.), *The Margin Fades: Geographical Itineraries in a World of Islands*, Institute of Pacific Studies, University of the South Pacific: Suva, pp. 29-48.

_____ (1996), 'Manufacturing in Fiji: Mixed Results', *Pacific Economic Bulletin,* Vol. 11, No. 1, pp. 47-62.

Chapman, M. (1991), 'Pacific Island Movement and Socio-economic Change: Metaphors of Misunderstanding', *Population and Development Review*, Vol. 17, No. 2, pp. 263-292.

Connell, J. (1980), *Remittances and Rural Development: Migration, Dependency and Inequality in the South Pacific*, Development Studies Centre, Australian National University: Canberra.

_____ (1981), 'Migration' Remittances and Rural Development in the South Pacific', in Jones, G.W. and Richter, H.V. (eds.), *Population, Mobility and Development,* Development Studies Centre, Australian National University: Canberra, pp. 229-255.

_____ (1986), 'Small States, Large Aid: The Benefits of Benevolence in the South Pacific', in Elridge, P., Forbes, D.K. and Porter, D. (eds.), *Australian Overseas Aid,* Croom Helm: Sydney and London, pp. 57-78.

_____ (1988), *Sovereignty and Survival: Island Microstates in the Third World,* Department of Geography, University of Sydney: Sydney.

_____ (1991), 'Island Microstates: The Mirage of Development', *The Contemporary Pacific*, Vol. 3, No. 2, pp. 251-287.

_____ and Brown, R.P.C. (1995), 'Migration and Remittances in the South Pacific: Towards New Perspectives', *Asian and Pacific Migration Journal,* Vol. 4, No. 1, pp. 1-33.

Crocombe, R. (1992), *Pacific Neighbours: New Zealand's Relations with Other Pacific Islands,* MacMillan Brown Centre for Pacific Studies: Christchurch.

Faeamani, Sione'U (1995), 'The Impact of Remittances On Rural Development in Tongan Villages', *Asian and Pacific Migration Journal,* Vol. 4, No. 1, pp. 139-155.

Fairbairn, T.I.J. (1985), *Island Economies: Studies from the South Pacific,* Institute of Pacific Studies, University of the South Pacific: Suva.

_____ (1987), 'Subsistence Economy and Policy Options for Small Island economies', in Hooper, A., Britton, S., Crocombe, R., Huntsman, J. and Macpherson, C. (eds.), *Class and Culture in the South Pacific*, Centre for Pacific Studies, University of Auckland, and Institute of Pacific Studies, University of the South Pacific: Auckland and Suva, pp. 56-69.

Gibson, L. (1991), 'The Politics of Aid in the South Pacific: Australasia and the Islands', *Review,* Vol. 19, pp. 3-7.

Grynberg, R. (1993), 'Trade Liberalisation in the Post-Cold War Era and its Implications for the Fiji Sugar Industry', *Journal of Pacific Studies,* Vol. 17, pp. 132-160.

_____ (1995), *The Impact of the Sugar Protocol of the Lomé Convention on the Fiji Economy,* Economics Division Working paper 95/8, Research School of Pacific Studies: Canberra.

_____ and Powell, M. (1995), *A Review of the SPARTECA Trade Agreement,* Economics Division Working paper 95/4, Research School of Pacific Studies: Canberra.

Hau'ofa, E. (1987), 'The new South Pacific Society: Integration and Independence', in Hooper, A, Britton, S., Crocombe, R., Huntsman, J. and Macpherson, C. (eds.), *Class and Culture in the South Pacific*, Centre for Pacific Studies, University of Auckland, and Institute of Pacific Studies, University of the South Pacific: Auckland and Suva, pp. 1-12.

_____ (1993), 'Our Sea of Islands', in Waddell, E., Naidu, V. and Hau'ofa, E. (eds.), *A New Oceania,* School of Social and Economic Development: Suva, pp. 2-16.

James, K. (1991), 'Migration and Remittances: A Tongan Village Perspective', *Pacific Viewpoint*, Vol. 32, No. 1, pp. 1-23.

Knapman, B. (1986), 'Aid and the Dependent Development of Pacific Island states', *Journal of Pacific History*, Vol. 21, No. 3, pp. 139-152.

Krishnan, V., Shoeffel, P. and Warren, J. (1994), *The Challenge of Change: Pacific Island Communities in New Zealand 1986-1993*, Institute for Social Research and Development: Wellington.

Larner, W. (1990), 'Labour Migration and Female Labour: Samoan Women in New Zealand', *Australian and New Zealand Journal of Sociology,* Vol. 27, No. 1, pp.19-33.

Loomis, T. (1990), *Pacific Migrant Labour, Class and Racism in New Zealand*, Avebury: Aldershot.

Luke, T.W. (1993),'Localised Spaces, Globalished Places: Tracing the Pacific Rim', *Journal of Pacific Studies*, Vol. 17, pp. 38-56.

Macpherson, C. (1992), 'Economic and Political Restructuring and the Sustainability of Migrant Remittances: The Case of Western Samoa', *The Contemporary Pacific*, Vol. 4, No. 1, pp. 109-135.

McCall, G. and Connell, J. (eds.) (1993), *A World Perspective on Pacific Islander Migration: Australia, New Zealand and the USA.,* Centre for Pacific Studies, University of New South Wales: Kensington.

Michal, E.J. (1993), 'Protected States: the Political Status of the Federated States of Micronesia and the Republic of the Marshall Islands', *The Contemporary Pacific*, Vol. 5, No. 2, pp. 303-332.

Munro, D. (1990),'Transnational Corporations of Kin and the Mirab System: the Case of Tuvalu', *Pacific Viewpoint*, Vol. 31, No. 1, pp. 63-66.

Neemia, U. (1992), 'Decolonization and Democracy in the South Pacific', in Crocombe, R., Neemia, U., Ravuvu, A. and vom Busch, W. (eds.), *Culture and Democracy in the South Pacific,* Institute of Pacific Studies, University of the South Pacific: Suva, pp. 1-8.

Overton, J.D. (1996), Restructuring Oceania: Regional Reconfigurations of Economic and Political Relations in the Pacific', in Yue-man Yeung (ed.), *Global Change and the Commonwealth,* Chinese University of Hong Kong: Hong Kong.

Raganivatu, A. (1996), 'In League with Britain', *Pacific Islands Monthly*, Vol. 66, pp. 7-44.

Robinson, G. (1995), 'New Zealand's Trading Policy in an Age of Globalisation: GATT, APEC and CER', *Pacific Viewpoint*, Vol. 36, No. 2, pp. 129-141.

Scheyvens, R. and Overton, J. (1995), 'Doing Well Out of Our Doing Good: A Geography of New Zealand aid', *Pacific Viewpoint*, Vol. 36, No. 2, pp. 195-210.

Sevele, F. (1987), 'Aid to the Pacific Reviewed', in Hooper, A., Britton, S., Crocombe, R., Huntsman, J. and Macpherson, C. (eds.), *Class and Culture in the South Pacific*, Centre for Pacific Studies, University of Auckland, and Institute of Pacific Studies, University of the South Pacific: Auckland and Suva, pp. 71-76.

South Pacific Commission (1993), *South Pacific Economies: Statistical Survey*, No. 13, South Pacific Commission: Noumea.

_____ (1995), *Overseas Trade 1991 - Statistical Bulletin of the South Pacific*, No. 45, South Pacific Commission: Noumea.

Stanwix, C. and Connell, J. (1995), 'To the Islands: The Remittances of Fijians in Sydney', *Asian and Pacific Migration Journal*, Vol. 4, No. 1, pp. 69-87.

Sutherland, W. (1982), 'SPARTECA and Continued Problems of Dependence', *Review*, Vol. 9, pp. 4-11.

Vete, Mele Fuka (1995), 'The Determinants of Remittances among Tongans in Auckland', *Asian and Pacific Migration Journal*, Vol. 4, No. 1, pp. 55-68

Walker, A. and Brown, R.P.C. (1995), 'From Consumption to Savings? Interpreting Tongan and Western Samoan Sample Survey Data on Remittances', *Asian and Pacific Migration Journal*, Vol. 4, No. 1, pp. 89-115.

Ward, R.G. (1989), 'Earth's Empty Quarter? The Pacific Island in a Pacific Century', *Geographical Journal*, Vol. 155, No. 2, pp. 235-246.

_____ (1993), 'South Pacific Island Futures: Paradise, Prosperity, or Pauperism?', *The Contemporary Pacific*, Vol. 5, No. 1, pp. 1-21.

Wartho, R. (1995), 'Conceptualising Oceania in the New World Disorders', *Pacific Viewpoint*, Vol. 36, No. 2, pp. 211-226.

Watters, R.F. (1987), 'Mirab Societies and Bureaucratic Elites', in Hooper, A., Britton, S., Crocombe, R., Huntsman, J. and Macpherson, C. (eds.), *Class and Culture in the South Pacific*, Centre for Pacific Studies, University of Auckland, and Institute of Pacific Studies, University of the South Pacific: Auckland and Suva, pp. 32-54.

# 5  New Zealand, National Identity and the Pacific Century

*Michael ROCHE*

## Introduction

The world of the 1990s would seem to offer empirical evidence to supporters of the 'end of the State thesis' and others advancing theorisations about the accelerating globalisation of economy and culture. New Zealand might be seen as exemplary in this respect, for successive governments since 1984 have vigorously embraced economic deregulation and state sector restructuring. The previously sheltered New Zealand economy has become more integrated into the world economy. Overseas investors have brought capital into New Zealand, a process hastened by an expansive state asset sales programme begun in the late 1980s. Legislative revision has simplified overseas investments and changed the immigration criteria. Concurrently New Zealand's foreign trade policy has proceeded along similar lines with involvement in the Cairns Group of agricultural exporting countries, supporting the GATT reforms and, via APEC, seeking greater economic engagement in the Asia-Pacific region in order to capitalise on the sustained economic growth in this area as the 'Pacific Century' dawns.

Official embracing of the globalised economy is also evident in changes to border functions, not only in terms of tariff reductions but through the CER (Closer Economic Relations) agreement with Australia (in effect creating a free trade zone across the Tasman), in harmonisation and mutual recognition of industry standards and codes between Australia and New Zealand as well as in the relaxation of visa requirements for overseas travellers in order to encourage commerce and tourism.

Some of the difficulties associated with the borderless economy have been driven home in recent months. In May 1996, Ministry of Agriculture (MAF) officials discovered unwelcome fruit fly larvae in fruits brought into the country by tourists and not declared to MAF Quarantine officials. More extensive field checks revealed isolated infestations of fruit flies in Mt. Roskill, part of the Auckland metropolitan area. Horticultural exporters faced immediate difficulties as importing regions placed a ban on fruits from within specific radii of the outbreaks (80 km in the case of Australia, 20 km for Taiwan, 15 km for Tonga and Japan and 7.2 km for USA). Given that horticultural crops contribute $NZ1.4 billion to export earnings, the potential damage is immense. Earlier in 1996, Ministry of Forestry officials discovered forest-dwelling moth species - regarded as a threat to timber exports. For an economy still heavily dependent on a range of primary product exports, the biological impact of such introductions in a borderless world is potentially catastrophic. While exotic introductions pose a real biological and economic threat and are worthy of closer attention, there are other implications of the borderless world that merit attention from a New Zealand perspective. These concern the manner in which the state-led pathway to globalisation has shaken and unsettled some prevailing notions of national identity among the New Zealanders, especially those of a European-settler descent.

For over a decade New Zealand has experienced traumatic social and economic transformations. Some of these changes, from an economic perspective have been outlined earlier (Roche 1994). This chapter, touches on the social turmoil of the last decade by attempting to make some sense of changing fortunes and meanings during an era of enormous economic and social transformations. And yet, many contemporary concerns and issues, arguably triggered by economic restructuring and deregulation in the 1980s, have developed into controversies which seem increasingly to be represented as lodged in a social and cultural realm.

These include, in no particular order, the referendum which supported replacing the First Past the Post (FPP) electoral system with a Mixed Member Proportional Representation (MMP) system; discussions about moving to a Republic; recommendations to end using the Privy Council as New Zealand's highest court of appeal; the Museum of New Zealand project; and immigration policy. Running across all these episodes and debates is a common thread in the form of an anxious and anguished re-examination of national identity by those of European (Pakeha) descent. This provides the major focus of this chapter: the impact of a borderless world on culture and identity. Not only does this appears to be a meaningful question for New Zealanders to think through but in a more general sense it encourages research on a globalising world to move out from economics and to pay attention to global-local relations.

**Economic Restructuring in the 1980s**

After Britain's entry to the EEC in 1973 the New Zealand government increasingly adopted interventionist regulatory strategies to try and sustain the economy. These efforts were exemplified by the Supplementary Minimum Prices agricultural subsidy scheme and the wages and prices freeze. As the economic crisis deepened, a snap election in 1984 saw a Labour Government returned to office. Labour's foreign policy, notably the anti-nuclear stance leading to the breach with the USA and the 'Rainbow Warrior' affair, arguably deserves a place in accounts of the end of the Cold War world order. At home, however, Labour followed an equally bold agenda and vigorously implemented a major programme of economic deregulation and state sector restructuring, surpassing, in some ways, the examples of Thatcherism and Reaganomics in introducing a neo-Liberal agenda (Britton, Le Heron, Pawson 1991). The subsidy regime was suddenly withdrawn from 1984 to 1986 with the objective of removing distortions to the market and forcing agricultural producers to be internationally competitive. New Zealand agricultural support remains the lowest in the OECD at a meagre 4 per cent in 1995 compared with 15 per cent in the USA, 49 per cent in the EU and 77 per cent in Japan. The embracing of market mechanisms and international competitiveness was to signal the commitment of New Zealand politicians to 'free trade' and the global economy.

Embracing globalisation does not, however, preclude searching for profitable markets in particular regions. State agencies and the private sector were, from the mid 1980s, increasingly identifying Asian economic growth rates as a sign of new markets to try and enter. The Asia 2000 Foundation initiative, for example, administers grant programmes in the areas of business, education/media, and culture/sport to foster greater New Zealand interest in Asia.[1]

Consistent with neo-Liberal positions and globalisation, the New Zealand Government has relaxed many 'boundary' rules and regulations relating to travel, investment and foreign exchange. Gone were the tight foreign exchange controls of the 1970s and early 1980s when overseas travel funds were pegged to a predetermined amount obtainable only a week before travel on presentation of tickets at your bank. In the horticultural arena strenuous efforts were made to open Japan to New Zealand apple imports, which in part required persuading Japanese officials that selected regions were fire blight free (Le Heron and Roche 1995). One indicator of the open nature of the New Zealand economy is that ownership of the local stock market in 1994 was 51 per cent in overseas hands (Scott 1994). Of the direct overseas investors in New Zealand some have arrived via the state's asset sales programme. For example, Telecom was sold in 1990 for $NZ4,250 million to a consortium of Ameritech, Bell Atlantic, Fay Richwhite and Freightways (NZ).  In the forestry sector, Rayonier (NZ) Ltd a subsidiary of US-based parent company purchased cutting rights to 97,453 ha of state forest for $NZ366 million in 1991.  International Paper Ltd, the world's second ranked pulp and paper company has entered via the purchase of a shareholding in the local company of Carter Holt Harvey.

Critics of economic deregulation and state sector restructuring have made sustained efforts to challenge the intellectual foundations of the neo-Liberal experiment, though with little apparent success.  Opponents of the Government's strategy were concerned about the uneven social impact of the move to market mechanisms; the replacement of the 'universality' of state welfare provisions by a targeted 'safety net' approach also attracted criticism.  The demands placed on church welfare services, pressures on food banks in major metropolitan areas and discussions on poverty all suggest greater social inequality in the 1990s (Varcoe 1996).

It is pertinent, at this juncture, to look at the impact of economic restructuring on national identity.  The focus is on the successive representations of national identity shared by the white-settler population, which is numerically the largest group by the mid-19th century.  The critical feature of contemporary European (Pakeha[2]) New Zealander's identity rests on the colonial past.  Thus, for example, Kelsey (1995:172) observes that:

'The dominant New Zealand identity is a fictional construct based on a colonial supremacism, patriarchal values, and derivations of British culture.'

and Berg and Kearns (1996:100) also note that:

'In the case of New Zealand, we suggest that nationalist and statist ideologies lead to a representation of New Zealanders in terms of the beliefs, attitudes, and cultural practices of a bourgeois pakeha masculine subject.'

For this group (as opposed to Maori and other minority groups) the formation of a national identity would seem to rest on a pioneering past (particularly bush settlements), decisive episodes on the battlefields (notably the Gallipoli Campaign in World War 1) and in a particular economic and social relationships with Britain - ('home' to some whose parents have migrated and whose children might not ever return to visit).  The end of the Dominion capitalist relationship between New Zealand and Britain brought on by the entry to the EEC would, doubtless, have initiated a slow reassessment of national identity (Sinclair 1986).  This process was accelerated markedly by the events of the 1980s both in terms of external challenges and domestic realignments felt through the reassertion of Maori sovereignty (Awatere 1984; Walker 1990).

Some research would suggest that this turmoil is consequent upon the political commitment to globalisation. The Government's desire to reposition New Zealand with respect to the Asia-Pacific economies implies an associated redefinition of national identity and that this alternate sense of identity also clashes with the strands of meaning in older versions of Pakeha national identity. This leads Bell, (1996:192) to reflect that:

'The effect of all of this on national identity has been profound. The population has moved from a certainty about our identity as a welfare state with an egalitarian ethos of collective responsibility to a new insecure situation couched in new language: 'level playing field' (battlefield?) 'windows of opportunity' and so on. Inevitably there has been growing understanding about destiny and identity.'

Other scholars writing in a more expansive fashion inlude Poggi (1990:27) who observes that:

'Generally speaking, a successfully constructed national identity facilitates communication between the people sharing about it, creating a backdrop of shared assumptions and understandings to their interactions.' '... More specifically, it can be argued that if strangers meeting in the market share a strongly felt sense of nationhood, this induces among them something of that sense of trust that in local communities is based on extensive, prolonged, mutual acquaintance, and this facilitates their entering into contractual arrangements with each other.'

Reflecting on the allied theme of nationalism in the late 20th century historian, Hobsbawm (1993:169) reflects that it 'is simply no longer the historical force it was'. He continues to observe that 'the current phase of essential separatist and divisive 'ethnic' group assertion' has no positive programme or prospect and derides it as 'entirely irrelevant to the problems in the late twentieth century, for which it provides no general solution or, except by a rare and happy accident, no local solutions' (Hobsbawm 1993:170). Nevertheless he acknowledges that the force of sentiment in pressing for what he terms 'ethnic/linguistic' identity cannot be dismissed. His explanation for its nature and rationale brings the global economy to centre stage (Hobsbawn 1993:171).

'What is the nature of this cry of distress or fury? Time and again such movements of ethnic identity seem to be reactions of weakness and fear, attempts to erect barricades to keep at bay the forces of the modern world ... What fuels such defensive reactions, whether against real or imaginary threats, is a combination of international population movements with the ultra-rapid fundamental and unprecedented socio-economic transformations so characteristics of the third quarter of our century.'

Ultimately, Hobsbawm (1993) rejects the 'politics of identity' as a moving force of history, seeing it rather as a symptom of social disorganisation. However, his discussion most clearly focuses on Europe, including Eastern Europe, with some excursions into the former colonial empires. New Zealand in the 1990s, formerly a nineteenth century British settler economy is an already populated land and now positioned on the Asia-Pacific periphery, does not fit comfortably within Hobsbawm's (1993) discussion.

Debate continues about the future on nation states and the fate of national movements. Some see evidence revealing increasing globalisation of the economy as a sign of a decline in state sovereignty. Others, however, point to the emergence of regional economic and political alliances as signs that states can combat globalishing tendencies (Taylor 1994). These tendencies have been played out in New Zealand where the economy is globally integrated and where the government has made attempts to redefine New Zealand as part of a greater Asian World.[3]  Bell and McLennan (1995:5) note that:

'This claim is transparently linked to the Government's desire to  encourage foreign investment and ownership, provoking an opposing and popular argument that this represents an unacceptable decline in a national sovereignty'.

Another sociologist, Claudia Bell (1996:187), meanwhile pointedly observes that:

'Politicians' insistence on calling this country 'part of Asia' demonstrates that official identity is arbitrary and manipulatable.  Where expedient, regional orientation may be a component of national identity.'

and that

'The issues of national identity and the state comes up most often in New Zealand in discussions about international relationships for security and trade.'

Kelsey (1996:140) explores the association of identity with trust, community and markets as noted earlier by Poggi (1990) for New Zealand in the context of globalisation.

'The dictators of international competition, the quest for foreign investment and the ideology of the global free market set the parameters for national government decisions on employment, environment, fiscal monetary and social policy.  In a very real sense, globalisation increasingly renders national economics, politics, legal regulations, culture identity and even territorial boundaries relics of a bygone age.'

She continues to offer a reassessment of the fashion and direction in which the New Zealand Government is reorienting national identity and offers a blunt appraisal of what underpins such actions.  Initially, she observes that New Zealand now looks on East Asia collectively as a significant export market.  Subsequently, she also identifies the Asia 2000 Foundation initiatives of the National Government as a strategy with three objectives: firstly, to develop a framework for New Zealand links to Asia and secondly, to raise the level of business contacts and opportunities.  The last objective she sees as being quite different:

'The third includes a conscious strategy to reorient New Zealand dominant culture and identity away from the anachronistic colonial past towards its newer economic destiny with the Asia region.' (Kelsey 1996:142)

The element of economic opportunism inherent in such a policy has not escaped attention domestically or from overseas' scholars. Clearly, however, writers from a number of social science disciplines recognise significant social and cultural impacts stemming from New Zealand's rapid integration into a globalising world economy.

## Contesting Identity and Place

Geographers in New Zealand collaborated in a multi-authored book which sought to document the changes of the 1980s (Britton, Le Heron and Pawson 1991) and in a follow up exercise half a decade on, 'focused on the issues of the mid-1990s: globalisation, corporate strategies, labour flexibility, social policy, policies of consumption and sites of local action' (Le Heron and Pawson 1996:xviii). Interestingly and significantly, the new book includes a chapter, 'Sense of Place', which briefly discusses issues of national identity in the context of immigration policy and Maori identities. Pawson (1996:348) reflects on the recent attempts to 'reinvent the national image with the adoption of the 'clear green' pose' but simultaneously stresses that these images and identities are 'hotly contested'. The reasons for this are two-fold:

'This is the result not only of the post - 1980s transparency of the country to external influences, and the uneven domestic impacts of economic restructuring. It is also due to the recovery from within of previously obscured narratives of place.' (Pawson 1996:348)

The dismantling of the universal welfare state and economic deregulation along with new immigration policies introduced in the mid-1980s, produced new political debates and tensions. These social and economic reforms have tended to reinforce the marginalisation of Maoris, Pacific Islanders and women. Simultaneously, Maori and iwi (tribal) groups have restored the Treaty of Waitangi to the fore so that the Government, usually distanced by its being referred to as 'The Crown', has attempted to redress historically based grievances, particularly in the areas of land and fisheries (Spoonley 1995; 1995a). Three ongoing events in New Zealand illustrate something of the current conflicts. These are the future of the Privy Council, planning for the Museum of New Zealand, and the immigration policy.

*The Privy Council*

On 10th April 1996, the National Government announced that it proposed to introduce legislation which would abolish the right of appeal to the Privy Council in Britain and reorganise the Court of Appeal so that it would become the highest court in New Zealand. The Privy Council originated as an inner advisory committee to the Sovereign on matters of state. The first New Zealand appeal to the Privy Council dates from 1849, nine years after the establishment of the Crown Colony. Since then 235 appeals have been made of which 84 have been allowed, 137 dismissed and 14 withdrawn. The appeals have been over-whelmingly for civil cases only (Mahoney 1996). New Zealand remains the largest of 14 countries still allowing appeals to the Privy Council. Australia, Canada, Malaysia and over 30 other countries have severed these links. This issue is not new, having been discussed in the Royal Commission on Courts in 1978 and advocated by retiring Presidents of the Court of Appeal in 1987 and 1994. Labour's Justice Minister, Sir Geoffrey Palmer, indicated his support for such moves in 1987. The Solicitor-General in reporting to the Government in favour of reorganising the Court of Appeal and severing the Privy Council connection, has drawn attention to the financial costs of taking cases to the Privy Council. Legal experts also point to differences of philosophy in the area of commercial laws between the New Zealand Court of Appeal's emphasis on fairness and equity and the Privy Council's emphasis on the certainty and predictability, including strict interpretation, of written agreements (Plunkett 1996; Clifford 1996). The Attorney-General's motives for favouring this reform are believed to be in other areas, notably concerns that Privy Council rulings cannot be ignored by the New Zealand government. In the past under First-Past-the-Post (FPP) such decisions could be overturned comparatively easily by an Act of Parliament. Under Mixed-Member-Proportional (MMP) and the prospect of minority governments such recourse may not be possible hence the desire to end the Privy Council link (Plunkett 1996).

Response from the legal profession was considered and focused on a perceived shortcoming of the new proposal, namely that New Zealand, unique amongst 'Westminster style' democracies would have only one court of appeal. Many newspapers featured editorials that supported the removal of 'another prop to New Zealand's colonial past' while simultaneously reporting Maori concerns about the severing of a link regarded as eroding the Treaty of Waitangi. Moves to sever the Privy Council link mean different things to different groups. Some Pakeha would see it as a sign of the growing maturity of New Zealand as a nation state; that New Zealand courts should be the final court of appeal. For the Maori, however, the same announcement may be read as a calculated move to break the relationships between Maori and the Crown initiated by the signing of the Treaty of Waitangi between chiefs and Captain Hobson, representing Queen Victoria, in 1840. Furthermore, denial of privy Council appeals can be interpreted as a means of creating conditions where future governments could back away from the Treaty claims process and adherence to the 'principles of the treaty' currently embodied in some pieces of legislation.

The breaking or retention of this link to Britain contributes quite different meanings to both the Pakeha and the Maori sense of identity. Furthermore, there are a number of Pakeha identities at stake, with some gaining reinforcement from a severing of the Privy Council ties and others in favour of the *status quo* and the imperial legacy who might feel losers in terms of their sources of national identity.

*Museum of New Zealand*

After much concerted effort dating back to 1984 the Government agreed in 1986 to fund a Museum of New Zealand to be housed in a new building on the Wellington waterfront to open early in 1998. Construction of the $280 million building is now well advanced and will provide spacious accommodation compared with the cramped and inadequate Dominion Museum. A 1992 Act of Parliament (New Zealand Statutes 1992, No. 19, Clause 4) established the museum to:

> 'Provide a forum in which the nation may present, explore and preserve both the heritage of its cultures and knowledge of the natural environment in order to better understand and treasure the past to enrich the present; and to meet the challenges of the future.'

The committee considering the Bill recommended that the Museum should have one name, The Museum of New Zealand Te Papa Tongarewa[4] rather than two distinct English and Maori names (New Zealand Parliamentary Debates 1992:522, 6496). In applauding this change, Hon. Peter Tapsell, the Member for Eastern Maori commented:

> 'the museum should endeavour to ensure that it both expresses and recognises the mana and significance of Maori first, European second, and other major traditional cultures. There is not a single Maori in New Zealand who believes, or would say that no other cultural groups have made a contribution to New Zealand's heritage. However, every Maori would insist that Maori made the first and greatest contribution, and that contribution has remained with us. It is our hope that all New Zealanders will come to see that as part of our heritage of and as part of the heritage of all New Zealanders as a whole.' (NZPD 1992:522, 6498)

Labour Member of Parliament, Margaret Austin, supported the intent of the Bill, for example:

'What better way to celebrate the turn of the century in New Zealand than with the completion of a project of this importance that demonstrates to New Zealanders and to the world our taonga and our cultural heritage.' (NZPD 1992:522, 6501)

and later during the second reading she remarked that:

'the museum expresses and recognises the mana and significance of Maori, European, and other major traditions and cultural heritages and that the museum provides the means for every such culture to contribute to it effectively as a statement of New Zealand identity.' (NZPD 1992:523, 7443)

The Member of Parliament for Northern Maori, Dr. Bruce Gregory, highlighted that the English and Maori segments of the name had different connotations and joined with his colleagues in suggesting that:

'the Bill highlights cultural aspirations, and attempts to unify aspects of our society that relate to history, and to the treasures that have been so eloquently talked about in the house tonight.' (NZPD 1992:523, 7448-9).

The debate surrounding the passage of the bill endorsed a bicultural thrust, although this was usually expressed in the context of comments about the Museum of New Zealand (MONZ) contributing to national identity without any contradictions being perceived. Initial reactions of support were tempered by concerns raised by provincial galleries and museums about iniquitous funding for a Wellington-based project. Some of these concerns were addressed in the legislation and required MONZ to co-operate with other museums (Rudman 1996). Former Prime Minister, Sir Wallace Rowling, who chaired the Museum organising committee, signalled as far back as 1990 that MONZ would seek to break new grounds in terms of dispensing with order department/collection based models of museum organisation. For Rowling, MONZ's role in terms of cultural identity was paramount (in Rudman 1996):

'Every country should have a cultural focus. We are building something for the 21st century, a people place, a place of national turf where it is all happening... The target will be to achieve in both practical and aesthetic terms a manifestation of how New Zealanders see themselves, and in ways that will enthral and inspire. The very soul of the nation will be exposed.'

The way in which MONZ is endeavouring to develop concepts and displays were at once innovative and controversial. Museum Chief Executive, Cheryl Southeran was quoted as saying:

'... the furore swirling around the museum about too much Maori content is not strictly about balance in the museum at all. It's about the whole issue of national identity and living together ... This is a vigorous debate about national identity and we would be doing something wrong if we were not positioned in that debate actively.' (Sotheran in Rudman 1996)

Letters to the editor in Wellington newspapers *(The Dominion and Evening Post)* record a continuing increasingly antagonistic debate about MONZ centring on claims about imbalances in space, interpretation and political correctness.[5] One left wing journalist and *Dominion* columnist was quick to make links between culture and the global economy. In Trotter's (1996) view MONZ was reflecting a 'world culture' perspective which deconstructed dominant western views. At the same time he observed that national cultures continue to endure while world culture is abandoned to sophisticated international authorities:

'What has gone unnoticed by the ordinary person in the street is the curious relationship developing between World culture and global economic change. As the ability of the nation state to control its own destiny is undermined by the rise of international financial markets, so too is the integrity of national culture ... the sense of being culturally besieged is fuelling national identity crises all over the western world.' (Trotter 1996)

These comments appeared along with a small news item as newspaper debate over MONZ was reaching a new high. It noted that a survey conducted by the Museum Directors Federation and the New Zealand Tourism Board indicated that over half the international visitors to museums said they wanted to see Maori culture but only 42 per cent reported noting it *(The Dominion, 1996)*.

The MONZ project has posed some difficult questions for professional historians involved in developing the Pakeha history exhibitions. Chief Historian of Internal Affairs, Jock Phillips, who worked on the MONZ project outlined some of the issues to historians earlier this year (Phillips 1996). He observed that one of the proposed themes for research was national identity and outlined the strongly negative reactions from the Maori History and Art and History teams, noting:

'That the nation as a collectivity should be expressed made the historians and scholars at the museum uncomfortable. They suggested that the promotion of national identity was too monocultural an aim, too crippling of diversity, too dangerous in imposing and reinforcing stereotypes.' (Phillips 1996:6)

At the same time, Phillips (1996) noted the museum was 'publicly promoted and funded as a route to national identity' leading to the problem of how to explore and affirm national identity while taking account of the historical committee concerns about such a project. The result has been the planning of three exhibitions which will suggest three different approaches to questions of identity:

the peopling of New Zealand (New Zealand as a nation of immigrants);
interaction with a distinctive environment (the land shaping the people); and
exhibiting ourselves (histories of the ideas of national identity). Amongst the
diversity and pluralism, Phillips (1996) identifies two larger universal threads
about Pakeha national identity embedded in the exhibition. The first of these
relates to the immigration experience, of upheaval, voyage and establishing new
roots. In Phillip's (1996) words:

> 'this experience is a key to New Zealand identity since it happened to every pakeha
> New Zealander on his/her ancestors. It is a founding trauma which must be at the core
> of identity. The fact that we are a migrant people, attempting to make a new home,
> must be the central truth to our identity.'

Secondly, the settlers did not arrive into an empty land.

> 'Further as a migrant people settling an inhabited land we as pakeha must come to
> terms with the fact that our settlement here and our identity as New Zealanders
> necessarily rests on a history of conflict with the tangata whenua.' (Phillips 1996:21)

In summing up, Phillips expressed his fears about the complexity of the task:

> 'In planning the history exhibitions, I have tried to balance public expectations that the
> museum will solve New Zealand's identity - crisis with my own integrity as a historian.
> It has been a huge and perhaps impossible assignment.' (Phillips 1996:26)

The wider complaints carried in newspaper letters to the editor and other stories
suggest the difficulty of the task; that many 'New Zealanders' feel MONZ is
devoting too much space to Maori projects. These critics will, doubtless, be
troubled by the Pakeha history exhibitions as well, because the old stable and
easily grasped national myths will not be reproduced.

The reaction to MONZ, as exemplified by ongoing press and TV coverage,
points to a (Pakeha) national identity under threat. Berg and Kearns (1996) in an
extended study of contemporary contests over place naming and identity rhetorics
of race, culture and nation, emphasise that a straight forward Pakeha-Maori split
is too simplistic. A detailed examination of the MONZ project may well reveal
on ongoing contest in which 'the specific interests of a hegemonic Pakeha
masculinity are asserted as universal national interests applicable to all New
Zealanders' (Berg and Kearns 1996:117). The current state of affairs is,
doubtless, some way from the confidence and exuberance with which Rowling (in
Rudman 1996) had announced the project as exposing the 'very soul of the
nation'. Instead, the Museum project reveals a serious gap between museum
management and (Pakeha) public expectations and what Phillips (1996) sees as
the essential place of immigration and conflict in Pakeha identity.

**Immigration Policy**

Although expressions of concern (mostly from Auckland) were at most 'a definite protest against the loss of economic sovereignty' (Trotter 1996), in the last six months, however, immigration has become a subject of heated debate accompanied by increasingly frequent accusations of racism.[5] Current debates over immigration policy centre around changes made in the last decade to replace some country preference with a points system in 1991 (Brooking and Rabel, 1995) along with liberalising visa requirements. This, as Bedford (1996, 350) notes, was 'an important component of the Fourth Labour Government's approach to reducing the significance of boundaries in international mobility.' The points system had facilitated the entry of migrants with skills and capital from non-traditional source areas leading Bedford (1996:351) to suggest that:

'immigration from Asia has become the major driving force in the contribution which international migration of non-New Zealand citizens makes to population change in New Zealand.'

New immigrants in the 1980s arrived as part of the internationalisation of the economy. Bedford (1996:304) notes, for instance:

'The attraction of Asian and European migrants to New Zealand lies in large part in opportunities to invest in development of the country's natural resources.'

In addition, he draws attention to official recognition of the value of dispensing with 'association' as a desirable outcome of immigration in favour of the contribution of ethnic heritage and diversity. By 1996, the change is of such magnitude that a return to the pre-1980s status quo is impossible, generating a source of difference that the Pakeha population had had to face up to (in conjunction with a more visible and assertive Maori presence). Grief (1995:19) suggests the 'immigration policy has always been enshrouded in controversy and tied to an economic strategy'. However, he observes that if New Zealand chooses to reject Asia and tries to return to a fortress New Zealand society, the 'economic future is very bleak'.

Many writers point to the connection between immigration policy and globalisation as it relates to issues of national identity on the part of Pakeha New Zealanders. For example:

'It therefore seems highly probable that future policy and dominant attitudes towards immigration and cultural diversity will be determinedly the outcome of that larger debate about the meaning of New Zealand national identity' (Brooking and Rabel 1995:49).'

and Ip (1995:199) notes that:

'In many ways, mainstream New Zealanders' wariness towards the new Asian immigrants is but a manifestation of their own fundamental unease about their identity ... The British Empire is no more... New Zealand has to decide what the country should become. With the Tangata whenua increasingly vocal and aware of their own history and future and a largely homogenous European population statistically in the majority, how is New Zealand trying to come to terms with her geopolitical position as an Asian-Pacific nation? Where Asian immigration is concerned, New Zealand has a fundamental conflict between her historical heritage and her geo-economic realms. The physical presence of the new Asian migrants is a constant reminder of this issue, which many people are not yet ready to face up to.'

Currently, tensions have been heightened, especially through the New Zealand First political parties' promotion of an immigration debate in the run up to the 1996 (MMP) elections. In an effort to make an emphatic response the Race Relations Conciliator, Rajen Prasard, authorised full page newspaper advertisements depicting racists as small brained/small minded. Berg and Kearns (1996:100) note that New Zealand First leader, Winston Peters 'seems to cross back and forth between Maori and Pakeha subjectivities.'

The Privy Council and MONZ can be discussed in terms of both Maori and Pakeha senses of identity. The immigration policy also has different implications for Maori and Pakeha, some of which have been recorded earlier. Although Phillips (1996) identifies the immigration experiences of New Zealanders of European origins as central to historical senses of identity, the late 20th century migration, triggered by the creation of an immigration policy consistent with a market driven economy, has produced the latest jolt to the comfort zone of Pakeha identity. Popular constructions of immigration would seem to focus on 'Asian' migrants, especially those with assets, who have concentrated in Auckland. Taking a historical perspective the inevitability of changing identities is apparent once Britain looked to the EEC.

## Discussion

To date, geographers in New Zealand have asked few questions about national identity/identities (exceptions include Berg and Kearns 1996; Pawson 1996). Researchers in other disciplines have, in contrast, paid growing attention to these issues. Examples, from other disciplines are historians (Sinclair 1986; Phillips 1996); sociologists (Bell 1996; Bell and MacLennan 1995), philosophers (Novitz and Willmot 1988), and lawyers (Wilson and Yeatman 1995; Kelsey 1996). There is an implicit and sometimes explicit territoriality in some of this work, and closer connections with processes driving economic change are sometimes absent.

The mainstream geographical writing on national identity uses nationalism as its reference point. Thus, Hoosen (1994) for example, points to what he regards as the absence of adequate theorisation about the importance of territoriality to nationalism. This leads him to posit in the immediate aftermath of the fall of the Berlin Wall and the collapse of the Eastern Bloc that:

> 'the return of geography, like the return (not the end) of history, is therefore a major factor to be reckoned with in evaluating the phenomena of national identity across the world in the closing years of this century and beyond.' (Hoosen 1994:378)

Too frequently, however, the reader is left feeling that 'the return of geography' extends only so far as providing a vantage point from which to enjoy the spectacle of Marxist scholars struggling to account for a resurgence of nationalist feelings in continental Europe.

The writings of some 'new cultural' geographers, in contrast, may offer more insight. Smith's (1993) comparison of nation building and immigration policy in Canada and the United Kingdom provides a useful starting point. She notes:

> 'Immigration policy and nation building therefore must be two sides of a single coin. Immigration controls which are always socially and economically selective, may be regarded as one expression of a political idea of who is, or could be eligible to receive citizenship entitlements of residence and citizenship.'

Contrasting British and Canadian immigration policy ('control' compared to 'regulation') gave rise, she suggests, to two contradictory visions of nationhood. For Britain, immigration legislation has functioned to produce a stable vision of nationhood based on exclusion and control compared with Canada emphasising regulation and selection of suitable migrants to emphasise vision of growth and change. New Zealand, since the late 1980s, has arguably put in place an immigration policy consistent with the goals of increasing the openness of the New Zealand economy and facilitating the imports of skills and capital. If this assessment is accurate, then it may go some way to explaining why the economic changes nationally and globally (especially Britain's closer engagement with the EU and the Asia-Pacific initiatives of the government) have such an impact on destabilising old ideas of national identity.

The New Zealand economy has been so changed by the events of the last decade that it is difficult, if not impossible to imagine a return to the former intervention strategies. There is a political commitment to globalisation for several reasons. Firstly, continued support of the neo-Liberal economic agenda; secondly, the dependence on exports produce, albeit more are value added than in the earlier decades; and thirdly, a desire to diversify the export markets and products which has led to the participation in the Asia-Pacific centred economic growth. Politically, some of these moves can also be read as the growing maturity of New Zealand as a nation and the forging of political and economic alliances not dependent on the older colonial relationships.

There are several messages from the New Zealand experience with globalisation. It reveals that globalisation is usually described in terms of increasing capital flows, expansion of offshore financial market, uptake of computerised information technology and finally, moves towards new regional groupings. Its achievement does not necessarily carry with it the goodwill of the population. In New Zealand, the 'reforms' of the 1980s were not only economically far reaching, but deeply unbalancing of national identity, rendering Pakeha New Zealanders vulnerable to assertions of sovereignty by Maori and producing further unease over the 'globalised' identity that seems to be favoured by politicians pushing for closer economic involvement in Asia.

## Conclusion

Many significant questions require attention. In particular, although a number of writers draw a connection between economic restructuring and changes to national identity, the relationship is under-theorised. To proceed along this pathway in the New Zealand setting will require that attention be paid to at least some of the following:

• The relationship between economy and identity as mediated by the state
• Recognition of the touch stones of national identity and an examination of the fashion in which the state might seek to promote a national identity
• A reworking of the globalisation-localisation literature with a view to an understanding of the identity and territoriality
• Establishment of a dialogue amongst economic geographers interested in globalisation and new cultural geographers. Goodwill, mutual respect and a shared interest will be necessary to this task.

Vanishing borders and globalisation by their very nature invite an internationalist, outward looking attitude and stance. Linking globalisation with identity serves as a reminder that an outward extension from one perspective may be an 'incursion' into the home territory of another. That such 'incursions' in a borderless world have a cultural as well as an economic dimension is perhaps likely to be overlooked, especially when the view is from the boardroom. External incursions can also mobilise indigenous peoples to reassert their identities and rights over natural resources which further destabilises latter day colonial national identities.

# Notes

1   Additional funding including a one-off grant of $2 million and an extra $1.8 million for 1996-99 were announced in May 1996. Foreign Minister, Don McKinnon, indicated the Government's desire to secure the Asia 2000 Foundation so it could attract financial support from private companies. The importance of the Asian export markets was reflected in the appointment of business leaders to the board (*Evening Post*, 14th May 1996).

2   The choice of words and even use or non-use of capitals provides strong positional signals. The title of this chapter is intended to signal that the focus is on a generalised European settler descended population's sense of national identity. The term, Pakeha is used to identify New Zealanders of European descent. Some European New Zealanders take strong exception to this term, objecting to its capitalisation, or seeing historical insults in the etymological meaning of this Maori word which is defined as 'imaginary beings resembling men, with fair skins' (Walker 1990:94). Others will use Pakeha as a means of asserting that their links to the 19th Century migration experience are now effectively broken and as a sign of New Zealand's political and national identity. This position has been concisely explored by historian and writer, Michael King (1985:12).

> 'I make no apology for use of the terms Maori and Pakeha. Some have argued there is no 'Maori' culture in New Zealand, only an analysis of New Zealand Polynesian tribal traditions... Others regard Pakeha as a pejorative expression and opt for European. I cannot agree that it makes sense to identify as European those whose physical and cultural origins are one, two or even four of five generations removed from Europe.'

Some Maori writers use Aotearoa instead of New Zealand as a sign of their identity, status and Tangata whenua and as a means of asserting their own Tino Rangatiratanga. Some Pakeha writers who wish to signal their congnisance of the post colonial-nature of society use Aotearoa/New Zealand. In the 1980s, Spoonley (1995:99) notes, some Pakeha 'have moved from seeing themselves as 'colonial' (in relation to the British) to a perception of themselves as 'colonisers' in relation to the Maori.'

3   It is not suggested that Pakeha national identity has been immutable nor that it has not been the source of doubt and anxiety in the past. Britain's entry to the EEC in 1973, for example, heralded the end of an era of Dominion capitalism and witnessed some new expressions of an independent foreign policy under the third Labour Government (1972-75). The last decade, however, has witnessed a greater number of potentially more destabilising events than in earlier years.

4   Te Papa Tongarewa, literally 'treasures of the earth'.

5   The fate of an 19th Century European furniture collection has become a symbolic touch stone for those seeing MONZ as virtually excluding things European from the Museum (Fulton 1996). Historians have also publicly challenged each other's views. Thus Graham Butterworth writes 'the project has been captured by the politically

correct.' Her (Southeran's) bland use of the key words 'colonialist', 'partnership' and 'challenging' are giveaways (*The Dominion*, 21st March 1996) leading Jock Phillips, the Government's Chief Historian and the history concept leader for MONZ to caution against drawing incorrect conclusions and urging people to withhold judgement until the museum opens (*The Dominion*, 27th March 1996). Phillips (1996) own evaluation of the connections between MONZ and identity was the subject of his Beaglehole address at the New Zealand History Conference in 1996.

## Postscript

In early December 1996 a coalition comprised of National, ACT, New Zealand First and United became the government in the aftermath of the first MMP election. In a matter of weeks it became clear that plans to sever the link with the Privy Council would not proceed. The press at around this same time noted that the MONZ project was expected to cost $NZ317 million to complete, nearly $40 million in excess of original estimates.

## References

Awatere, D. (1984), *Maori Sovereignty*, Broadsheet: Auckland.

Bell, A. and McLennan, G. (1995), 'National Identities: From the General to the Pacific', *Sites*, Vol. 30, pp. 1-8.

Bell, C. (1996), *Inventing New Zealand Everyday Myths of Pakeha Identity*, Penguin: Auckland.

Berg, L. and Kearns, R. (1996), 'Naming as Norming: 'Race' Gender and the Identity Politics of Naming Places in Aotearoa, New Zealand', *Environment and Planning D: Society and Space*, Vol. 14, pp. 99-122.

Britton, S., Le Heron, and Pawson, E. (eds.) (1991), *Changing Places: A Geography of Restructuring*, New Zealand Geographical Society: Christchurch.

Brooking, I. and Rabel, R. (1995), 'Neither British nor Polynesian: A Brief History of New Zealand's Other Immigrants', in Grief (ed.), pp 23-49.

Clifford, J. (1996), 'A High Court New Zealanders are Privy to', *Sunday Star Times*, 14th April.

Fulton, D. (1996), 'Treat Elgar Collection with Pride', *The Dominion*, 19th April.

Grief, S. W. (ed.) (1995), *Immigration and National Identity in New Zealand*, Dunmore Press: Palmerston North.

Hobsbawm, E.J. (1993), *Nations and Nationalism since 1870: Programme, Myth, Reality*, Canto: Cambridge, 2nd edition (1st published 1990).

Hoosen, D. (1994), 'Afterwords - Identity Resurgent - Geography Revived', in Hoosen (ed.), pp. 371-374.

_____ (ed.) (1994), *Geography and National Identity*, Blackwell: Oxford.

Ip M. (1995), 'Chinese New Zealanders: Old settlers and New Migrants', in Grief (ed.), pp. 371-374.

Jackson, P., and Penrose, J. (eds.) (1993), *Constructions of Race, Place and Nation*, UCL Press: London.

Kelsey, J. (1995), 'Some Reflection on Globalisation Sovereignty and the State', *Sites*, Vol. 30, pp. 165-172.

_____ (1996), 'Globalisation and the Demise of the Colonial State Option for Decolonisation in Aotearoa/New Zealand', in Trainer, L. (ed.), pp. 137-160.

Le Heron, R. and Pawson, E. (1996), *Changing Places: New Zealand in the Nineties*, Longman: London.

Le Heron, R. and Roche, M. (1995),'A 'Fresh' Space for Food's Place', *Area*, Vol. 27, No. 1, pp. 23-33.

Mahoney, D. (1996), 'Privy Council for a Final Judgement', *Evening Standard*, 12th April.

*New Zealand Parliamentary Debates* (NZPD) (1992).

*New Zealand Statutes* (1992), Museum of New Zealand Te Papa Tongarewa, Novitz, D. and Willment, W.E. (1989), *Culture and Identity in New Zealand*, P. Books: Wellington.

Novitz, D and Willmont, W.E. (1989), *Culture and Identify in New Zealand*, P. Books: Wellington.

Pawson, E. (1996), 'Sense of Place', in Le Heron, R. and Pawson E. (eds.), pp. 347-384.

Perry, N. (1994), *The Dominion of Signs*, Auckland University Press: Auckland.

Phillips, J.O.C. (1996), *Our History, Our Selves, The Historian and National Identity*, Beaglehole Lecture.

Plunkett, P. (1996), 'What Might Replace the Privy Council', *The Dominion*, 11th April.

Poggi, G. (1990), *The State: Its Nature, Development and Prospects*, Polity: Cambridge.

Roche, M. (1990), 'Perspective on the Post 1984 Restructuring Of Forestry in New Zealand', *Environment and Planning A*, Vol. 22, pp. 941-959.

_____ (1990a),'The New Zealand Timber Economy 1840-1935', *Journal of Historical Geography*, Vol. 16, No. 3, pp. 295-313.

_____ (1994), 'Britain's Farm to Global Producer? Food regimes and New Zealand's Changing Links within the Commonwealth', Paper presented at the Commonwealth Geographical Bureau Conference, Hong Kong.

Rudman, B. (1996),'Museum Expose the Soul of the Nation', *Sunday Star Times*, 14th April.

Scott, L. (1994), *Ownership Structure of the New Zealand Stockmarket*, Doyle Patrson Brown: Wellington.

Sinclair, K. (1986), *The Native Born: The Origins of New Zealand Nationalism*, Massey Memorial Lecture 1986, Massey University Occasional Publication No. 8.

Smith, S.J. (1993), 'Immigration and Nation-building in Canada and the United Kingdom', in Jackson, P. and Penrose, J. (eds.), pp. 50-80.

Spoonley, P. (1995), 'Constructing Ourselves: The Post-colonial Politics of Pakeha', in Wilson, M. and Yeatman, A. (eds.), *Justice and Identity Antipodean Practices*, Bridget Williams Books: Wellington, pp. 96-115.

_____ (1995a), 'The Challenges of Post-colonialism', *Sites*, Vol. 30, pp. 48-68.

Taylor, P. (1994), 'The State as Container: Territorially', *Progress in Human Geography* Vol. 18, pp. 151-162.

The Dominion (1996), 'Tourist Demand Maori Culture', 16th March.

Trainer, L. (ed.) (1996), *Republicanism in New Zealand*, Dunmore Press: Palmerston North.

Trotter, C. (1996), 'Museum Should Heed Orwell's Words', *The Dominion*, 23rd March.

Varcoe, J. (1996), 'Food Banks', in Le Heron, R. and Pawson, E. (eds.), pp. 242-243.

Walker, R. (1990), *Ka Whawhai Tonu Matou Struggle Without End*, Penguin: Auckland.

# 6 Visa-waiver and the Transformation of Migration Flows Between New Zealand and Countries in the Asia-Pacific Region, 1980-1996

*Richard BEDFORD and Jacqueline LIDGARD*

## Introduction

One of the most obvious indicators of the 'vanishing border' is the removal of a requirement to obtain a visa before travelling to another country. The proliferation of visa-waiver arrangements between pairs of countries has transformed the nature of migration between these countries. New Zealand has a very liberal visa-waiver policy by comparison with other traditional countries of immigration such as Australia and the United States. This chapter explores the development of this policy as part of the wider transformation of New Zealand's immigration policy, and the drive to 'locate' New Zealand more firmly in the Asia-Pacific region. An integral component of New Zealand's multi-faceted push to be recognised as 'part of Asia' is the promotion of a greater awareness of Asian cultures and contexts amongst New Zealanders, and New Zealand's attractions and opportunities amongst Asians. The extensive interchanges of 'tourists', or short-term visitors travelling at will without the need to apply for visas, is seen to be essential for developing this awareness.

## Facilitating Travels in the New Zealand Context

International passenger travel has exploded in the past decade, and nowhere more dramatically than in Southeast and East Asia. For instance, the region is forecast to account by 2010 for 400 million passengers yearly, or half the global total, from 122 million passengers and a third of world traffic in 1993 (*New Zealand*

*Herald*, 11th June 1996). Facilities to cope with the demand for travel across national boundaries are barely coping as the burgeoning middle classes of the Asian 'tiger' economies seek the pleasures of travel to other countries. A global airline industry alliance, the Air Transport Action Group, estimates that Asia-Pacific nations will have to spend US$200 billion on airport extensions or new facilities by 2010. Other studies suggest a bill twice this size by 2005 (*New Zealand Herald*, 11th June 1996).

The demands placed on Asian airports are not just a function of an awakening interest amongst domestic populations in international travel, including emigration. They are also linked, obviously, to the popularity of Asian countries as destinations for tourists, business people and, where tight immigration regulations allow, immigrants from other parts of the world. Facilitating the movement of millions of people entering and leaving countries is a major logistical problem facing customs and immigration authorities.

An international trend is to try and minimise the paper work which travellers have to complete as part of the process of crossing national boundaries. A common strategy adopted to capture more tourists is to remove the need for entry visas to be obtained before departure for overseas destinations. Usually this requirement is dropped as a result of reciprocal visa-waiver agreements between two countries. In the case of most countries which are members of the European Community, the strategy adopted has been a common customs and immigration border. Once an international traveller has negotiated the right to cross this border in one country, there is no restriction on travel to other countries subscribing to the Schengen Agreement. In the case of North America, Canadian and US citizens can easily negotiate the land border dividing their countries; people of other nationalities have to complete more formalities. The Trans-Tasman Travel Arrangement allows New Zealanders and Australians unrestricted access to both countries. To all intents and purposes, international borders have 'vanished' for millions of travellers in some parts of the world - selected millions, because not everyone has the same rights and privileges of entry.

New Zealand is unusual in the Asia-Pacific region because of a willingness by successive governments to enter into bilateral visa-waiver agreements. In part, this is due to the fact that New Zealand is a long way from anywhere except Australia and some small Pacific states. It has no land borders with neighbouring states and is not subject to some of the pressures associated with illegal migration which characterise flows into many Asian countries. However, it is not just isolation, and the fact that there are no common land borders, which has encouraged the visa-waiver system. Much more important is the way in which immigration policy is used to facilitate both the access which New Zealanders can gain to countries overseas, as well as the desired foreign policy objectives of New

Zealand governments.

Indeed, many of the visa-waiver agreements have been negotiated to ensure that peripatetic New Zealanders can travel more easily to places in which they are interested. Another way in which New Zealand's interests are served, especially in the broad arena of strengthening bilateral trade and capital flows, and establishing stronger cultural and social links, is through offering different types of visa-waiver agreements as components of bilateral packages during negotiations between national leaders. Two examples of the way immigration policy is used to further New Zealand's foreign policy imperatives in the recent push into Asia are given in the latter part of the chapter.

New Zealand has had a significant net gain of population over the past 15 years from what is termed in the official statistics as 'short-term' migration. Between 1st April 1981 and 31st March 1996 the total net gain to the country's population through international migration (+76,800) was, apparently, due to a surplus of short-term arrivals over short-term departures. There was actually a small net loss of permanent and long-term migrants (-150) during the 15 years because the loss of New Zealanders leaving the country for 12 months or more (-237,650) exceeded slightly the gain of non-New Zealanders arriving to stay for at least a year (+237,500). 'Immigration' (the arrival of people intending to settle or to stay for a reasonably long time in New Zealand) merely served to replace the 'emigration' of New Zealanders. There was no overall growth in population due directly to permanent and long-term migration. The aggregated net gain came from differences between numbers of short-term arrivals and departures.

In New Zealand's case at least, then, it is quite misleading to examine the demographic impacts of international migration with reference to permanent and long-term migrants only. The highly diverse and complex short-term flows, which encompass the movement behaviour of tourists, friends and relatives, business men and women, entertainers, conference participants, and students amongst others, have a very important role to play in population gains (and losses) from different parts of the world.

The argument in the chapter is presented in three sections. The first reviews briefly the history of New Zealand's visa-waiver agreements, with particular reference to the development of these sorts of links with Asian countries since 1986. In the second section, two Asian examples are examined to illustrate the ways in which foreign policy initiatives, rather than immigration policy imperatives, can influence the development of schemes facilitating flows of tourists, business people and, most recently, young travellers seeking to augment their savings by temporary work while on holiday. The third section turns to the statistical evidence of the contribution which short-term migration from different parts of the world has been making to overall net migration gains (and losses) in

New Zealand since 1981. Particular attention is focussed on flows which have been influenced by visa-waiver arrangements introduced since 1986.

## Visa-waiver Arrangements and the Vanishing Border

The history of visa-waiver arrangements in New Zealand goes back to the end of the Second World War and the passing of the New Zealand Citizenship Act in 1948. This Act defined much more precisely who was entitled to New Zealand citizenship. All British subjects born in New Zealand, naturalised in New Zealand, or ordinarily resident in New Zealand for at least one year, became New Zealand citizens automatically as of 1st January 1949 (McKinnon 1996). Before this date New Zealanders had a common British nationality, along with residents of Canada, Australia and other 'Dominions' in the British Empire.

### The Early Arrangements with European Nations

The introduction of New Zealand citizenship did not change much the patterns of migration to New Zealand from countries within the British Commonwealth. There were few controls over migration from the United Kingdom, Canada and especially Australia. Pacific Islanders living in countries administered by New Zealand (the Cook Islands, Niue, Tokelaus and Western Samoa) had special privileges, while movements from other Pacific countries were linked to the nature of New Zealand's strategic, social and economic interests. Links with Asian countries were relatively weak in the 1940s, although relationships with some Commonwealth countries in the region, especially Malaysia (or Malaya as it was then) and Singapore, developed during the 1950s under the Colombo Plan.

The New Zealand Citizenship Act did necessitate the negotiation of more formal arrangements regarding the entry of people from non-Commonwealth countries. The first group of such countries to gain some special privileges with regard to entry of their citizens to New Zealand included a number of former allies in the Second World War - France (1947), Sweden (1948), Switzerland (1948), Denmark (1949), Netherlands (1949) and Norway (1950). Arrangements were reached between the government of New Zealand and the governments of these countries to waive the requirement for visas for tourists and business people visiting the other country for less than a specified maximum period (usually three months but in the case of some countries, for example, France up to six months). These arrangements were enshrined in high-level Exchanges of Notes which continue to have the status of Treaties. Details of the specific conditions of each visa-waiver agreement can be found in the New Zealand Treaty Series.

The formalisation of bilateral visa-waiver arrangements between New Zealand and selected European countries did not result in any significant increase in the movement of visitors in either direction immediately after they were implemented. Until the 1960s, tourist and business travel between New Zealand and countries in Europe involved a lengthy and time-consuming journey by sea. However, the arrangements did symbolise a 'special relationship' between the countries concerned and, once international air travel made New Zealand (and Europe) much more accessible to tourists, the visa-waiver arrangements facilitated considerably the process of negotiating international borders.

In addition to these early visa-waiver arrangements, there were also agreements with certain countries over the mutual abolition of fees for visas. The first agreement of this kind was with the United States (1937, amended 1949). Visas were still required, but there would be no charge for the issuing of these. During the 1950s and 1960s, a number of European countries were added to the fee-waiver list: Federal Republic of Germany (1955), Israel (1958), Turkey (1958), Italy (1961), Greece (1961), and the USSR (1967). Other European countries to be included in the visa-waiver list after 1950 were Luxembourg (1951), Monaco (1952), Austria (1958), Federal Republic of Germany (1972), Finland (1973) and Iceland (1974).

## The Inclusion of Selected Asian Countries

The first Asian countries to be included in the privileged visa-waiver/fee-waiver systems were Japan (visa-waiver, 1970) and the Philippines (fee-waiver, 1962). In the case of Japan, it seems that it was access by New Zealanders to Japan that stimulated the Exchange of Notes between the New Zealand Ministry of Foreign Affairs and the Japanese Embassy on 15th May 1970 concerning the abolition of visas for visits of up to thirty days (extended to 90 days, at the request of Japan, in 1976). In the case of the Philippines, the Exchange of Notes on 12th and 14th June 1962 concerning the mutual abolition of visa fees for visits not exceeding 59 days was covered by a Treaty. The development of a movement of students between the Philippines and New Zealand (student visa fees for visits of up to two months were also abolished) may have been a factor in the negotiation of this particular arrangement.

Through the 1970s, only a small number of new agreements were negotiated, partly because of a significant tightening of immigration policy after 1974, and partly because of a concern from the late 1970s that the existing Immigration Act (1964) needed substantial re-writing to meet the needs of New Zealand in the late twentieth century. Attempts were made to introduce a new Act in the early 1980s, but these foundered in the political confusion which surrounded the last years of the highly interventionist Muldoon government. It was not until August 1986 that a substantive review of immigration policy was published (Burke 1986), and just over a year later a new Immigration Act (1987) came into force.


## The Immigration Policy Review, 1986

Late in 1985 the New Zealand government advised governments of those countries with which they had visa-waiver arrangements already in force that they were standardising these with a view to having a more consistent policy regarding privileges extended to visitors. It was noted in the *Review of Immigration Policy, August 1986* that 'in the year to 31st December 1985 over 600,000 people, or about 90 per cent of visitors other than New Zealand residents, were able to enter New Zealand without visas or prior entry requirements' (Burke 1986:30). The government saw no need to change the temporary entry arrangements that governed this free flow across New Zealand's border, although there was seen to be considerable scope for bringing much greater consistency to the multiplicity of tourist visa arrangements.

In the *Immigration Policy Review, August 1986* the following statement is made concerning visa-waiver provisions from the beginning of 1986:

> From 1st January 1986 visa free entry arrangements with the countries of Western Europe, Japan, Canada and the United States, and the period of initial stay authorised, have been standardised at three months. (In recognition of treatment accorded New Zealand travellers in Britain, United Kingdom citizens will continue to be granted six-month periods of stay on arrival). It remains open to all visitors to apply for an extension of stay up to a total of 12 months should they so wish. One consequence of this move is that reciprocal arrangements can now be negotiated with Spain and Portugal to permit visa-free entry for New Zealand tourists and business visitors. The Government will examine the scope for extending visa-free entry to other countries, particularly to major tourist sources, as soon as more effective screening systems are available and new immigration legislation is in force (Burke 1986:30-31).

An important caveat added to the standardisation of visa-waiver arrangements was the removal of restrictions on visitors seeking work while in New Zealand. Immigration policy in force until 1986 made it illegal for visitors to seek work while in New Zealand without specific authority to do so. The Labour Government, however, decided that people already in New Zealand as visitors could take up employment incidental to their holiday, subject to certain conditions. From the beginning of 1986, the 23 District Offices of the

Department of Labour were authorised to issue work permits to visitors who had a written employment offer which could not be satisfactorily filled from job seekers on the local register of unemployed people. The main reason given for this liberalisation of visitor access to work in New Zealand was the long-standing tradition of New Zealanders going overseas, especially to the United Kingdom, and gaining 'overseas experience' in work as well as in social and cultural contact. The importance of the amended working visitor policy was seen to lie 'not so much in the economic impact as in the contribution it makes to the creation of international understanding and knowledge of other cultures, particularly amongst younger people' (Burke 1986:31).

## Visa-waiver Arrangements in the Late 1980s

The significance of the 1986 policy review for the visa-waiver system is that it favoured a substantial extension of these sorts of arrangements to countries which were important sources of tourists travelling to New Zealand, or destinations for New Zealanders travelling overseas. Late in 1986 a number of Pacific Island countries were included (Fiji, Kiribati, Nauru, Tonga, Tuvalu, Western Samoa) - all countries with which New Zealand had special work permit schemes or long-established economic, education, religious or medical links. The extension of visa-free access to New Zealand for citizens of Fiji, Tonga and Western Samoa was short-lived. In February 1987, the visa-waiver arrangements, which had been unilaterally declared by New Zealand in December 1986, were terminated, largely because of a fear of non-compliance with the three month time limit for a visitor's visa. There was a substantial growth in visitor numbers after the requirement for a visitor's visa was waived. The government was not prepared to wait and see if these people returned to the islands within three months. They feared an explosion in the numbers of 'overstayers'.

Only one Asian country, Singapore, was included in the December 1986 set of arrangements. For three others, Malaysia, Indonesia and Thailand, arrangements for visa-waiver were included in the First Schedule of the Immigration Act (1987). The standard provision of free entry for up to three months applied. It should be noted that, as with the arrangements with Pacific countries in 1986, these visa-waiver provisions for Asian tourists were a unilateral move by New Zealand, not requiring the agreement of any other party. Bilateral negotiations were to come later in the case of some countries. In fact, later in the 1980s New Zealander visitors were granted visa-free entry to all three countries, although not for a period as long as three months.

**Visa-waiver in the 1990s**

During the early 1990s the visa-waiver system came under intense scrutiny during discussions between the Australian and New Zealand governments about the possibility of establishing a common customs and immigration border for the purposes of facilitating passenger entry into the two countries. A serious problem for Australia in these negotiations was the fact that the great majority of visitors to New Zealand could enter without a visa. All visitors to Australia, except Australian and New Zealand residents, required a visa. The Trans-Tasman Travel Arrangement, which permits New Zealanders and Australians free access for any length of time to both countries, is something of a policy anomaly for the Australians.

The Australian authorities endeavoured to persuade their New Zealand counterparts to abandon several of its bilateral visa-waiver arrangements. This was not considered to be an option by New Zealand. As noted earlier, many of these arrangements have the status of treaties, and to abolish them would require a unilateral decision by the New Zealand government which could only be interpreted as an 'unfriendly' act by the other party. The New Zealand government had no intention of jeopardising the various opportunities visa-waiver arrangements afforded New Zealanders, or the significant tourist traffic which had escalated sharply with the advent of mass international air travel during the 1980s in particular. By 1990 tourism was one of the largest industries in New Zealand, in terms of contribution to GDP. The New Zealand government saw this industry, and the various bilateral arrangements which contributed to its growth, as essential for the development of the national economy into the 21st Century.

The common border discussions foundered in 1993 when the Australian Prime Minister suddenly withdrew from negotiations over access of New Zealand airlines to the Australian domestic market. In the ensuing 'cooling' of trans-Tasman relations, the Ministry of Foreign Affairs concluded visa-waiver arrangements with the Korean and Brunei governments. These arrangements came into effect in July 1993. A reciprocal agreement was reached with the Republic of Korea and signed in August 1994. Attempts by the Taiwan government to get similar provisions for Taiwanese visitors during 1994 were not successful, however. Under an agreement with the People's Republic of China (PRC) in 1972, New Zealand recognised the government of the PRC as the sole government of China, and accepted that all official contacts between New Zealand and Taiwan would cease. None of the OECD countries has visa-waiver arrangements with Taiwan. As far as the Taiwanese are concerned, this is not a satisfactory arrangement, especially given the significance of Taiwan as a source of tourists for New Zealand, and the fact that New Zealanders have free entry to the country for up to 14 days.

## The Situation in 1996

By June 1996 New Zealand had visa-waiver arrangements with 33 countries. Twenty-one of these are with countries in Europe[1], 7 are with countries in Asia (Brunei, Indonesia, Japan, South Korea, Malaysia, Singapore, Thailand), 5 are with countries in the Pacific (Kiribati, Nauru, Tuvalu, French Polynesia and New Caledonia), and 2 are with North American countries (Canada and the United States of America). In addition, there is the special Trans-Tasman Travel Arrangement which covers all forms of population movement between New Zealand and Australia.

These arrangements covered the entry of almost 90 per cent of the 1.5 million overseas visitors (excluding New Zealand residents) who came to New Zealand in the year ended 31st March 1996. They also ensured that most of the 956,000 New Zealand residents, who departed for short stays overseas during the same period did not have to apply for visas. There is little doubt that visa-waiver provisions have contributed positively to the development of tourism in New Zealand. It is a moot point, however, whether they have had a profound impact on the volume of tourist flows into (and out of) the country. Australia, with its strict policy regarding visa requirements, had also experienced massive growth in tourist numbers.

The significance of visa-waiver provisions in a range of bilateral contexts is recognised in a review of visitor policy which aims to produce a consistent framework for the assessment of visa-waiver arrangements and related temporary working holiday schemes. The New Zealand Immigration Service (NZIS) is determined to get an acceptable framework in place to ensure a more consistent approach is applied to proposals for visa-waiver schemes and associated bilateral arrangements. Foreign policy initiatives, however, continue to play an important part in developing these relationships as the recent examples of working holiday schemes with Malaysia and the Republic of Korea illustrate.

## Foreign Policy Initiatives

During the 1990s there has been increasing pressure from the Ministry of External Relations and Trade (later the Ministry of Foreign Affairs and Trade) for removal of the requirement for citizens of a number of Asian countries to obtain visas before visiting New Zealand. This pressure became intense around 1992 as the New Zealand economy began to grow rapidly, and Asian immigration picked up sharply as a result of the introduction of a points system in November 1991. It was argued by representatives of the tourist industry, amongst others, that the requirement for citizens of these three countries to obtain visas before visiting New Zealand was adversely affecting tourism, investment and trade. A waiver of visas for tourists and entrepreneurs would demonstrate that the New Zealand government was prepared to take firm action to back up the case for working more closely with Asian nations. There has also been a push for the extension to important trading partners on the Asia-Pacific rim of other 'special arrangements', such as the working holiday scheme.

## The Working Holiday Scheme

The working holiday scheme was initiated in the 1970s with the United Kingdom following the tightening of immigration regulations in New Zealand. This scheme allowed young New Zealanders to work in the United Kingdom (and, at that time, in many countries in Europe) for up to two years. The arrangement was not fully reciprocal, although provisions for UK citizens to work in New Zealand while on holiday have been in existence for many years. During the 1980s reciprocal working holiday schemes were negotiated with Canada and Japan.

By 1992 the Ministry of External Relations and Trade (MERT) was pushing for similar arrangements with several European countries, as well as Malaysia. In the case of the European countries, it was recognised that the development of a common border in Europe, and the gradual tightening up of regulations governing work for short-term visitors, was making it virtually impossible for New Zealanders, seeking to gain 'overseas experience', to work in Europe. MERT was keen to promote the bilateral working holiday schemes as a way of allowing young New Zealanders to gain direct experience of work methods and practices in other countries, as well as to broaden their cultural understanding of the different peoples who were now travelling to New Zealand as tourists in much larger numbers.

### The Malaysian Working Holiday Scheme

Malaysia was chosen as the first country in Southeast Asia for a working holiday scheme, largely because of long-standing education and defence ties, the widespread use of English as a second language, some common professional qualifications, the potential for economic links to be strengthened, and a proposal by the Prime Minister of New Zealand to make an official visit in 1994. The Ministry of Foreign Affairs and Trade (MFAT) endeavoured to get a reciprocal agreement arranged early in 1994, but it became clear that this would take some considerable negotiation with the Malaysian authorities. Malaysia has very strict policies on the issue of any form of work permit to foreigners, and the proposed working holiday scheme was a novel idea for the immigration authorities.

The New Zealand Immigration Service's initial response to the scheme was guarded because at that time there was no clear framework in place for assessing the merits of such schemes in terms of a coherent policy for short-term entry. It was to take almost two years of consideration and negotiation before an agreement was finally reached, and an Exchange of Letters was signed in March 1996 by the New Zealand Minister of Foreign Affairs and the Malaysian Minister of Education.

The Malaysia Working Holiday Scheme is not likely to result in a substantial increase in population movement between the two countries. Indeed, by mutual agreement, the number of citizens from each country who can participate in the scheme each year is restricted to 100. However, the working holiday arrangement is considered to be an important extension of bilateral relations between the two countries. As the Prime Minister of Malaysia, the Honourable Dato Seri Dr Mahathir Bin Mohamad, pointed out on 26th March 1996, while on an official visit to New Zealand:

> 'Of special significance is the signing of the instrument on 'The Working Holiday Arrangement' which would allow citizens of both countries to enjoy an extended holiday in each other's country whilst engaging in some form of employment. New Zealand is the only country that Malaysia has entered into such an arrangement. I can confidently say that the scheme is a practical one that would go a long way to generating better understanding and co-operation between the peoples of our two countries. I hope the scheme can be implemented as soon as possible.'

The working holiday scheme is a land-mark event for both countries. In the case of New Zealand, it is the first agreement with one of the Newly Industrialising Countries (NICs) in Asia which allows a small number of 'young' (18-30 years) Malaysian tourists to obtain work for up to six months while on holiday. The Malaysian Government, in turn, has agreed to allow up to 100 New Zealand citizens a year, who are holidaying in Malaysia, to seek employment to supplement their travel funds.

*The Korean Working Holiday Scheme*

Prime Ministerial exchanges and the arrangements they bring in the form of trade, investment, education, and migration concessions, are important components of the geopolitics of re-alignment of economies and cultural identities. In May 1996 the Prime Minister of New Zealand, the Honourable James Bolger, made an official visit to the Republic of South Korea. One of a number of initiatives which the Prime Minister raised during his talks with South Korean President Kim was a working holiday scheme. Australia had a working holiday scheme with the Republic of Korea that was working well. Canada had also commenced a working holiday scheme with Korea on 1st January 1996. In early May Mr Bolger and President Kim did agree, in principle, to establish a reciprocal working holiday scheme, on the understanding that the details would be worked out subsequently by officials in the two countries. This scheme, like the one negotiated with the Malaysian government, is to be based on the premise that the establishment of working holiday schemes allows young New Zealanders the opportunity to acquire invaluable experience of countries that are becoming increasingly important to New Zealand in terms of trade, regional co-operation, and the changing cultural mix of New Zealand society. The common argument in favour of such schemes is that 'increasing exposure at the personal level will serve to enhance mutual understanding'.

In order to encourage this exposure at the personal level, barriers to movement between countries have to be reduced as much as possible. In New Zealand's case, removing the requirement to have a visitor's visa and, in the case of young travellers from selected countries, granting a work visa or permit, is a key element of strategies to facilitate travel. It remains to examine how such strategies have impacted on population movement to New Zealand in recent years. The next section explores some dimensions of short-term migration to New Zealand, with particular reference to changes in arrival flows, and the impact of short-term movement on net migration gains and losses.

**Visa-waiver and Short-term Migration, 1982-1996**

At the beginning of the 1980s, the total number of arrivals in New Zealand was just under 1 million (970,260 for the year ended 31st March 1981). By the mid-1990s this number had grown to just under 2.5 million (2,464,700 for the year ended 31st March 1996). In the early 1980s the movements of New Zealand and Australian citizens comprised just over two thirds of this total (68 per cent). By the mid-1990s this share had fallen to 52 per cent. Almost half of all the arrivals in the country in the year ended 31st March 1996 (hereafter referred to simply as 1996)[2] were travelling on passports for countries other than New Zealand and Australia.

## The Explosion of Asian Arrivals

The biggest percentage increase in share of arrivals for a major world region, between the year ended 31st March 1981 and the year ended 31st March 1996, is for the Asian countries on the Pacific rim: Southeast and East Asia. In 1981, countries in this region were the source of only 39,700 arrivals (just over 4 per cent of the total), while in 1996 they totalled 518,800 - 21 per cent of the total. In the case of the other three major sources of New Zealand's arrivals (excluding Australia) - Europe, North America and the Pacific Islands - the percentage shares in 1981 and 1996 were, respectively, Europe (including the United Kingdom) 14.0 (1981) and 14.6 (1996); North America (Canada and the USA) 10.0 (1981) and 7.8 (1996); and the Pacific Islands 2.6 (1981) and 2.3 (1996). It is clear that population movements between countries on the Asian Pacific rim and New Zealand have grown much more substantially and rapidly in relative terms than is the case with movement to New Zealand from other parts of the world. Indeed, since 1992, arrivals from East Asian countries as a group have exceeded the number of Australian citizens entering New Zealand.

It is hardly surprising that 'migration from Asia' became a very topical political issue in the New Zealand in the mid-1990s. The significant changes made to New Zealand's immigration policy in 1986 have truly transformed the nature of New Zealand's links, through people, into the global economy and society. It is from 1986 that the growth in number of arrivals from countries in the Asia Pacific rim really began to take off. In 1986 the number of arrivals from East and Southeast Asia totalled 84,000. A year later, after the change in immigration policy in August 1986, they totalled 111,850 - an increase of 33 per cent in one year. This compares with an overall increase in total arrivals of 19 per cent. The only region to have a larger annual increase in arrivals was the Pacific Islands (40 per cent) where the short-lived visa-waiver experiment with Fiji, Tonga and Western Samoa produced a massive increase in short-term migration.

Over the four years between 1st April 1987 and 31st March 1991 the number of arrivals from East and Southeast Asia increased by a further 81 per cent compared with a 34 per cent increase in total arrivals and only a 2.5 per cent increase in arrivals from Pacific countries. Contributing significantly to the booming Asian visitor and migrant flows were the extension of visa-waiver privileges to a number of Southeast Asian countries in 1987 (Malaysia, Thailand and Indonesia), and the development of an immigration consultancy industry to market New Zealand as a desirable destination for migrants as well as visitors.

The immigration policy changed again substantially in 1991 with the introduction of a points system. This development, coupled with the extension of visa-waiver privileges to citizens of the Republic of Korea in 1993, saw the number of arrivals from Asian countries on the Pacific rim to increase by a further 156 per cent between 1st April 1991 and 31st March 1996. This compares with a 39 per cent increase in total arrivals during the six years. Arrivals from countries with which New Zealand has visa-waiver arrangements accounted for 75 per cent of the total citizen arrivals of East and Southeast Asian countries.

### Visa-waiver and the Arrival Boom

The timing of the boom in short-term as well as permanent and long-term migration to New Zealand from Asian countries is very closely tied to the negotiation of visa-waiver agreements and the introduction of new immigration policies. In August 1986 citizens of Singapore were included in the list of nationalities covered by visa-waiver provisions. The number of short-term arrivals from this country almost doubled in a year - from 6,800 in 1986 to 13,400 in 1987 (Figure 6.1). In the case of Malaysia, visa-waiver provisions came into force after the passing of the new Immigration Act in November 1987. During the year ended March 1987 there were a total of 5,750 short-term arrivals from Malaysia; for the year ended 31st March 1988 this number had risen to 10,700 (Figure 6.1).

Not all countries granted visa-waiver provisions in the late 1980s produced such dramatic growth in short-term arrivals. In the cases of Thailand and Indonesia, both of which were included in the visa-waiver provisions of the 1987 Immigration Act, there was not much change in the trend of arrivals in New Zealand (Figure 6.2). Real growth in numbers of short-term arrivals from these countries, especially Thailand, came in the 1990s, particularly between 1994 and 1996. It has taken some time for the tourist markets in these two countries to develop because these countries have not had particularly close economic or social links with New Zealand in the past.

The most spectaclar growth in arrival numbers since the introduction of the points system in 1991 has been in two East Asian countries: the Republic of Korea and Taiwan (Figure 6.3). Citizens in Korea have been granted visa-waiver under an arrangement approved in New Zealand in 1993, but the New Zealand

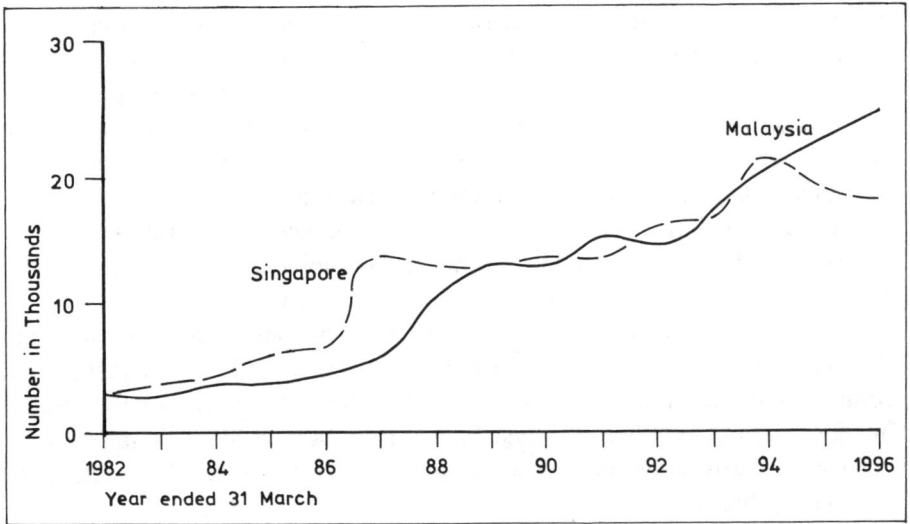

**Figure 6.1   Short term arrivals:  Malaysia and Singapore, 1982-1996**

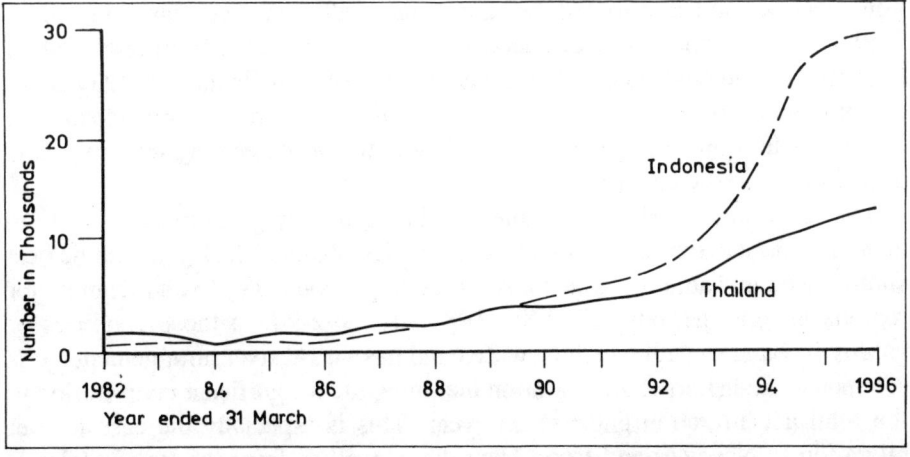

**Figure 6.2   Short term arrivals:  Thailand and Indonesia, 1982-1996**

government, along with all of the OECD countries, have not extended formal recognition to the government of Taiwan through a treaty on visa-waiver. It is interesting to note that despite the absence of visa-waiver provisions, Taiwan was the first of the two countries to experience a visitor boom to New Zealand. The number of short-term Taiwanese arrivals virtually doubled between 1988 and 1989, largely as a result of the activity of immigration consultants promoting New Zealand in Taiwan. The number of arrivals continued to grow rapidly through to 1995 when a change in the points system had the effect of dampening Permanent/Long Term (PLT) migration from Taiwan.

Visitor numbers from Korea took off in 1992, largely as a result of the rapid expansion of Korean migration to New Zealand after the introduction of the points system in 1991. For the next 3 years numbers doubled every year - by far the most rapid increase in the number of arrivals from any country through the 1990s (Figure 6.3). By 1996 Koreans (125,300) were the fourth largest arrival group by nationality after the Australians (330,000), citizens of the United Kingdom and Ireland (201,500) and Japan (169,000). In all of these countries visa-waiver provisions have contributed to the removal of an effective international border.

**Visa-waiver and Immigration**

In addition to fuelling tourist flows, visa-waiver provisions have facilitated the process of immigration to New Zealand. As noted earlier in the chapter, between 1st April 1981 and 31st March 1996 the short-term population movement to and from New Zealand contributed the equivalent of all of the net migration gain of 77,000 for the period. The permanent and long-term gains from immigration (237,500) were more than offset by the emigration of New Zealanders (237,650). This may seem something of a contradiction, but a very common practice in New Zealand is for quite a large number of visitors to stay on as long-term migrants once they get to the country.

The contributions which permanent and long-term migration and short-term migration make to the net gains and losses in New Zealand each year can be best summarised in Table 6.1 which covers the migration flows to and from major regions in three periods: 1982-86, 1987-91, 1992-96. In those countries or groups of countries with which New Zealand has visa-waiver arrangements, it is common to find short-term migration making quite a significant contribution to the total net migration gains in any year. This is especially the case for net migration to New Zealand from Australia as well as from the Pacific Islands (where New Zealand's 'special relationships' have had an important impact on migration), and from North America (the USA and Canada). Following the introduction of the points system in 1991, PLT net immigration became much more significant than net gains from short-term migration for citizens of countries in Asia, Europe (including the United Kingdom), and Africa and the Middle East (Table 6.1). However, in the late 1980s net gains from short-term migration in all three regions were also significant (Table 6.1).

An important observation is that the role of short-term migration has become increasingly significant in recent decades, both in terms of volumes of travelers as well as in terms of the ease of crossing international borders. Visa-waiver, then, has not just been important for facilitating short-term visitors to New Zealand; it has also the eased the crossing of international borders on a long-term basis.

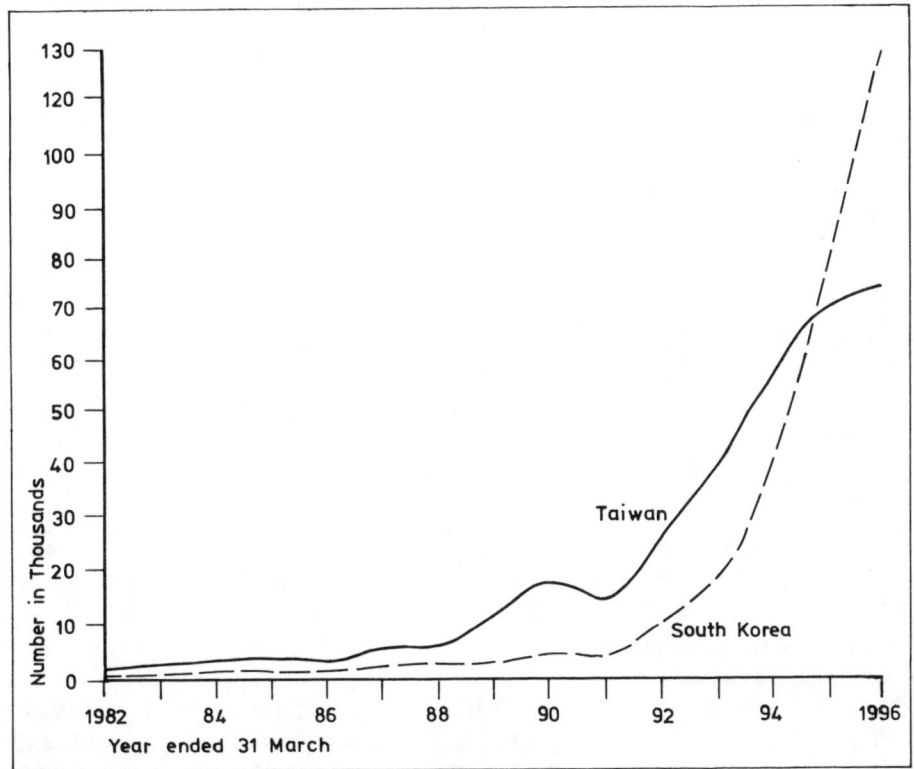

**Figure 6.3   Short term arrivals:  Taiwan and South Korea, 1982-1996**

**Table 6.1   Contribution of permanent/long-term (PLT) and short-term migration to net migration, 1981-1996**

| Nationality | March years | | |
|---|---|---|---|
| | 1982-1986 | 1987-1991 | 1992-1996 |
| *Australia* | | | |
| Total | 2,799 | -2,272 | 35,147 |
| PLT | 6,264 | 5,887 | 8,914 |
| Short-Term | -3,465 | -8,159 | 26,233 |
| *Pacific Islands* | | | |
| Total | 13,879 | 30,351 | 9,687 |
| PLT | 6,893 | 10,547 | 3,969 |
| Short-Term | 6,986 | 19,804 | 5,718 |
| *Asia* | | | |
| Total | 10,021 | 42,058 | 73,146 |
| PLT | 6,893 | 29,168 | 74,357 |
| Short-Term | 3,128 | 12,890 | -1,211 |
| *Europe* (including UK) | | | |
| Total | 15,115 | -5,599 | 19,586 |
| PLT | 17,202 | 15,956 | 27,999 |
| Short-Term | -2,087 | -21,555 | -8,413 |
| *Americas* | | | |
| Total | 3,519 | -405 | 5,656 |
| PLT | 2,407 | 3,124 | 3,533 |
| Short-Term | 1,112 | -3,529 | 2,123 |
| *Africa/Mid East* | | | |
| Total | 1,586 | 4,204 | 15,369 |
| PLT | 795 | 2,125 | 11,350 |
| Short-Term | 791 | 2,079 | 4,019 |
| All Countries (excluding New Zealand citizens) | | | |
| Total | 3,103 | -2,086 | 75,793 |
| PLT | -31,418 | -46,981 | 78,243 |
| Short-Term | 34,521 | 44,895 | -2,450 |

## Conclusion

It appears that the question of vanishing borders as a significant development in the context of a new international order for the 21st Century is a paradoxical issue as noted by the Malaysian Minister of Foreign Affairs, Datuk Abdullah Haji Ahmad Badawi, in his opening address of this conference:

> 'You will have to grapple with the paradoxes of our times. On the one hand, there is the reality of the global market place which sees borders as barriers to the free flow of peoples, capital, technology, ideas and profit. On the other hand, there are many others who see borders as a necessary bulwark protecting their hard won identities as peoples and nations, and as a 'safety barrier' against the domination of other more powerful peoples and nations. And there are yet others who see borders as geographical entities which need to be expanded, thereby inviting conflict with neighbouring territories and peoples.'

This chapter has revealed such a paradox in the case of New Zealand's international border in the context of migration flows. On the one hand, an important New Zealand response to the forces of globalisation, especially since the mid-1980s, has been to remove certain restrictions over the negotiation of permission for people to cross the international border through visa-waiver arrangements. On the other hand, the development of an increasingly liberal approach towards the documentation of short-term movement of citizens of other countries into New Zealand has been accompanied by some quite vociferous debate about the policy imperatives which are making the border more porous.

In the case of international migration, it is clear that the extent to which a border 'vanishes' or becomes highly visible is subject to considerable manipulation by policy makers. When there is a public outcry about international migration, as there has been in all of the traditional countries of immigration on the Pacific rim in recent years, then regulations governing inward flows are modified. This happened in New Zealand in October 1995; it happened recently in Australia when the immigration quota was reduced by 11,000; it is the subject of some heated debate in the United States and Canada. As the Malaysian Minister of Foreign Affairs put it, 'when you speak of 'vanishing borders'... you ... have to address the complex inter-play between sovereignty as symbolised by national borders and inter-dependence as dictated by the forces of international economic and trade relations as well as the advancements in technology especially in the area of communications.' The ambiguous role of borders in international migration in the Asia-Pacific region in the 21st Century is better reflected in the question of whether borders have vanished rather than in a statement which assumes that national borders will, indeed, disappear. That said, visa-waiver arrangements and other bilateral agreements designed to facilitate the flows of people between countries are certainly making borders more porous than they were a decade ago.

## Acknowledgement

This study forms part of two larger research projects, the Demographic Crossroads Programme and the New Demographic Directions Programme, which are being carried out at the University of Waikato with financial support from the Foundation for Research, Science and Technology. The authors gratefully acknowledge the assistance provided by the staff in the Policy Division of the New Zealand Immigration Service, especially with the documentation of visa-waiver arrangements and work permit schemes. Particular mention should be made of support provided by Mr Peter Leniston, Ms Pauline O'Brien, Ms Anita Reedy and Mr John Roseveare. The advice, support and assistance of Dr Elsie Ho and Ms Joanne Young, members of the project's migration research team, continues to be greatly appreciated.

## Notes

1  These countries are Austria, Belgium, Denmark, Finland, France, Germany, Great Britain, Greece, Iceland, Ireland, Italy, Liechtenstein, Luxembourg, Malta, Monaco, Netherlands, Norway, Portugal, Spain, Sweden, Switzerland. Note that British passport holders, who have evidence of the right to reside permanently in the United Kingdom, qualify for visits of up to six months, visa free, irrespective of the country they live in. This provision covers a significant number of visitors from places like Hong Kong, South Africa and other former British colonies.
2  Unless otherwise stated, all years referred to in this section end on 31st March; they are not calendar years.

## References

Burke, K. (1986), *The Immigration Policy Review, August 1986*, Wellington, Appendices to the Journal of the House of Representatives, G. 42, Government Printer.
McKinnon, M. (1996), *Immigrants and citizens: New Zealanders and Asian Immigration in Historical Context*, Institute of Policy Studies, Victoria University of Wellington.

# 7  Vanishing 'International' Borders:  The Implications for Reconstruction and Development in Southern Africa

*Christian M. ROGERSON*

## Introduction

The grand design of apartheid planners involved the creation of an array of 'independent' Black Homelands which would be geographically separate or distinct from the political space of so-called 'White' South Africa (Lemon 1976). More specifically, the failed apartheid project encompassed the territorial division of South African space and the making of a set of new 'international' boundaries that would demarcate ten ethnically discrete so-termed black Homelands or Bantustans (Figure 7.1).  At its most advanced state of evolution, by the early 1980s, this grand design of apartheid planners resulted in the internal Balkanisation of South Africa and the establishment of the political 'independence' of four of these ethnic states, namely of Transkei, Bophuthatswana, Ciskei and Venda (Drummond 1991). These artificial 'international' borders, however, were unrecognised in international law, being the products of the apartheid regime. With the emergence of a new democratic South African political dispensation, symbolised by the inauguration of President Nelson Mandela in 1994 and the signing of South Africa's new constitution in 1996, these artificial states and their illegitimate international boundaries have been swept aside.  In addition, after the historic democratic elections of 1994, South Africa's pariah status in the global community was terminated along with the ending of economic and political sanctions.

These dramatic transformations that recently have taken place in South Africa are re-shaping the geo-political and economic landscape of Southern Africa

(Rogerson 1996). Central to the changes that are remoulding the spatial fabric of the sub-continent is the new South African government's commitment to transcend the apartheid legacy and to re-make the country's economy and society. At the heart of the legislative programmes of the democratic government is the national Reconstruction and Development Programme (RDP) designed as 'an integrated, coherent socio-economic policy framework' for informing development planning in general and for 'the building of a democratic, non-racial and non-sexist future[1] (ANC 1994:1). Moreover, the architects of the RDP acknowledge that in the long term 'sustainable reconstruction and development in South Africa requires sustainable reconstruction and development in Southern Africa as a whole' (ANC 1994:116). Although some of the initial impetus associated with the RDP as an agent of transformation and redistribution has given ground in 1996 to a new policy emphasis on economic growth as the national prime tool of change (Caliguire 1996), the RDP remains still a powerful vision for casting new geographies of development in South and Southern Africa into the next century (Rogerson 1996).

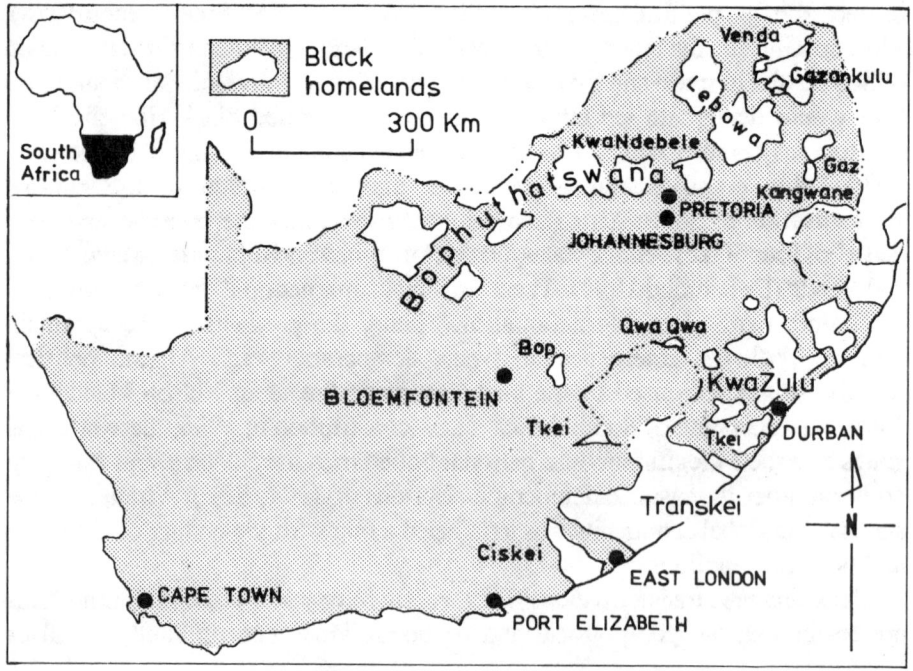

**Figure 7.1   The grand design of apartheid planning**

The objective in this chapter is to raise several key aspects of the developmental implications in South Africa and the Southern African region of the vanishing 'international' borders which had been erected by apartheid planners. Two key sets of themes are discussed. First, an examination is undertaken of some of the spatial developmental changes occurring *within* post-apartheid South Africa as a consequence of the dismantling of the Homelands and their re-integration into a non-racial democracy. Second, the discussion widens to the *external* impact of South Africa's apartheid-created vanishing borders. Issues of concern relate to the shifting competitive position of neighbouring countries for investments and to the emergent roles of a democratic South Africa in the new international regional groupings both within Africa and beyond. Overall, it is contended that the vanishing international borders in South and Southern Africa, associated with the death of apartheid, are forging the bases for a fresh geo-political and economic dispensation across the sub-continent as part of the new emergent international order into the 21st century.

## New Geographies in South Africa

Apartheid social engineering gave birth to new (often inhuman) geographies in South Africa which are a legacy that the democratic government seeks to challenge and overcome (ANC 1994). The post-apartheid government faces a geographical rationalisation of past fragmented boundaries, including the thorny issue of re-incorporating the Homelands or Bantustans (Drummond 1991). The management of reconstruction and development has involved the demarcation of nine new provinces, the essential building blocks of the new South Africa, with new legislative and executive powers and the forging of new relationships between the centre and the new provinces (Rogerson 1994).

A coherent spatial development framework has yet to emerge for planning reconstruction and development in post-apartheid South Africa. Nevertheless, the broad contours of a new spatial dispensation appear likely to align South Africa to global policy trends which premise national economic success and social reform on dynamic urban development (Heymans 1995). Emphasis is placed in official planning documents on the imperatives of market-driven patterns of spatial development and on the importance of new local economic development processes to replace the 'top-down' centralised spatial planning initiatives which dominated the apartheid years (South Africa 1995a; 1995b). In terms of the 'vanishing international borders' that are associated with the dismantling of the Homelands, key sets of changes regarding the location of industrial activities and casino tourism are re-shaping the development of South

African space. A vital historical aspect of attempts to legitimise the separate political status of the artificially created 'states' under apartheid was the government-sponsored efforts to furnish the Bantustans with an economic base through programmes of industrial decentralisation and casino development (Rogerson 1988; 1990; 1991; Pickles 1991). In this section the focus is upon interpreting aspects of the emergent geographies of development within the new South Africa which are linked to modifying or changing these former apartheid programmes.

## *From 'Factories in the Field' to the De-Industrialisation of the Homelands*

From the late 1950s the South African government pursued an active regional development policy which targeted the decentralisation of manufacturing into the country's peripheral areas (Rogerson 1988). The goals of regional development policy were conflated with those of apartheid social engineering as the decentralisation programme focussed on promoting a selection of industrial 'growth points' bordering or within the Bantustans. During the early 1980s a more vigorous regional industrial development programme (RIDP) was introduced, designed to siphon industries away from South Africa's major metropolitan areas (most importantly, the Pretoria-Witwatersrand-Vereeniging region) into Bantustan growth points (Rogerson 1991). This period was a watershed in terms of regional development planning as the packages of incentives on offer to lure local and international investors into the Homelands were deemed among the most generous available anywhere in the world (Rogerson 1988).

The effects of the state decentralisation programme have been the source of much controversy and debate. In developmental terms, attention is drawn to the programme's failure to achieve local linkages, the insecure and highly exploited work conditions of the predominantly female industrial workforce, and the footloose nature of much investment that occurred in the Bantustans (Rogerson 1988; 1991). Nonetheless, it is clear that the generous incentives offered to local and foreign investors were responsible for the emergence of a new geographical landscape of localised rural industrialisation in South Africa (Pickles 1991). Many growth points in the rural periphery, such as Isithebe, Fort Jackson or Phuthithadjaba, recorded extraordinarily rapid rates of manufacturing expansion as new 'factories in the field' sprang up as features of the new apartheid-engineered geographies of several Bantustans (Pickles 1991). The economic health of these 'new industrial spaces', artificially fostered by apartheid planning, was threatened, however, during the years of late apartheid as mounting criticism was directed at South Africa's decentralisation strategy and a revised Regional

Industrial Development Programme (RIDP) phased into operation in 1991 (Rogerson 1994; 1995). This revised strategy survived the democratic political transformation and remained in operation until November 1996 when it was replaced by a new tax holiday programme which incorporated a spatial component (*Engineering News*, 6th December 1996).

Essentially, the 1991 RIDP shifted from the past approach of selective growth points and instead introduced a package of graded incentives that ostensibly interfered less with the market, thereby encouraging greater economic and financial efficiency rather than the support of inefficient firms (Rogerson 1994). In financial terms, the 1991 RIDP was far more modest in the incentives made available to potential investors than its predecessor. The key aspect of the new programme, however, was that it removed the spatial discrimination which formerly favoured the official Bantustan growth points and replaced it with a pattern of incentives which are graded across different zones of the country (Rogerson 1991; 1994). The 1991 RIDP marked a major policy reversal from the old programme which underpinned apartheid planning. No longer was industrial decentralisation to be encouraged in the manner in which it was originally conceptualised (that is, firms relocating from the space of 'White' South Africa to the Bantustans and their borders) and functioned for almost three decades. The revised decentralisation strategy de-emphasised the importance of industrialisation in the Bantustans with the consequence of dramatically reducing the competitiveness of these regions for new industrial investments (Rogerson 1995; Rwigera 1995).

Although vigorous efforts were made to 'sell' the growth points of the former Bantustans to potential investors, it is clear that the 1991 RIDP exerted a negative impact on patterns of new industrial investments in these regions. Several studies disclose mounting evidence of manufacturing enterprises uprooting their operations and leaving Homeland growth points, often relocating to areas in and around South Africa's metropolitan regions (Rogerson 1994; Harrison 1995; Rwigera 1995). Moreover, other 'fly-by-night' enterprises, notably run by many Taiwanese or Israeli investors, have closed down completely their South African operations following the withdrawal of the lucrative investment concessions (Rogerson 1991). Accordingly, having lost their competitive edge in terms of available incentives, many of the former Bantustan regions have experienced stagnation, if not a dramatic downturn in their industrial employment base. For example, in the former territory of Ciskei the haemorrhaging of the industrial base has been sharp with a loss recorded of 33 per cent of the region's manufacturing base between 1990 and 1992 (Harrison 1995). Moreover, it was observed that from the inception of the 1991 RIDP to the middle of 1994 'not a single industrialist had applied to locate in the

Transkei' (Rwigera 1995:528). Nevertheless, it must be acknowledged that not all the decentralised Homeland factories were marginal operations and that many factories will survive into the post-apartheid era of reduced incentives (Rogerson 1994).

One key policy issue that emerges from the 'bleeding' of industrial jobs in many Homeland areas concerns the future of those poor communities now affected negatively by the withdrawal of their former preferential investor status. Many of these communities represent populations who were often victims of forced removals under apartheid social engineering programmes. The danger is that these same communities may be victims once more, this time, ironically, from the consequences of the ending of apartheid (Rogerson 1995). This issue is re-emphasised by the limited number of former Homelands growth points that were included in the list of locations that qualify for tax holidays under the democratic government's programme for promoting new industrial investments, which was announced in November 1996 (*Engineering News*, 6th December 1996).

*Casino Development:  From Forbidden Fruit to Democratic Order*

Another area of economic development that was heavily influenced by apartheid Homelands planning and which is now experiencing major restructuring as a result of the changes produced in the new democracy is the geography of casino tourism. Under apartheid South Africa's Calvinistic puritanism and anti-gambling codes, strict legislation had been enacted to completely ban the operations of casinos within the country (Rogerson 1990). Accordingly, during the 1970s the lucrative gambling trade of Southern Africa was therefore monopolised by the casino developments which took place in the regional 'pleasure periphery' of Botswana, Lesotho and Swaziland (Crush and Wellings 1983).

This situation was radically changed, however, with the South African government's grant of nominal 'independence' to several of the Bantustan areas, *viz.*, Transkei (1976), Bophuthatswana (1977), Venda (1979) and Ciskei (1981). As independence redefined the functions of these areas in South African space, it created opportunities for the opening up of the gambling industry in these areas (Rogerson 1990). A flurry of new casino resorts (the most well-known and spectacular is the large Sun City complex in Bophuthatswana) were constructed in the late 1970s and the early 1980s to serve as purveyors of the 'forbidden fruit' denied to South Africans by the country's anti-gambling codes. But beyond the Sun City complex and other resorts in Bophuthatswana, several other major casino tourism developments occurred particularly in Transkei and Ciskei. By

1990, nine major casino complexes were established in the so-called independent Homelands. The financial success of these new casino complexes in these areas was, to some extent, at the expense and downgrading of the casino developments and tourism industries in Botswana, Lesotho and Swaziland (Rogerson 1990).

With the re-integration of the Homelands into the new South African political order, the gambling industry is experiencing a radical shake-up. Of key importance is the ending of the monopoly enjoyed by the Homeland areas on the operations of gambling. In the immediate aftermath of political change, large numbers (estimated to be 'in the thousands') of illegal casinos opened up operations throughout South Africa, in particular in the lucrative markets offered by the country's largest cities (*Sunday Times*, 3rd September 1995). During 1995 and 1996, however, the central government moved to crack down and close down the activities of these illegal casinos in line with the introduction of national legislation designed to regulate the gambling industry.

The new national gambling legislation provides for the establishment of 40 gambling casinos throughout the country (*Sunday Times*, 3rd September 1995). In terms of geographical distribution, of central significance has been the allocation of licences between South Africa's nine provinces. Powers have been given to the provincial governments to regulate the specific geographical location of casinos within their areas. The final map of casino development in post-apartheid South Africa is still not drawn. Nonetheless, the provincial allocation of the casino licences has been finalised with six to Gauteng; five each to the provinces of North West, Kwazulu-Natal, Eastern Cape and Western Cape; four each in Free State and Mpumalanga; and three each in Northern Cape and Northern Province. Already evident from this provincial allocation of licences is that some of the casino developments in former Homeland areas will have to be rationalised and disposed of (*Financial Mail*, 10th November 1995). Of greater long-term significance, however, is the potential reduction in casino tourism in these areas as a consequence of the wider geographical distribution of casino resorts in the new South Africa.

**New Geographies in Southern Africa and Beyond**

The unfolding of apartheid planning impacted externally beyond South Africa's borders, especially upon the neighbouring and economically peripheral states of Southern Africa (Rogerson 1981; Atkinson 1992). In particular, aspects of the changing economic landscape of countries such as Botswana, Lesotho, Swaziland or Mozambique cannot be understood in isolation from the economic forces for restructuring which have emanated from apartheid South Africa. Equally, the removal of apartheid has witnessed the opening of a set of new regional developmental opportunities and problems during the phase of reconstruction and development.  In this chapter two themes are explored: the external impact of South Africa's vanishing international borders upon the group of immediate neighbouring countries, and the changing prospects for new regional economic groupings both within Southern Africa and beyond.

## *Vanishing Borders and the Southern African Periphery*

In seeking to nurture an economic base in the Homelands, the apartheid government boosted the investment attractions of these areas, particularly relative to the advantages of surrounding countries (Rogerson 1981; 1990). At the heyday of the attractions and investment packages offered to international and local manufacturers to locate in the Homelands, it was evident that in the peripheral countries of Southern Africa industrial development was taking place at only a slow pace (Atkinson 1992). Indeed, in the case of Swaziland, partly as a consequence of the Bantustan industrial promotion, a process of deindustrialisation was clearly under way in the early 1980s as several companies relocated their operations from Swaziland to the South African Homelands (Miles 1997).

The mid-1980s saw a turning point in the industrial fortunes of South Africa's neighbouring states. The imposition of tightening international sanctions on South Africa, as a result of its apartheid policies, precipitated a new trend towards the re-industrialisation of the peripheral countries of Southern Africa. This was accompanied by several examples of foreign and South African capital relocating their plants away from South Africa into neighbouring countries (Atkinson 1992; Miles 1997).  Although a trickle of plant relocations occurred in Botswana, the vast majority of movement and transfers took place to either Lesotho or Swaziland.  In Lesotho, the decision taken to exploit its temporary relative advantage over South Africa resulted in the emergence of an infant clothing and textile industry which was based almost entirely on female labour (Baylies and Wright 1993).  In Swaziland, prominent international investors that shifted operations from South Africa included Coca Cola, Cadburys and Kirsch Industries, a South African consortium. Moreover, Swaziland benefitted also from a stream of Taiwanese textiles enterprises setting up operations or relocating from South Africa (Atkinson 1992). Overall, in common with Lesotho, 'Swaziland played the market to her best advantage while enjoying the fruits of disinvestment in South Africa in the late 1980s' (Miles 1997:133).  In the case of both countries, it is apparent that without sanctions and disinvestment their favourable internal climates 'would not have attracted the investment that it did' (Atkinson 1992:180).

The sweeping away of apartheid and the Homelands poses problems for the long-term stability of these fledgling new industrial developments (Atkinson 1992:180). For Lesotho the lifting of sanctions on South Africa 'entails the loss of a large element of comparative advantage, and, given Lesotho's geographical position and poor infrastructure, it is possible that many firms will choose to relocate across the border' (Baylies and Wright 1993:590). A parallel climate of uncertainty prevails in Swaziland where there is great concern over 'the threat to investments posed by the new South Africa' (Miles 1997:134). As Miles (1997:134) argues: 'The allure of Swaziland as locus of investment has dulled. The once comparative advantages the country had have ceased to hold up in an environment of stiffer international competition'.

Although some aspects of the internal changes in South Africa, accompanied by the removal of the Homelands borders, might rebound to the detriment of manufacturing growth in these peripheral states of Southern Africa, new growth and investment opportunities also are in evidence. For example, the Korean multinational, Hyundai, has announced plans to establish in Botswana a motor-car assembly operation with a planned capacity of 60,000 cars per year in Botswana (*The Star* Business Report, 25th June 1996). The new completely knocked down (CKD) plant in Gaborone, which is presently geared almost exclusively for the South African market, will provide 1,000 new employment opportunities and establish the motor industry as the country's second largest foreign exchange earner after minerals exports (*Financial Mail*, 7th July 1995 and 2nd February 1996). Nonetheless, with the South African market as the project anchor, it is hoped that the new facility in Gaborone may emerge in future as Hyundai's world right-hand drive assembly hub (*Engineering News*, 13th December 1996).

Finally, one of the most promising dimensions of post-apartheid change is the renewed prospects for cross-border international development projects which might involve co-operation between South Africa and the surrounding states. Among the first of these cross-border projects is the Lesotho Highlands Water Project, the agreement for which dates back to 1986, to provide water resources from Lesotho to South Africa's industrial heartland (Lesotho Highlands Development Authority 1994). At the heart of this particular project is the construction of the enormous Katse and Mohale dams (completion date 2003) and associated tunnels in the Lesotho Highlands which will store water for onward feeding to South Africa's thirsty cities (*Financial Mail*, 22nd December 1995). In this second phase of the Lesotho Highlands water project the South African government is seeking a greater measure of control over the financing, employment spin-offs and development initiatives associated with this water transfer scheme than was possible in the project's first phase, conceived and brokered in the period of South Africa's isolation from the international community (*Star* Business Report, 6th August 1996).

A second major cross-border project launched in 1996 is for establishing the Maputo Development Corridor (*Engineering News*, 16th February 1996; *Financial Mail*, 29th March 1996). This mega-project involves a programme of joint South Africa-Mozambique cooperation designed to revitalise the tourism, agriculture, mining and manufacturing bases of both South Africa's eastern Mpumalanga province and of war ravaged southern Mozambique (Figure 7.2). The South Africa-Mozambique corridor is the first of several such development corridor initiatives which presently are under discussion in post-apartheid Southern Africa (Harrison and Todes 1996).

Planning for the Maputo Development Corridor project involves major cross-border infrastructural improvements including a new toll-road from Witbank (in Mpumalanga) to Mozambique's capital, the upgrading of Maputo harbour and new telecommunication linkages between South Africa and Mozambique (Mpumalanga Development Corporation, 1996). Maputo port currently handles only 5 per cent of regional traffic as a result of civil unrest and political instability. The project aims to restore the formerly important role of Maputo in the Southern African regional economy to handle 40 per cent of shipping and cargo for South Africa's industrial heartland (Gauteng). The upgrading of Maputo harbour is to be a joint initiative between the Mozambique government and South African parastatal and private investors. In addition to securing a reliable outlet for exports from South Africa, the project is linked to the broader concerns of reconstruction in Mozambique and Southern African cooperation (Harrison and Todes 1996:71). Once complete, the Maputo Development Corridor promises to be a 'major potential player in world markets' (*Engineering News*, 28th June 1996). Because of the significance of this mega-project for the whole Southern Africa region, interest in linking into this development corridor through the establishment of feeder corridors has been shown both by the governments of Swaziland and Botswana (*Engineering News*, 28th June 1996). Again, these proposed feeder corridor developments will demand cross-border cooperation between the democratic South African government and the surrounding countries.

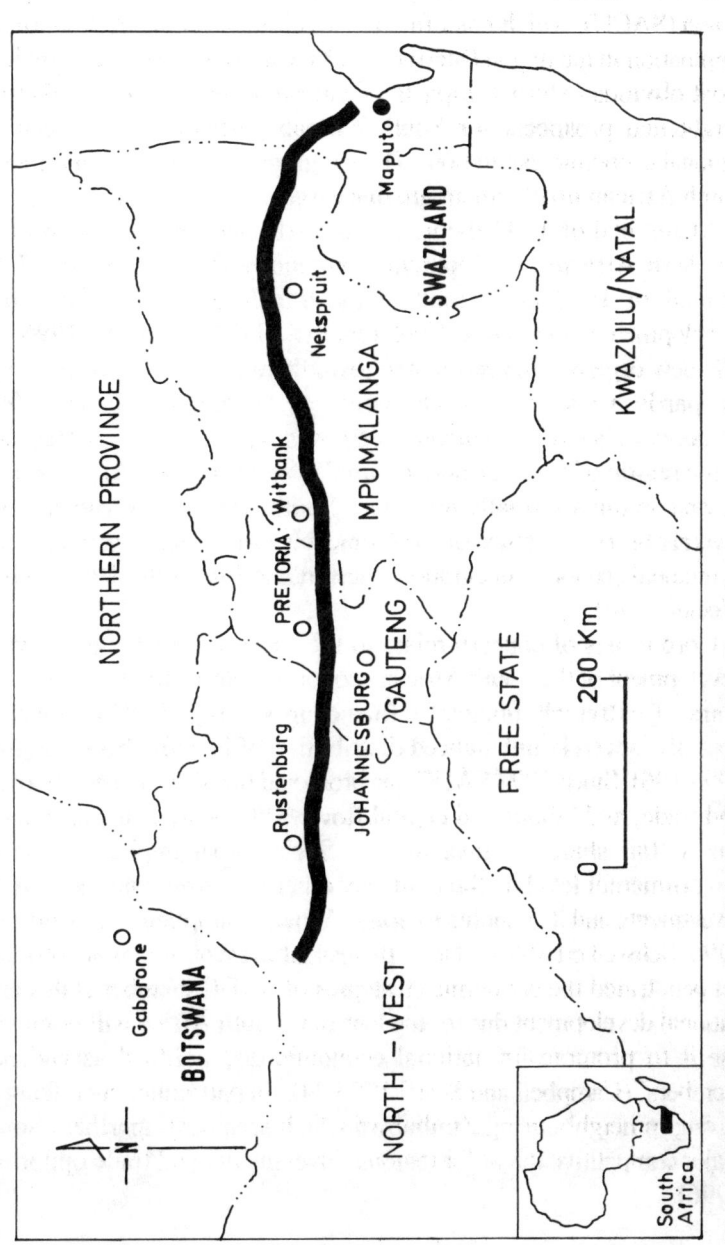

**Figure 7.2   The Maputo African Development Corridor**

*Regional Economic Associations: Africa and Beyond*

Regional economic associations in Southern Africa are not new phenomena. Indeed, South Africa has long been a member of the Southern African Customs Union (SACU), which has often been viewed as an instrument of South African domination in the region (Stewart and McCarthy 1995). Nevertheless, among the most obvious external impacts of vanishing borders in Southern Africa is the heightened prospects for South African participation in fresh initiatives for regional economic integration. Three regional associations and their potential for South African involvement are discussed.

At the end of 1994 the new South African government formally joined the Southern African Development Community (SADC) (Figure 7.3), which was formed in 1992 as a result of the transformation of the Southern African Development Coordination Conference (SADCC) (Lindeke 1996; Weeks 1996). The new organisation reoriented towards regional co-operation was constituted as 'partly a response to the demise of apartheid' (Lindeke 1996:61) for its predecessor's explicit *raison d'etre* was 'to counter the destabilising influence in the region of the apartheid regime' (Weeks 1996:106). Despite the euphoria of welcoming a formally non-racist South African government into the SADC, several observers warned of the formidable difficulties that remain in the pathway of regional economic integration (Stewart and McCarthy 1995; Schweikert 1996; Weeks 1996).

Core issues of concern relate to the sheer size and higher level of economic development of the South African economy relative to other countries prompting fears of extremely unequal influence in setting SADC regional policy and of possibly 'severely unbalanced distribution of benefits from integration' (Weeks 1996:106). Since 1992 SADC has promoted the idea of cross-border investments and trade, and labour and capital flows with the idea that each member country has a 'fair share' of investment. Such a goal implies a managed policy at governmental level as the tendency otherwise would be the gravitation of such investments and its benefits to South Africa (Campbell and Scerri 1995; Lindeke 1996; Schweikert 1996). Nevertheless, at present, regional co-operation has not yet penetrated the economic strategies of SADC member states as a priority for national development due to 'the fear that South Africa will dominate SADC and use it to promote its national economic and political ascendancy over other members' (Campbell and Scerri 1995:24). In particular, such fears are especially strong in neighbouring Zimbabwe which sees post-apartheid South Africa as a major competitive threat for regional investments and trade opportunities (Naude 1996).

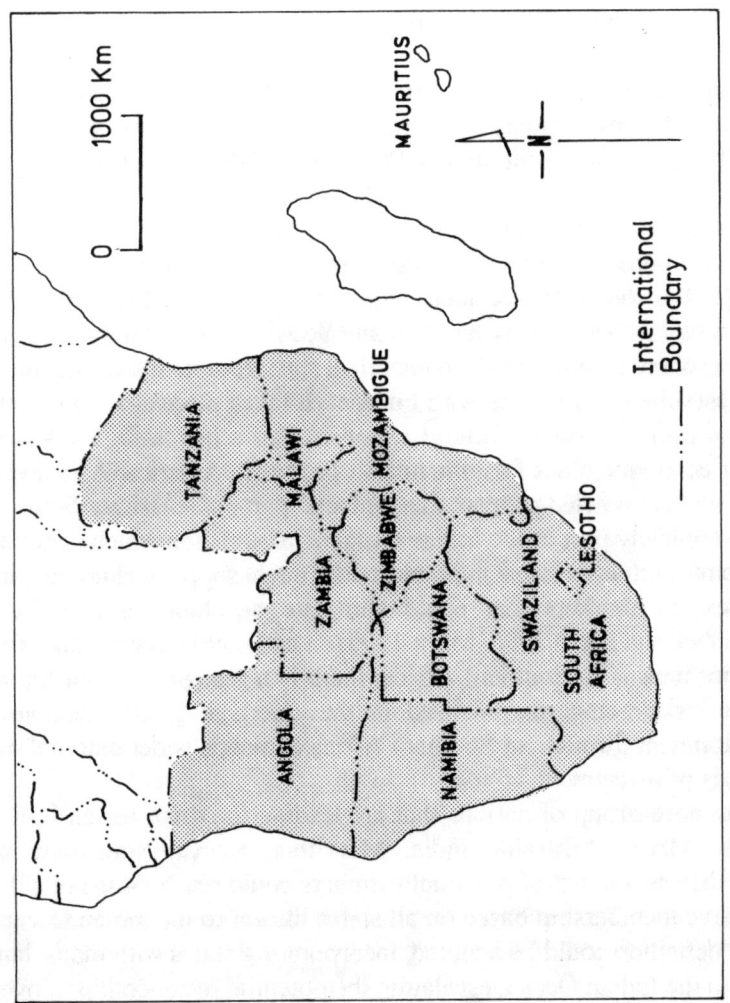

**Figure 7.3   The Southern African Development Community**

In addition to SADC, South Africa has been courted as a potential member of the larger African grouping, the Preferential Trade Area (PTA) for Eastern and Southern Africa which in December 1994 became the Common Market for Eastern and Southern Africa (COMESA). Like the SADC, the PTA responded to the new international opportunities created by the breakdown of apartheid and upgraded its integration efforts with plans to form an economic community (Stewart and McCarthy 1995). The reborn COMESA currently comprises a diverse group of 18 members stretching from Lesotho to Sudan. The history of PTA's 'rather bleak performance' means, however, that it is unlikely to be an attractive partner for South Africa (Schweikert 1996:54). Although efforts are being made to galvanise the COMESA objectives of a common market 'it is considered by most commentators in South Africa as the least viable of regional groupings in Southern Africa' (Campbell and Scerri 1995:25). Moreover, 'because its aims are similar to those of SACU, there is an inherent conflict between the two organisations which, because of South African backing for SACU, can only result in the failure of COMESA' (Campbell and Scerri 1995:25).

The most ambitious proposal for South Africa to participate in new initiatives for international economic co-operation is the concept of forging an Indian Ocean Rim (IOR) economic association (Figure 7.4), which was first seriously discussed only in November 1993 (Campbell and Scerri 1995). South Africa's interest in the concept of an IOR marks an important shift from its traditional preoccupation with establishing linkages with Europe. It takes place against a background of several events, most importantly South Africa's increasing exclusion from the major economic blocs forming in Europe, North America, Asia and the Pacific and an acknowledgement that, albeit part of Africa, South Africa is geographically part of the Indian Ocean Rim, a region which contains potential economic partners of great importance who might supply technology, investments and export markets that could stimulate development and reconstruction (Campbell and Scerri 1995; Marx 1995). Lastly, although South Africa's prime commitment is to Southern Africa, there is a recognition that the region as a whole risks being marginalised in the emergent global economy and that development throughout Southern Africa demands wider external markets and sources of investment.

The core group of nations that are leading the drive for an IOR comprised South Africa, Australia, India, Mauritius, Kenya, Singapore and Oman. Nonetheless, the list of potential members could reach 24 using a definition of inclusive membership based on all states littoral to the Indian Ocean. An even wider definition could be adopted, incorporating states with major land or water links to the Indian Ocean, escalating the potential membership to over 40 states

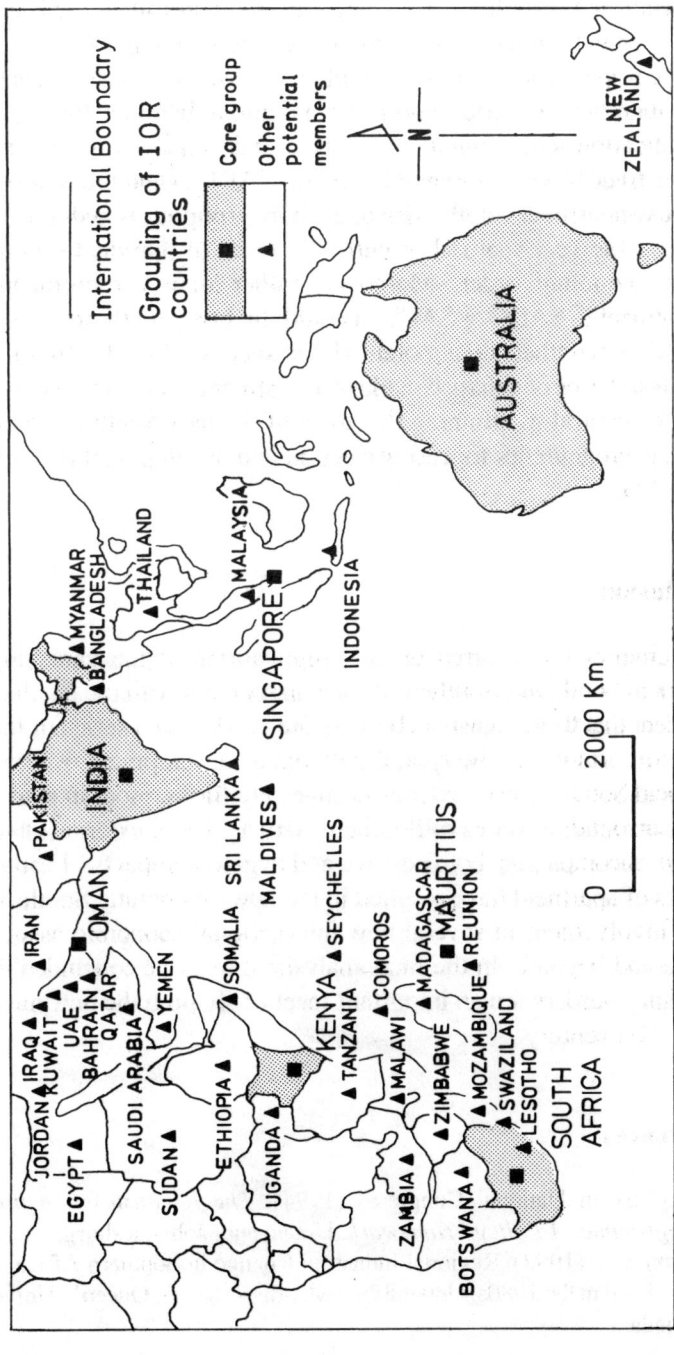

**Figure 7.4   The Indian Ocean Rim Economic Association**

(Campbell and Scerri 1995). Although there are many infrastructural and organisational problems that need to be confronted before such an IOR association is founded, it holds many potential benefits for an expanded South-South co-operation. Indeed, Campbell and Scerri (1995) suggest that it would offer member countries enormous potential benefits through intra-regional specialisation and economies of scale and enhanced leverage with powerful existing trade blocs (for example, EU or NAFTA) and international institutions. For post-apartheid South Africa, an IOR grouping is seductive as a means of escaping the very real risk it currently faces of marginalisation in the current global economic order. Moreover, rather than compromising its existing commitment to SADC or SACU, it could, by bringing these organisations within an IOR, strengthen their potential for success. Finally, by offering potential benefits in terms of enlarged markets, investments and technology flows, the IOR could be central to attaining the goals of the new South African government's domestic programmes for reconstruction and development (Campbell and Scerri 1995: 11).

## Conclusion

This chapter has centred on the implications of the vanishing international borders in South and Southern Africa, associated with the death of apartheid. It is evident that these vanishing borders are producing a series of internal changes, most importantly in the spatial patterns of development occuring within post-apartheid South Africa. External changes are furthermore in evidence, especially in the surrounding states of Southern Africa. These external changes have been uneven, encompassing both positive and negative impacts. Lastly, the vanishing borders of apartheid have resulted in the new democratic South Africa engaging in an involvement in several new international economic associations both in Africa and beyond. In the final analysis, it must be concluded that apartheid's vanishing borders are an important facet of shaping the new international order in the 21st century.

## References

ANC (African National Congress) (1994), *The Reconstruction and Development Programme: A Policy Framework*, Umanyano: Johannesburg.
Atkinson, C.J. (1992), Regional Industrial Change in Southern Africa: A Case Study of Swaziland in the 1980s, Unpublished MA dissertation, Queen's University: Kingston, Canada.

Baylies, C. and Wright, C. (1993), 'Female Labour in the Textile and Clothing Industry of Lesotho', *African Affairs*, Vol. 92, pp. 577-591.

Caliguire, D., (1996), 'Death of a Dream', *Democracy in Action*, Vol. 10, No. 3, pp. 5-6, 20.

Campbell, G.R. and Scerri, M. (1995), 'The Prospects for an Indian Ocean Rim (IOR) Economic Association', *South African Journal of International Affairs*, Vol. 2, No. 2, pp. 11-37.

Crush, J. and Wellings, P. (1983), 'The Southern African Pleasure Periphery', *Journal of Modern African Studies*, Vol. 21, pp. 673-698.

Drummond, J. (1991), 'The Demise of Territorial Apartheid: Re-incorporating the Bantustans in a 'New' South Africa', *Tijdschrift voor Economische en Sociale Geografie*, Vol. 82, pp. 338-344.

*Engineering News* (Johannesburg: Weekly).

*Financial Mail* (Johannesburg: Weekly).

Harrison, P. (1995), *Global Transformations and the Changing Geography of Production in KwaZulu-Natal*, Interim Report No. 5, Natal Town and Regional Planning Commission: Pietermaritzburg.

_____ and Todes, A. (1996), 'The Development Corridor Route: New Highways or Old By-ways?', *Indicator South Africa*, Vol. 13, No. 3, pp. 70-75.

Heymans, C. (1995), 'Cities: Engines of Prosperity or Sites of Decay?', *Indicator South Africa*, Vol. 12, No. 3, pp. 47-53.

Lemon, A. (1976), *Apartheid: A Geography of Separation*, Saxon House: Farnborough.

Lesotho Highlands Development Authority (1994), *Lesotho Highlands Water Project*. Department of Water Affairs and Forestry: Pretoria.

Lindeke, W. (1996), 'Southern African Development Community', *TransAfrica Forum*, Vol. 10, No. 1, pp. 59-70.

Marx, J. (1995) 'South African Foreign Policy in the New Era: Priorities in Africa and the Indian Ocean Islands', *South African Journal of International Affairs*, Vol. 2, No. 2, pp. 1-10.

Miles, M. (1997), Migration and Development in Post-colonial Swaziland: A Study of Women's Mobility and Livelihood Strategies, Unpublished PhD dissertation, University of Witwatersrand: Johannesburg.

Mpumalanga Development Corporation (1996), *Opportunities for Growth and Development in Mpumalanga*, Mpumalanga Development Corporation: KaNyamazane.

Naude, W. (1996), 'Macro-economic Change in Zimbabwe: Implications for South Africa', *Africa Insight*, Vol. 26, No. 1, pp. 57-64.

Pickles, J., (1991), 'Industrial Restructuring, Peripheral Industrialization and Rural Development in South Africa', *Antipode*, Vol. 23, pp. 68-91.

Rogerson, C.M. (1981), 'Industrialization in the Shadows of Apartheid: A World-systems Analysis' in Hamilton, FEI and Linge, G.J.R. (eds.), *Spatial Analysis, Industry and the Industrial Environment: International Industrial Systems*, John Wiley: Chichester, pp. 395-421.

_____ (1988), 'Regional Development Policy in South Africa', *Regional Development Dialogue* 9, (Special Issue), pp. 228-255.

_____ (1990), 'Sun International: The Making of a South African Tourism Multinational', *GeoJournal*, Vol. 22, pp. 345-354.

_____ (1991) 'Beyond Racial Fordism: Restructuring Industry in the 'New' South Africa', *Tijdschrift voor Economische en Sociale Geografie*, Vol. 82, pp.355-366.

_____ (1994), 'Democracy, Reconstruction and Changing Local and Regional Economic Planning in South Africa', *Regional Development Dialogue*, Vol. 15, pp. 102-118.

_____ (1995), 'Forgotten Places, Abandoned Places: Migration Research Issues in South Africa' in Baker, J. and Aina, T.A. (eds.) *The Migration Experience in Africa*, Nordiska Afrikaininstitutet: Uppsala, pp. 109-121.

_____ (1996), 'Towards Reconstruction and Development in Southern Africa', *GeoJournal*, Vol. 39, pp. 1-2.

Rwigera, H.B. (1995) 'South Africa's Revised Industrial Incentives: An Assessment', *Regional Studies*, Vol. 29, pp. 519-531.

Schweikert, R. (1996), 'Regional Integration in Eastern and Southern Africa', *Africa Insight*, Vol. 26, No. 1, pp. 48-56.

South Africa, Republic of 1995a: *Rural Development Strategy of the Government of National Unity*, Government Gazette No. 16679, 3rd November, Government Printer: Pretoria.

South Africa, Republic of 1995b: *Urban Development Strategy of the Government of National Unity*, Government Gazette No. 16679, 3rd November. Government Printer: Pretoria.

*Star* (Johannesburg; Daily).

Stewart, J.B. and McCarthy, C.L. (1995), 'An Appropriate Model for Joint Regional Action in Southern Africa after Apartheid', *Development Southern Africa*, Vol. 12, No. 3, pp. 401-411.

*Sunday Times* (Johannesburg: Weekly).

Weeks, J. (1996), 'Regional Cooperation and Southern African Development', *Journal of Southern African Studies*, Vol. 22, No. 1, pp. 99-117.

# PART III

# REGIONAL COOPERATION: THE POLITICAL DIMENSIONS

# 8 India, ASEAN and the New Geopolitical World Order

*Chandra Pal SINGH*

## Introduction

In the closing years of the twentieth century the world appears to be moving towards a world system where the borders between and among the nation-states may be vanishing. The driving force behind the elimination of barriers and borders are the compulsions of mobility of goods and capital across countries and continents. The major carriers of these trends are the multinational corporations and the communication revolution which is spreading fast in different degrees in different parts of the world. Yet, in spite of the communication facility of the internet, the transfer of capital over the modern channels of satellites and computers, unprecedented growth of the tentacles of multinational corporations, possessiveness over territory and territorial limits, national rivalries in economic and political decision making, and maintaining sovereign control over nationals and aliens has not reduced significantly. There is, however, a trend of some of the nation-states willing to give up very reluctantly and grudgingly some of their sovereignty in favour of regional groupings of countries, for the sake of securing better economic and security benefits for themselves and their citizens.

This is an era of multipolarity and the compulsions of competition between the rival economic centres for a larger share of the spoils from global resources, which is the motor behind the drive for the elimination of barriers to the mobility of goods and capital and for the growing monopolisation of economic activities within national boundaries and its trans-nationalisation world-wide. At the time of increasing globalisation, it is also associated with a counter process of more protection to businesses and industries within national boundaries and the sharpening of trade disputes (Varadarajan 1996), a process which became the election plank of the BJP party and government in India to protect indigenous industry and trade. For instance, the cancellation of the Enron project and its rehabilitation later after suitable modification to the project was to take care of the indigenous interests by the BJP government in the state of Maharashtra in India.

These changes have come about since the end of the Cold War in 1990. Earlier security considerations were given primacy over economic relations by individual states. At the close of the twentieth century the roles have reversed. Economic relations have become of primary importance over security considerations in the conduct of international relations among nation-states. This chapter analyses the current geopolitical and economic situation in the world and attempts to look at the interlinkages of India as a nation-state with the supranational organisation of ASEAN with which the country makes a contiguous boundary, and how security and economic compulsions have necessitated reordering of their mutual relations.

## Global Geopolitics

Five years after the end of the Cold War, the outlines of the new world order and a definitive pattern of international relations have begun to be clear. There have been remarkable changes in the global economic and geopolitical world order during this period. The Soviet Union, the second pole of the bipolar world, has disappeared leaving behind it a considerably weakened Russia and about a dozen new CIS countries; China has brought about dramatic changes in its economic policies and, militarily, it is regarded as the new superpower; the United States under a new Democratic President has maintained leadership of the First World and on the economic front, it has forged a new grouping, NAFTA, over the North American continent; the Asia-Pacific rim countries and most countries of Southeast Asia registered unprecedented economic boom placing them among the fastest growing economies in the world, and most of them joined the ASEAN Regional Forum (ARF) to take care of their security concerns after the withdrawal of the U.S. forces from the region; India adopted economic policies in conformity with the trend of globalisation that changed the course of economic development in the country, a direction which is likely to be maintained even after a change of government. Throughout the world, realpolitik appeared to have taken the back seat for some time and its place was taken over by economic considerations. The world economy was in the throes of evolution in a new direction during this period, more favourable to the newly emerging Asia.

Geopolitically, the collapse of the former Soviet Union left behind a unipolar world dominated by U.S. hegemonism. It had several consequences for the world order, the most significant of which was the reduction of the United Nations to the dictates of the hegemony. Along with its European and Japanese allies, it could call the shots anywhere and everywhere in the world, as was demonstrated by events in Iraq and Bosnia. At the end of the Cold War, the UN was reduced to 'mendicancy' (as the Secretary General has observed) with some 70 member nations, led by the U.S. not paying (US$1.4 billion from U.S. alone) both the budgetary dues and those for peace-keeping operations. And, in turn, the UN itself is indebted to many members who supplied forces and equipment for peace-keeping operations. In other words, instead of a better world order at the end of the Cold War, it is now worse in some respects - at least so far as the UN is concerned. In consequence, the organisation is worse off in a unipolar world than in a bipolar one.

Another consequence of the ongoing U.S. dominated world order is the increasing interference by the U.S. and its friends in the internal affairs of Third World nations through different organs of the United Nations. Many excuses are given for doing so, such as the alleged violation of human rights, the replacement of non-democratic regimes by a democratic system (of the Western model), the replacement of oppressive regimes (for example, allegedly in Iraq) by better (if not necessarily democratic) leadership, demand for 'good government' (of the Western conception) and so on. In principle, they might seem reasonable, but in practice, these judgements are self-righteous, selective and discriminatory, especially in respect of Third World countries. To make things worse, the Non-Aligned Movement (which once spearheaded the opposition to the Cold War and its deleterious consequences) has weakened and there appears to be no other movement or conference to remind the world community of the potential of the revival of the Cold War.

Some of the structures of the Cold War continue to remain intact. For instance, one of the major post-Cold War developments is the survival of NATO, a notorious Cold War symbol, while its Communist counterpart - the Warsaw Pact - has been dismantled. The former Warsaw Pact members are now keen to join NATO, both on their own and at the encouragement of NATO. So it seems likely that soon all of them (including Poland with common borders to the Russian Federation) are likely to join this organisation. Initially, Russia protested against this likelihood, but it was persuaded by NATO to join in a 'Partnership for Peace' - a clear sign of Russia's dependence on Western economic assistance. No doubt, this is a Western move to pre-empt the revival of the old Soviet domination over Central and Southern Europe. Another most recent instance of change in the world scene of the post-Cold War era is the dramatic replacement of the UN peace-keeping force in Bosnia by the NATO forces (Rajan 1996).

Among the tectonic changes that have accompanied the end of the Cold War, a significant yet little noticed shift has taken place in the maritime trade of the world. Consequent to the disintegration of the USSR and the shift away from competitive nuclear weapons-led security and stability, the world is moving towards the frenzy of the free market and free trade. A shift has taken place from the economic predominance of Europe and North America to the growing economic importance and probably the future economic predominance of the whole Asian region, particularly the Asian land mass and big populations of India and China. With the emergence of Asia-Pacific and South Asia as regions of high economic growth, the global maritime focus has shifted imperceptibly from the Atlantic and Pacific Oceans to the Pacific-Indian Ocean combine. Prevailing geopolitical and geoeconomic trends suggest that the arc from the oil-rich Persian Gulf through the Indian Ocean to the Sea of Japan is the new silk route of today (Uday Bhaskar 1995).

**Tripolar Focus**

There are three centres of accumulation in the world today: North America, the European Union and Asia. In each of these centres, the dominant players are trying to strengthen their hold over their region's trade and investment. In the Americas, NAFTA is firmly established and Chile is on the verge of becoming its fourth member. The financial crisis in Mexico has only led to its further economic integration with the U S. Over a quarter of the trade between the two countries now takes place as book transfers between U.S. parents and Mexican subsidiaries.

The EU has begun to extend in two directions: eastward towards Eastern Europe, and southward towards the Mediterranean. The Euro-Med Summit in Barcelona in November 1995 was a step in the direction of the EU's desire to build a Euro-Mediterranean Free Trade Area (EMEA) by the year 2010. Within a month, the EU leaders formally announced the start of negotiations aimed at establishing a free trade agreement with Mercosur, the trade bloc that links Argentina, Brazil, Paraguay and Uruguay.

Both for the European Union and the U.S., Asia is likely to be tough to deal with. For one, the U.S. itself is considered by many as an interloper in the Asia-Pacific region. The trend in Asia appears to be that while the U.S. may think the APEC to be its trump card, Asian countries, on average, trade with one another more and are reluctant to grant concessions to an outsider. This fact was commented upon by the International Herald Tribune that for the first time a 'major international economic group incorporating the U.S. has so strongly resisted the post-war Anglo-Saxon model of trade liberalisation. This means that President Clinton's grandiose plans for free trade areas in Asia and Latin America are now in serious trouble' (Varadarajan 1996). Japan is spearheading the resistance to the binding rules and deadlines which the U.S. wants and many Asian countries are siding with Tokyo. As far as the European Union is concerned, APEC is a device to cut it off from Asia. Hence, it is keen to forge links with the ASEAN countries and a EU-ASEAN summit is likely to take place.

While these developments are taking place four major processes affecting global change can be identified:

- The spread of information technology: The whole world economy is now moving into a stage at which the most important controlling system is that of electronic communications and in which everything else has to respond to the development of the technology and the structure of that area
- This economy of electronic communications is accompanied by a transfer of technology which will revolutionise the entire gamut and which the developing countries are able to develop. There is a genuine world economy in which technology transfer is almost instantaneous
- The shift of power is taking place from Europe and North America to the predominance of the whole of Asian region with three major foci - East Asia including China and Japan, Southeast Asia, and South Asia with India being predominant there
- Democratic systems are being triumphant over the totalitarian systems, both in terms of economic organisation and internal administration of the state (Singh 1993), proving independent human initiative and action to be more productive than controlled human action in command economies.

## Security Issues

There is reasonable expectation that in the next 25 years Asia will become the centre of gravity of the globe in the economic, strategic and political fields. It is expected that the G-7 countries of 2025 AD are likely to be China, U.S., Japan, Germany, India, Indonesia and Korea. Asia again becomes important in a situation where nuclear weapons play a role as a currency of power in international relations. Five (Russia, China, India, Pakistan and Israel) out of the eight nuclear powers (U.S., Britain and France being the other three) are in Asia. Sixty per cent of the global population is in this continent. All the major energy sources are also located in Russia, the Middle East, Central Asia and South China. In terms of the world market for goods produced in industrialised countries, it is not the Asia-Pacific rim only but the entire rim of the Asian continent along the Pacific and Indian Ocean which will be the globe's main market.

With the rapid development of Asian countries their energy requirements are bound to shoot up and these will have to be met by tapping the new potential in Central Asia or the South China Sea. Not surprisingly, there are already struggles to take control of these resources. This explains, too, the U.S. interests in the Central Asian Republics and the ASEAN region.

Analysts point out an inherent contradiction in the U.S. policies towards Asia. Even as the U.S. asserts that it will fight the emergence of any power that challenges its position as the leading manager of the international system, it is doing everything to inhibit the growth of countervailing power centres in Asia which will balance the rapidly developing Chinese power. American policies towards Japan, Russia and India appear to be self-defeating and are likely to lead to a confrontation between the U.S. and China in the not-too-distant future, the beginning of which could be seen in the setting off of yet another acrimonious round in bilateral relations of the two countries over the alleged copyright violations by China. The Americans announced about US$3 billion worth of retaliatory tariffs on Chinese exports to the United States as on 16th May 1996, while China retorted by a similar announcement against American imports and suspension or freezing of further negotiations on some Sino-U.S. contracts to be finalised. Even though the two sides return from the brink at the last minute, these irritations between the two countries can have long term effects on not only the relations of the two countries but also on their multilateral relations, thus, complicating the global scene. The future of Asia will depend largely on the stability and peaceful transition to political pluralism in China. Should that not happen for some reason or other, there are possibilities of either China emerging as the most powerful authoritarian military power or its breaking down. Both possibilities are likely to have far reaching impact on the whole of Asia, including India and Southeast Asia.

## India and ASEAN - in a Unipolar World

Scholars in India believe that the historical relationship of India with Southeast Asia was a very substantial one. That warrior, priestly and commercial communities from India actually travelled across the seas to Southeast Asia to establish political, religious and economic institutions and values which constitute a prominent feature of the past of these regions. Recent historical research, partly in the countries of Southeast Asia and partly also in metropolitan academies in the first world, takes a slightly different view of the nature and character of Indian influence in the region. It is argued that the dissemination of Indian influence and culture was a more 'passive' business than it was imagined earlier. That the whole process rested on the physical movement of very small diasporic communities which carried with them the 'high traditions' of Indian civilisation and grafted them on the societal fabric of Southeast Asia without any fundamental changes in the existing scheme of things in these parts (Kumar 1995). In other words, the 'Hinduisation' of Southeast Asia, or the conversion of this region to the Buddhist worldview were low-key and gentle processes which did not involve any serious social or political dislocation, nor did it involve substantial physical migration of communities from India. Perhaps the only exception to this was the location of small mercantile communities in the coastal regions of Southeast Asia in the classical and medieval centuries.

During the 19th Century a substantial change occurred in the nature of Indian diasporas across the seas to foreign lands. From the late 18th Century till the middle of the 20th Century, India was an integral constituent of a world-wide British Empire, as were several countries of Southeast Asia. From the Ganga Basin as well as the riverine regions of Tamil Nadu, substantial numbers of landless peasants went to work in other British colonies. Such diasporas also drew in their wake members of the commercial and liberal professions, who migrated initially to serve their countrymen but established themselves later on as frugal and competitive social groups in the countries they had adopted as their own. The social classes drawn into these diasporas - impoverished peasants and enterprising men from the liberal and commercial professions - also moved to Sri Lanka, Southeast Asia, the East and the West Indies, as members of a far-flung imperial system with its metropolitan centre in Great Britain.

The currents that were transforming the social and political consciousness of the people within India, under colonial aegis, also affected members of the diasporic communities in their newly located foreign homes. The diasporic communities of the colonial era were equally active in the second half of the 20th Century. There were some seminal changes in the composition of these communities at this juncture. A new sort of Indian - a product of a society with a sophisticated capacity for generating professional skills - made his presence felt overseas in the second half of the 20th Century. Throughout the developed world, therefore, there exists today a substantial number of highly skilled Indians who are contributing significantly to the economic growth of the polities in which they are located, no less than they contributing to their ethnic and cultural diversity (Kumar 1995). These skilled communities, together with the older commercial diasporas of the colonial period, make non-resident Indian (NRIs) among the wealthiest social groups in their new homelands.

Apart from the contribution of the Indian diasporas drawn from a highly pluralistic society inhabiting over a territory of sub-continental scale, India was also instrumental in affecting the society and politics of the states of Southeast Asia in various other ways. Buddhism which originated in India is the major religion of most of these countries today. The juxtaposition of Buddhism with Taoism and Confucianism, along with Islam and Christianity, has created the complex religious culture of the region, giving rise to pluralistic societies in many of its countries (Singh 1993). The sea routes to Southeast Asia from the ports of peninsular India brought the people of the two neighbouring regions into close contact with each other for a long time in the not too distant past (Panikkar 1955). The indivisibility of sea and physical proximity of the two regions remain major factors in their close relationship. Sometimes the fact that the Union Territories of India - Andaman and Nicobar Islands - are within a distance of 250 to 500 kilometres from the coasts of Myanmar, Thailand, Malaysia and Indonesia is overlooked. The southernmost of these islands, Nicobar, is even closer - less than 100 kilometres from the Sumatran coast. If Southeast Asia has close cultural affinity with China through the land and sea connections, it is similarly connected with India through the Bay of Bengal and overland through Myanmar with northeast India, which is in close proximity to Thailand, Cambodia and China. Geography has placed Southeast Asia and India as contiguous regions, and events whether economic, social, political and environmental in one are bound to affect the other.

Besides, a common colonial experience and heritage bind India with Southeast Asia, where a majority of countries were governed by Britain. The colonial structures of economy, languages that served as lingua franca among the diverse people within and outside these countries, institutions of governance based on European moral and legal systems, transport and communications networks, etc. are some of the examples of the common heritage in India and Southeast Asia. India led these countries in obtaining freedom from colonialism, which paved the way for their joining together under the Non-Aligned Movement. But within almost a decade of achieving independence for themselves Malaysia, Singapore, Thailand, Indonesia, and the Philippines formed the Association of Southeast Asian Nations (ASEAN) in 1967 to originally look after the business interests of its members. Brunei joined it in 1984 after attaining independence, while Vietnam joined it as recently as mid-1995. Defence issues remained a matter between individual countries and outside powers, notably the U.S. and Britain. However, the end of the Cold War, the rise of China, the relative decline of Russia and the U.S. defence cutbacks brought security questions to the fore and the ASEAN

Regional Forum (ARF) came into existence on 25th July 1993 at their annual meeting at Singapore to take care of the security concerns of the member states. Over a period of time, several countries from and outside the Pacific rim of Asia were allowed to become 'dialogue partners' of ASEAN. They included the U.S., Japan, South Korea, Australia, New Zealand, Canada and the European Union. Besides, China, Russia, Vietnam (till its becoming a member), Laos and Papua New Guinea were made observers or consultative partners.

India was the only regional power of any consequence which was not included in the ARF regional grouping. This was a country which was playing a leading role in Southeast Asia till the 1960s. The exclusion of India is attributed by some analysts to the foreign policy failures of India during the peak of the Cold War in a tilt towards the Soviet Union and its policies in the 1980s towards Cambodia and Vietnam (Singh 1996). It was after prolonged and behind the scenes diplomatic efforts that India became a full dialogue partner of ASEAN in December 1995, and it was as recently as mid-May 1996, that the way for India's participation in the ARF was finally cleared. This is to some extent a recognition that India has a role to play in the security matters of Southeast Asia. With the membership of the ARF, India and Southeast Asia could forge closer economic ties, explorations for which have been going on among the business and industrial community from the countries concerned in the wake of the liberalisation of economic policies pursued by India. But considering that Vietnam, Laos, Cambodia and Myanmar are yet to be fully absorbed within the regional fold, India's economic integration with Southeast Asia is still a long way away and this linkage may not prove to be a short-cut to prosperity in India.

## Some Economic Indicators of India and ASEAN

On December 25th, 1995 the Organisation for Economic Co-operation and Development (OECD) released a study which predicted that the six 'Asian Dragons' - Singapore, Malaysia, Hong Kong, South Korea, Taiwan and Thailand - will remain the 'major engines' for world trade and commerce over the next two years, despite their own somewhat moderate growth rates. That 'moderate' growth rate will be between 6 and 7 per cent a year on an average for the six Dragons. These economies expanded at average rates of 7.6 per cent in 1994 and an estimated 7.8 per cent in 1995. Much of the slowdown in their growth in the coming couple of years will be because China has been consciously slowing its growth, which was 11.8 per cent in 1994 and is expected to be 8.9 per cent in 1996 (Table 8.1). Meanwhile India's growth rate has barely touched 6 per cent

**Table 8.1   Selected economic indicators of India, ASEAN and other countries**

| Country | Areas (sq. kms) | Population (million) 1995 | GDP (US$ million) 1993 | GDP per capita (US$) 1993 | Base Year | Growth rate of GDP (per cent per annum) | | | | | | | |
|---|---|---|---|---|---|---|---|---|---|---|---|---|---|
| | | | | | | Average (1981-90) | 1990 | 1991 | 1992 | 1993 | 1994 | 1995 | 1996 |
| 1. India | 3287263 | 935.74 | 262810 | 290 | 1980 | 3.4 | 5.4 | 0.9 | 4.3 | 4.3 | 5.3 | 6.1 | 7.0 |
| ASEAN | | | | | | | | | | | | | |
| 2. Brunei | 5770 | 0.27 | 4001 | 14530 | - | - | 3.2 | 3.3 | - | - | - | - | - |
| 3. Indonesia | 1904570 | 195.28 | 136620 | 730 | 1983 | 5.5 | 7.2 | 7.0 | 6.5 | 6.5 | 7.4 | 7.1 | 7.1 |
| 4. Malaysia | 329750 | 19.95 | 60141 | 3160 | 1978 | 5.2 | 9.7 | 8.7 | 7.8 | 8.3 | 8.5 | 8.5 | 8.0 |
| 5. Philippines | 300000 | 70.01 | 54593 | 830 | 1985 | 1.0 | 3.0 | 0.6 | 0.3 | 2.1 | 4.3 | 5.0 | 5.5 |
| 6. Singapore | 641 | 2.99 | 55372 | 19310 | 1985 | 6.3 | 8.8 | 6.7 | 6.0 | 10.1 | 10.1 | 9.0 | 8.5 |
| 7. Thailand | 513120 | 58.79 | 120235 | 2040 | 1989 | 7.1 | 4.9 | 6.0 | 8.6 | 8.1 | 8.8 | 8.5 | 9.0 |
| 8. Vietnam | 331690 | 74.54 | 11997 | 170 | - | - | - | - | - | - | - | - | - |
| 9. Cambodia | 181035 | 9.61 | 1580 | 170 | - | - | - | - | - | - | - | - | - |
| 10. Laos | 236800 | 4.88 | 1308 | 290 | - | - | - | - | - | - | - | - | - |
| 11. Myanmar | 678031 | 46.52 | 30707 | 700 | - | - | - | - | - | - | - | - | - |
| Total (ASEAN) | 4461386 | 482.84 | 476554 | | | | | | | | | | |
| OTHERS | | | | | | | | | | | | | |
| 12. China | 956096 | 1206.6 | 581109 | 490 | 1978 | 10.4 | 3.9 | 8.0 | 13.2 | 13.4 | 11.8 | 9.8 | 8.9 |
| 13. Japan | 377800 | 125.36 | 4693200 | 37560 | - | 3.6 | 4.8 | 4.3 | 1.1 | 0.1 | 0.8 | 2.1 | 3.4 |
| 14. S. Korea | 99020 | 44.83 | 337910 | 7670 | 1985 | 10.7 | 9.5 | 9.1 | 5.1 | 5.5 | 8.3 | 7.3 | 6.8 |
| 15. U.S.A. | 9809426 | 263.06 | 673400 | 25850 | - | 3.1 | 0.8 | 1.2 | 2.1 | 3.2 | 4.0 | 3.0 | 2.5 |
| 16. Canada | 9976136 | 29.46 | 574936 | 20670 | - | 3.4 | 0.2 | 1.7 | 0.7 | 2.4 | 4.2 | 3.6 | 3.0 |
| 17. Australia | 7713358 | 18.02 | 310050 | 17510 | - | 3.5 | 0.6 | 0.6 | 2.7 | 2.8 | - | - | - |
| 18. Germany | 3789618 | 81.91 | 1908570 | 23630 | - | 2.2 | 5.7 | 5.0 | 2.2 | -1.1 | - | - | - |

*Source:*   Compiled from Statistical Yearbook for Asia and Pacific (1994); Economist Intelligence Unit (1995-1996); International Monetary Fund Annual Report (1994); Asian Development Bank Outlook (1995 and 1996); Pacific Economic Outlook Outlook 1991-92; U.S. National Committee for Pacific Cooperation (1991); Handbook of International Trade and Development Statistics (1994); Spectrum (1994); Encyclopaedia Britannica (1997)

after four years of reform and may slow down after the outcome of the recent general elections, at least till a stable government is in office.

In size, both in terms of area and population, India is much larger than any of the ASEAN countries. But it is for this very reason largely that it is poorer in terms of per capita income, or purchasing power parity. Singapore, the richest ASEAN country, has a per capita income of US$19,850 in 1993, which was 66 times higher than that of India at US$300 (Sarma and Mehta 1995). More important, leaving aside the Philippines, the rate of growth of GDP was also lower in India (1980-93). As compared to ASEAN, the share of the primary sector in the GDP was much higher in India. As regards the share of manufactures in GDP, India was much less industrialised than any of the ASEAN country. It is also important to note that the contribution of services to GDP was high in India at 41 per cent in 1993 but it was still higher in the ASEAN countries, ranging from 42 per cent in Indonesia and Vietnam to 63 per cent in Singapore.

Most ASEAN countries derive a large share of their income from the external sector, though it varied from one country to another. Whereas exports constituted as much as 169 per cent of the GDP of Singapore in 1993 on one extreme, they were 28 per cent in Indonesia, on the other. Even allowing for the size, exports as a percentage of GDP of India were much lower at 11 per cent in 1993, though they were barely 4 per cent in 1970. The higher degree of openness of the ASEAN countries is also reflected in the share of imports in their GDP. Imports as a percentage of GDP in 1993 varied from 19.4 per cent in Indonesia to 154.5 per cent in Singapore, against 10.1 per cent in India. Imports also recorded a higher growth in ASEAN, in the range of 4.5 per cent to 9.7 per cent per annum during 1980-93, than in India (4.2 per cent).

Unlike most ASEAN countries, India is a large importer of fuel. Still, per capita energy use was much lower in India (242 kg of oil equivalent) than the ASEAN countries (ranging from 5,563 kg equivalent in Singapore and 1,529 kg of oil equivalent in Malaysia to 321 kg of oil equivalent in Indonesia). At the same time, GDP produced per kg of oil equivalent is also much lower in India (US$1.2) than in ASEAN countries (ranging from $3.6 in Singapore to $2.2 in Malaysia), indicating the inefficient use of energy in India. This suggests that India can learn in terms of energy management from ASEAN countries. This seems to be one of the vital areas of co-operation from India's point of view.

It is not surprising therefore that despite the economic growth rate the per capita income and expenditure in India has been low and the ranking of the country in the Human Development Index has remained very low and stagnant over the years. Yet these figures and cross-country comparisons conceal many vital facts about the economic strength of India which are attractive to investors and businessmen. Though all the approximately one billion people in India cannot really be called 'consumers', there is enough affluence among about 300 million, especially among the top 10 per cent, which make India a huge market. The scramble for getting a foothold in the emerging market of India by the major car manufacturers of the world in the past one year is a case in point. When one looks at the Indian economy, one can see that India comprises three economies: pre-industrial, industrial and information age - each belonging to a different period of change in the whole pattern of production. India still has a large economy which belongs essentially to the factory age. It has a growing economy and a very important one, which already belongs to the information age. So, India is already involved in every stage and level of this historic development (Lord Rees-Mogg 1966). India also has a professional academic and business class of somewhere around 250 million people. It is a formidable force as it becomes deployed in the most modern methods of economic management. Technology will always be transferred at its most advanced level. Millions of Indians are actually using it every day although they may probably not be aware of it, electronic software which had not been designed in 1990. This explains why the latest World Bank Report (1996) identifies South Asia was the fastest growing developing region over the past decade, following the pace set by East Asian economies, with an average GDP growth of 5.1 per cent. Of this, India accounted for 80 per cent of the region's GDP. This country continued to draw substantial benefits from the trade and investment liberalisation undertaken after the 1991 balance of payment crisis. In the fiscal year ending March 1995, India maintained economic growth at 6.3 per cent. Inflation at the end of March 1996 was less than 5 per cent.

## Conclusion

It is within this environment, within each of the countries of Southeast Asia and South Asia, as well as at the global level, that the two regions have to assess their future interlinked as it is with each other, particularly the role of the Indian Ocean in regional and global trade. The present pattern of trade through this Ocean is likely to see dramatic changes even by the turn of the next century. As Uday Bhaskar (1995) points out, of the global trade of US$7,480 billion at present, the intra-Indian Ocean region trade accounts for only US$912 billion. The merchandise trade within the region currently is a mere 22 per cent of this total trade. Of the total global trade levels of 1993 , about 40 per cent is estimated to transit through this 'new silk route' - or trade worth US$3 trillion traverses these sea-lanes. This value is enhanced by the fact that all vibrant economies of Asia -

Japan, China, India and ASEAN - will for the foreseeable future depend on the Indian Ocean's sea-lanes for their oil imports. Thus, the security and stability of the Ocean will engage the attention of the major powers. India can make a notable contribution to this both because of its geography and the professionalism of its naval forces.

With the economic power shift towards Asia, ASEAN is likely to play a key role between the Asia Pacific and the Indian Ocean rim countries. India, on the other hand, is placed between the two foci of the post Cold War attention of the U.S. in Asia, namely, China and the Pakistan-Iran-Afghanistan area. It has to protect its security interest from the fallout of the U.S. actions, such as wanton air intrusions, massive influx of terrorists, arms, narcotics and money and attempts at destabilisation. The decision of allowing India to join the Asean Regional Forum may prove to be useful both for the ASEAN and India in taking care of their security and trade interests in a dynamically changing regional and global situation in the post Cold War world.

# References

Asian Development Bank Outlook (1995 and 1996), Asian Development Bank.

Economist Intelligence Unit (1995-1996), *Country Profile, U.S.A., 1995-96*.

Encyclopaedia Britannica (1997).

Handbook of International Trade and Development Statistics (1994), UNCTAD.

International Monetary Fund Annual Report (1994).

Kumar, Ravinder (1995), 'India and South-East Asia', *Times of India*, 26th December.

Lord Rees-Mogg (1996), 'India as Economic Super Power', *Hindustan Times*, 24th March.

Pacific Economic Outlook 1991-1992.

Panikkar, K. M. (1955), 'Geographical Factors in Indian History', reprinted in Singh, C.P. (ed.), 1994, *Selected Readings in Political Geography of India*, Heritage: Delhi.

Rajan (1996), 'Cold Wars to Warm Wars', *Hindustan Times*, 21st January.

Sarma, Atul and Mehta, Pradeep Kumar (1995), 'A Place Among the Cubs', *Economic Times*, 6th September.

Siddharth Varadarajan (1996), 'Tossed into the Sea of Globalisation', *Times of India*, 5th January.

Singh, C. P. (1993), 'Democracy and Privatisation: A View from India', in Taylor, P.J. ed.), *Political Geography of the Twentieth Century*, Belhaven Press: London, pp. 257-261.

_____ (1996), 'Towards a New Equilibrium: India, Asia-Pacific and global Geopolitical Change', in Rumley, Dennis, *et al.* (eds.), *Global Geopolitical Change and the Asia-Pacific: A Regional Perspective*, Chapter 16 (forthcoming).

*Spectrum* (1994) (January).

*Statistical Yearbook for Asia and Pacific* (1994), ESCAP: Bangkok.
Uday Bhaskar, C. (1995), 'India and the World: Policy at Sea in the Indian Ocean',
    *Times of India*, 29th December.
U.S. National Committee for Pacific Cooperation (1991), PECC: San Francisco.
World Bank Report (1996).

# 9  Appraising the Possibility of Promoting Interdependent Development Between SAARC and ASEAN

*Ziaush Shams HAQ*

## Introduction

South Asian Association for Regional Cooperation (SAARC) and Association for Southeast Asian Nations (ASEAN), the two regional groupings of Asia, are quite different in terms of socio-economic, political and cultural profile. In this chapter, socio-economic indicators and perception of threat will be examined to analyse the prospects of cooperation between these two geographically contiguous Asian regions and also to appraise the potential benefits which may accrue to the member states of SAARC from such cooperation. An attempt will also be made to outline the manner in which ASEAN states reckoned with the problem of underdevelopment and to assess its applicability to the South Asian nations. In addition, this chapter will systematically outline the political dynamics which may either facilitate or endanger cooperation between ASEAN and SAARC. The chapter concludes with some insights regarding the possibility of promoting the dynamics of interdependence between the two regions.

## SAARC and ASEAN: A Socio-Economic and Political Profile

Table 9.1 indicates that the member states of both SAARC and ASEAN have diverse socio-economic and cultural characteristics. SAARC, for example, is constituted of large states such as India, with an area of 3,185,847 square kilometres and a population size of 849.5 million (1990 estimate); and other states such as Maldives with an area of merely 298 square kilometres and a

**Table 9.1   Basic indicators of SAARC and ASEAN states, 1990**

| | Area (sq. km.) | Population (million) | Life expectancy (years) | Adult illiteracy | | GNP per capita Annual average | | Annual average Rate of inflation (%) 1980-1990 |
| --- | --- | --- | --- | --- | --- | --- | --- | --- |
| | | | | Female | Total | US$ | Growth rate (%) | |
| **SAARC** | | | | | | | | |
| Bangladesh | 144,036 | 106.70 | 52 | 78 | 65 | 210 | 0.7 | 9.6 |
| Bhutan | 46,632 | 1.40 | 49 | 75 | 62 | 190 | n.a. | 8.4 |
| India | 3,185,847 | 849.50 | 59 | 66 | 52 | 350 | 1.9 | 7.9 |
| Maldives | 298 | 0.20 | n.a. | n.a. | 6 | n.a. | n.a. | n.a. |
| Nepal | 141,096 | 18.90 | 52 | 87 | 74 | 170 | 0.5 | 9.0 |
| Pakistan | 804,145 | 112.40 | 56 | 79 | 65 | 380 | 2.5 | 6.7 |
| Sri Lanka | 65,627 | 17.00 | 71 | 17 | 12 | 470 | 2.9 | 11.1 |
| Total | 4,387,681 | 1,106.10 | - | - | - | - | - | - |
| **ASEAN** | | | | | | | | |
| Brunei | 5,767 | 0.30 | n.a. | n.a. | 55 | n.a. | n.a. | n.a. |
| Indonesia | 1,904,839 | 178.20 | 62 | 32 | 23 | 570 | 4.5 | 8.4 |
| Malaysia | 332,456 | 17.90 | 70 | 30 | 22 | 2,320 | 4.0 | 1.6 |
| Phillippines | 300,078 | 61.50 | 64 | 11 | 10 | 730 | 1.3 | 14.9 |
| Singapore | 570 | 3.00 | 74 | 7 | 5 | 11,160 | 6.2 | 7.2 |
| Thailand | 514,132 | 55.80 | 66 | 10 | 7 | 1,420 | 4.4 | 3.4 |
| Total | 3,057,842 | 316.70 | - | - | - | - | - | - |

*Source:*   Compiled from World Bank (1992:218-219) and The Almanac (1991)

population size of only 200,000. Along similar lines, the socio-economic characteristics of the member states of ASEAN states display some prominent differences. Indonesia, the largest and most populous of the ASEAN states, has an area of 1,904,839 square kilometres and a population size of 128.7 million. On the other hand, Singapore, also an ASEAN member, has an area of only 570 square kilometres and a population size of 3 million. A closer examination of Table 9.1 provides additional insights regarding the socio-economic profile of the member states of SAARC and ASEAN. The ASEAN region, though comparable to SAARC in terms of total geographical area, displays a population size which is almost one fourth the population size of SAARC. As regards the income of the people in the South Asian region, it is at a rather low level.[1] In fact, with the exception of the East African region, there is no other region in the world where poverty is so widespread. The ASEAN region, by comparison, is much more prosperous. Incomes are at a substantially higher level and the Gross Domestic Product (GDP) are substantially more (Tables 9.1 and 9.2). In Singapore, an ASEAN member-state, income is even comparable to the income of OECD countries and its GDP is significantly higher than that of Bangladesh and is comparable to Pakistan's GDP - the third and second largest economies within SAARC respectively. Indications regarding the quality of life in the SAARC and ASEAN regions, are available, albeit indirectly, from the data on life expectancy and adult illiteracy, as shown in Table 9.1. Life expectancy in South Asia, with the exception of Sri Lanka, is clearly at a lower level than the ASEAN states. Added to this, with the exception of Sri Lanka again, most South Asian countries have a relatively high level of both adult and female illiteracy.

The level of productivity of SAARC states - in comparison with ASEAN states is shown in Table 9.2. Two important observations in Table 9.2 deserve specific mention. Firstly, during the 1965-1990 period, the GDP of the ASEAN states (considered collectively) increased at a more rapid rate relative to SAARC. Furthermore, the rank ordering, as provided in Table 9.2, suggests that although India obtained the first position (in terms of production power) in the grouping of ASEAN and SAARC states (considered collectively), the majority of South Asian states fared poorly. In terms of structure of production, both SAARC and ASEAN states manifest certain interesting (and, in some cases, similar) patterns. The picture which presents itself at the very outset in Table 9.3 is one of a trend towards a rising significance of the industrial sector in both the ASEAN and SAARC states. In the ASEAN region, however, the industrial sector developed at a much faster pace in comparison with SAARC.[2]

Macro data, as outlined in Tables 9.4 and 9.5, assist in providing insight into the socio-political realities and foreign policy alignment patterns of the various member states of ASEAN and SAARC. In terms of the form of government prevalent in the decade of the 1990s in these two geographically contiguous areas, namely, South and Southeast Asia, republics (and their variants of the Islamic, democratic people's or socialist form), tend to predominate. Other forms of government such as kingdoms and monarchies, however, also exist in this political landscape.

As regards the religious composition of society, a monolithic nature - in the form of an overwhelming predominance of a single religious group, is a distinct feature of almost all of the SAARC and ASEAN states. In the case of the SAARC states, a Muslim majority population exists in 3 states (Pakistan, Bangladesh and Maldives), and amongst the ASEAN states again, a Muslim majority is prevalent in Indonesia, Malaysia and Brunei. As regards the other states, a Hindu majority population is noted in 2 instances - India and Nepal; a Buddhist majority population exists in Bhutan, Sri Lanka, Thailand and Singapore; and Christians are noted to be the overwhelming majority in the Phillippines. The foreign policy implications of such a religious landscape in South and Southeast Asia manifest clearly in the form of membership/non

## Table 9.2  Production power of SAARC and ASEAN states

|  | GDP 1965 | (US$ millions) 1990 | Rank in SAARC | Rank in SAARC & ASEAN countries (combined) | Rank in the world |
|---|---|---|---|---|---|
| **SAARC** | | | | | |
| Bangladesh | 4,380 | 22,880 | 3 | 8 | 66 |
| Bhutan | n.a | 280 | 6 | 12 | Below 100 |
| India | 50,530 | 254,540 | 1 | 1 | 14 |
| Maldives | n.a. | 69.70 ('87) | 7 | 13 | Below 100 |
| Nepal | 730 | 2,890 | 5 | 11 | Below 100 |
| Pakistan | 5,450 | 35,500 | 2 | 6 | 53 |
| Sri Lanka | 1,770 | 7,250 | 4 | 10 | 90 |
| Total | 62,860 | 323,409.70 | - | - | - |
| | | | | | |
| **ASEAN** | | | | | |
| Brunei | n.a. | 7,930 | 6 | 9 | 85 |
| Indonesia | 5,980 | 107,290 | 1 | 2 | 27 |
| Malaysia | 3,130 | 42,400 | 4 | 5 | 47 |
| Philippines | 6,010 | 43,860 | 3 | 4 | 46 |
| Singapore | 970 | 34,600 | 5 | 7 | 54 |
| Thailand | 4,390 | 80,170 | 2 | 3 | 33 |
| Total | 20,480 | 316,250 | - | - | - |

*Source*:  Compiled from World Bank (1992:222-223) and Asiaweek, 17th May 1992

membership in the Organisation of Islamic Conference (OIC). Thus, akin to Bangladesh, Pakistan, Maldives within SAARC, Brunei, Indonesian, and Malaysia are also members of OIC (Tables 9.4 and 9.5).

A tilt towards the West is also a prominent feature of most of the SAARC and ASEAN countries. The other tendency observed in the foreign policy patterns, outlined in Table 9.4, is one of non-alignment. It is important to note, however, that although some countries such as Pakistan and Bangladesh claim to be non-aligned, they have, in functional terms, continued (with possibly only brief intervals) to associate closely with the West. This, however, is not true in the case of India and Sri Lanka. In discussing the 'Western tilt', it is important to mention specifically that, in contrast to the non-aligned tendencies noticed in South Asia, all the member states of ASEAN have traditionally had a definite Western tilt. Such a Western tilt can be better complemented if one takes into account the popularly identified source of threat in the ASEAN region. As seen in Table 9.5, the fear of Communism and mainland China stands out prominently amongst the ASEAN states. In fact, the creation of ASEAN itself in 1967 was in response to

**Table 9.3    Structure of production in SAARC and ASEAN, 1990**

|  | Agriculture | | Industrial | | Service, etc. | |
|---|---|---|---|---|---|---|
|  | 1965 | 1990 | 1965 | 1990 | 1965 | 1990 |
| SAARC |  |  |  |  |  |  |
| Bangladesh | 53.0 | 39.0 | 11.0 | 15.0 | 36.0 | 46.0 |
| Bhutan | n.a. | 44.0 | n.a. | 27.0 | n.a. | 29.0 |
| India | 44.0 | 31.0 | 22.0 | 29.0 | 34.0 | 40.0 |
| Maldives | n.a. | n.a. | n.a. | n.a. | n.a. | n.a. |
| Nepal | 65.0 | 60.0 | 11.0 | 14.0 | 23.0 | 26.0 |
| Pakistan | 40.0 | 26.0 | 20.0 | 25.0 | 40.0 | 49.0 |
| Sri Lanka | 28.0 | 26.0 | 21.0 | 26.0 | 51.0 | 48.0 |
| ASEAN |  |  |  |  |  |  |
| Brunei | n.a. | n.a. | n.a. | n.a. | n.a. | n.a. |
| Indonesia | 51.0 | 22.0 | 13.0 | 40.0 | 36.0 | 38.0 |
| Malaysia | 28.0 | 21.0 | 25.0 | 35.0 | 47.0 | 44.0 |
| Philippines | 26.0 | 22.0 | 27.0 | 35.0 | 47.0 | 43.0 |
| Singapore | 3.0 | 0.0 | 24.0 | 37.0 | 74.0 | 63.0 |
| Thailand | 32.0 | 12.0 | 23.0 | 39.0 | 37.0 | 65.0 |

Distribution of GDP (per cent)

*Source*:    World Bank (1992:222-223)

**Table 9.4   Typology of SAARC states**

| | Form of government | Religious composition of society (%) | Patterns noted in current foreign policy orientation | Popularity identified source of threat |
|---|---|---|---|---|
| Bangladesh | Peoples' Republic | Muslims (83.0) Hindus (17.0) | OIC member; Western-learning; non-aligned | Political instability: poverty; fear of India |
| Bhutan | Kingdom | Buddhists (75.0) Hindus (25.0) | Foreign policies defined by India | Underdevelopment: territorial claims by India and China |
| India | Democratic Republic | Hindus (83.0) Muslims (10.0) Christians (3.0) Sikhs (2.0) Others (2.0) | Non-aligned | Separatist tendencies; domestic unrest arising out of ethnic/ religious discord |
| Maldives | Republic | Predominantly Muslim | OIC member; Western-leaning | Fear of India |
| Nepal | Kingdom | Hindus (90.0) Buddhists (5.0) Muslims (3 Others (2.0) | Non-aligned; Western-leaning | Underdevelopment; fear of India and China |
| Pakistan | Islamic Republic | Muslims (97.0) Others (3.0) | OIC member; Western-leaning; non-aligned | Domestic unrest; separatist tendencies; fear of India |
| Sri Lanka | Democratic Socialist Republic | Buddhists (69.0) Hindus (15.0) Muslims (8.0) Christians (8.0) | Western-leaning; non-aligned | Ethnic problems and consequant separatists tendencies; fear of India |

*Source:*   Compiled from the Almanac (1991); Asia Yearbook (1992); and Japan and the Pacific Rim (1991)

**Table 9.5    Typology of ASEAN states**

| | Form of government | Religious composition of society (%) | Patterns noted in current foreign policy orientation | Popularly identified source of threat |
|---|---|---|---|---|
| Brunei | Sultanate | Muslims (60.0)<br>Christians (8.0)<br>Buddhists (32.0) | OIC member; Western-leaning; non-aligned | Territorial claims by Malaysia and Indonesia |
| Indonesia | Republic | Muslims (87.0)<br>Christians (10.0)<br>Hindus & Buddhists (3.0) | Non-aligned; OIC member; Western-leaning | Fear of China; separatist movement in Sumatra; Communism |
| Malaysia | Constituent Monarchy | Muslims (53.0)<br>Buddhists (17.0)<br>Chinese folk religion (12.0)<br>Hindus (7.0)<br>Christians (6.0)<br>Others (5.0) | OIC member; Western-leaning non-aligned | National integration problem; Communism; fear of China |
| Philippines | Republic | Christians (85.0)<br>Muslims (4.0)<br>Protestants (3.0)<br>Others (8.0) | Western-leaning, non-aligned | Domestic political unrest; Separatist movement; Communism |
| Singapore | Kingdom | Buddhists & Taoist (52.0)<br>Christians (18.0)<br>Muslims (16.0)<br>Hindus (5.0)<br>Others (9.0) | Western-leaning | Potential Malaysian and Indonesian territorial designs |
| Thailand | Kingdom | Buddhists (95.0)<br>Muslims (5.0) | Western-leaning | Domestic unrest; fear of China; Communism |

*Source:* Compiled from the Almanac (1991); Asia Yearbook (1992); and *Japan and the Pacific Rim* (1991).

such fears. The fear of China, due to border disputes, territorial claims and hegemonistic designs, is not alien to South Asia. This is amply clear in Table 9.4.

However, two additional factors serve to somewhat dilute this fear of China in the South Asian context. Firstly, the fear of India - in the context of South Asia and SAARC - has continued to be considered by some states such as Pakistan, and in more recent times, by others such as Bangladesh, Nepal, Sri Lanka and Maldives as being a compelling security concern. In fact, Pakistan, since its creation in 1947, has always felt that India had never, for a moment, abandoned its 'Akhand Bharat' designs.

In addition, poverty and economic underdevelopment are commonly considered by the South Asian populace as the principal threat to their national well-being. The earlier discussion on the socio-economic realities of South Asia suggests that such fears are not totally unfounded. It should also be noted in this context that the economic problems in South Asia have often contributed to domestic instability, fostered ethno-religious discord and provided leverage to separatist forces. This, in effect, had undermined the general politico-economic climate and served subsequently to make potential investors (domestic and foreign) somewhat uncomfortable. The cyclical forces thus generated and their adverse impact upon South Asia can hardly be overemphasised.

Additional insights regarding the economic bill - of- health and potentialities of the SAARC and ASEAN states, and the prospects for economic growth and development are available from Table 9.6. Prior to discussing these findings, it is important to mention an important feature of the ASEAN member states which distinguishes them from the SAARC states. ASEAN, in the truest sense of the term, is a 'merchandise trade oriented' society. Thus, for example, the ASEAN states in 1990, exported goods worth US$144,272 million and imported goods worth US$157,925 million. The export and import figures for the SAARC states (considered collectively) was much lower, viz. US$27,215 million and US$37,404 million respectively. Furthermore, it is important to note that the collective value of exports from the ASEAN states, as a percentage of their combined GDP, was 45.62 per cent. The corresponding figure in the case of the SAARC states was only 8.33 per cent.[3]

Table 9.6 shows changing pattern of imports and exports in terms of primary and manufactured commodities. Primary goods, as a proportion of the total merchandise exports, underwent a decline during the 1965-1990 period in the case of each and every SAARC and ASEAN member state. A similar trend, with some exceptions (Pakistan, Brunei and Thailand) is observed in the data pertaining to primary commodity imports. As regards manufactured goods, exports rose sharply in the case of all the members states of SAARC for which data was available. A consistent pattern, in the case of imports of manufactured goods was, however, somewhat less discernable both in the case of ASEAN and SAARC groupings.

**Table 9.6  Structure of merchandise exports and imports**

| | Export (% of total export) | | | | Import (% of total import) | | | |
|---|---|---|---|---|---|---|---|---|
| | Primary commodities | | Manufactured commodities | | Primary commodities | | Manufactured commodities | |
| | 1965 | 1990 | 1965 | 1990 | 1965 | 1990 | 1965 | 1990 |
| SAARC | | | | | | | | |
| Bangladesh | n.a. | 26.0 | n.a. | 74.0 | n.a. | 50.0 | n.a. | 50.0 |
| Bhutan | n.a. | n.a. | n.a | n.a. | n.a. | n.a. | n.a. | n.a. |
| India | 51.0 | 27.0 | 49.0 | 73.0 | 41.0 | 37.0 | 59.0 | 63.0 |
| Maldives | n.a. | n.a. | n.a. | n.a | n.a. | n.a. | n.a. | n.a. |
| Nepal | n.a. | 25.0 | n.a. | 75.0 | n.a. | 28.0 | n.a. | 72.0 |
| Pakistan | 64.0 | 30.0 | 36.0 | 70.0 | 28.0 | 42.0 | 72.0 | 58.0 |
| Sri Lanka | 99.0 | 53.0 | 1.0 | 47.0 | 53.0 | 34.0 | 47.0 | 66.0 |
| ASEAN | | | | | | | | |
| Brunei | n.a. | n.a. | n.a. | n.a. | n.a. | n.a. | n.a. | n.a. |
| Indonesia | 96.0 | 64.0 | 4.0 | 36.0 | 11.0 | 23.0 | 89.0 | 77.0 |
| Malaysia | 94.0 | 56.0 | 6.0 | 44.0 | 47.0 | 22.0 | 53.0 | 78.0 |
| Philippines | 95.0 | 38.0 | 5.0 | 62.0 | 37.0 | 30.0 | 63.0 | 70.0 |
| Singapore | 65.0 | 27.0 | 35.0 | 73.0 | 56.0 | 26.0 | 44.0 | 74.0 |
| Thailand | 97.0 | 36.0 | 3.0 | 64.0 | 20.0 | 22.0 | 80.0 | 78.0 |

*Source*:  World Bank (1992:246-249)

### Partners on the Road to Prosperity:  SAARC and ASEAN

The preceding analysis of the socio-economic and political profile of SAARC and ASEAN clearly suggests that there is, for all practical purposes, sufficient scope for cooperation between SAARC and ASEAN.  The patterns noted in the current foreign policy orientations of the SAARC and ASEAN states, as discussed in the previous section, indicate no major contradiction in the fundamental goals and objectives of these states.  Added to this, both regional groupings are motivated primarily by the purpose of promoting prosperity for their people.  In the case of SAARC, initiated by the late President Ziaur Rahman of Bangladesh, the focus was on functional areas such as science and technology, and also on education, sports, cultural exchanges, etc.[4]  The philosophical theme which has and continues to inspire and guide the prospects of SAARC - originates from the neo-functionalist school.  In other words, the basic premise is that if satisfactory relations can be facilitated between states in relatively non-controversial areas such as tourist travel, student and cultural exchanges, etc, this would, in itself, foster, in the long-run, better inter-state relations in the political realm also.[5]  The approach is to 'go-slow', and Article X(2) of the Charter which was adopted in the Dhaka Summit of the Heads of State on 7th and 8th December, 1985, kept 'bilateral' and 'contentious' issues outside the scope of SAARC.[6]  While the purpose of the planners of SAARC may have been to provide the 'aperitif' prior to getting bogged down with the 'main course' of political problems, critics of the SAARC approach to diplomacy and conflict resolution seem to suggest that by keeping 'bilateral' and 'contentious' issues outside the scope of SAARC, distrust, fears and other such sentiments, which constitute the 'main course' of political problems in South Asia, have persistently been excluded from the SAARC menu.  In a similar manner, compelling political problems such as the crisis in Kashmir, the Tamil dilemma, the Ganges water dispute with Bangladesh, etc., have continued to serve as irritants in inter-state relations in South Asia.  Added to the above impediments, SAARC's preoccupation with peripheral concerns such as student exchanges, tourism and cultural matters has, in essence, also contributed to a (conscious or possibly unconscious) neglect of critical areas of economic activities, such as attracting foreign investments, promoting trade and facilitating monetary cooperation with South Asia.[7]  Recently, the  member states of SAARC are aspiring to form a free trade zone entitled 'South Asian Free Trade Area', (SAFTA), by the early decades of the next century.  But progress to date in even implementing the mechanism of South Asia Preferential Trade Arrangement, SAPTA, is anything but satisfactory.  The above approach, as the discussions in the earlier section seem to suggest, has not contributed to facilitate significant economic progress and well-being in South Asia.  In contrast, however, several of the ASEAN states - have gradually entered the portals of the Newly Industrialised Countries (NICs).  Their economic strategies and political planning clearly deserve some discussions in this chapter as to ASEAN's approach to overcome the problems of underdevelopment, attaining the objective of sustained rapid economic development, and its applicability to the South Asian context.

ASEAN'S planning, in the socio-economic and political realm has traditionally evolved around the compelling fear of communism. And while, during the formative phase, some leaders of the ASEAN states, such as the former President Marcos of the Philippines, wished ASEAN to transcend into the field of defence (*FEER*, 8th February 1968), the approach which was adopted eventually by ASEAN emphasised economic well-being and prosperity as the best means to protect against Communism. In fact, ASEAN's creation itself was considered by the member states and also by the world community at large as primarily the emergence of an economic union, and to this day, ASEAN, despite some intra-regional rivalry and other preoccupations, has remained committed mainly to economic development. To attain the objective of sustained economic development, ASEAN has aggressively explored methods - both in the domestic domain and in the realm of international trade - to facilitate the economic uplift of Southeast Asia. The underlying ethos of the formula devised by ASEAN has focused on de-regulation, structural adjustment, industrialisation and preferential trading arrangements amongst the member states. Trade liberalisation within ASEAN, despite the adverse response of some sections of the private sector in the ASEAN states, remained the prime objective of ASEAN in the seventies. And in more recent times, it has been observed that, by the year 1993, a system entitled 'Common Effective Preferential Tariff' has been put into place in order to create a truly 'Free Trade Area' within ASEAN by the turn of this century (*Daily Star*, 2nd July 1992).

As regards the domestic economic policies which have propelled several ASEAN states to their current economic well-being, it may be worthwhile to highlight some of their prominent features. Indonesia adopted the approach of privatisation, de-regulation, structural adjustment and trade liberalisation -- and economic recovery was soon to follow. In the case of Malaysia, poverty eradication and the attainment of racial economic equality have continued as the principal goals of the government. And in attaining these objectives, increased measures towards privatisation has gone hand in hand with increased levels of government spending. The positive outcome of this policy is visible in the sustained GDP growth rates and in the average annual rate of inflation of only 1.6 per cent (which is considered as an outstanding achievement in even the OECD countries) during the 1980-1990 period. (Tables 9.1 and 9.2). While privatisation, preferential trading arrangements, de-regulation, structural adjustment and the other measures mentioned in the above paragraphs may be options which decision-makers in SAARC countries may consider adopting, the policy path adopted by Thailand - may be of particular relevance to the countries. Thailand, in trying to emerge out of the poverty pit, has focussed primarily on export-oriented industrialisation - based on a labour intensive approach and the use of indigenous raw materials. To the extent that the socio-economic realities of the member states of SAARC during much of the twentieth century were not too different from that of Thailand, these countries, in fact, should benefit by adopting, during the closing decade of the 20th Century, the Thai approach to development - in order to ensure that the countries of South Asia are not marginalised in the economic realm of the world in the 21st Century.

## Conclusion

The quest for economic prosperity, akin to the quest for security, is a complex phenomena. The discussion on the economic formula which has provided the ASEAN states with the hope for prosperity serves as one dimension of the question regarding how the SAARC states can attempt to not only cope with their current economic woes but also to strive for economic success. A satisfactory political climate is, however, essential in order to attain economic development. In the context of South Asia, a satisfactory state of intra-state relations is imperative for productive economic activity and for attracting foreign direct investments (FDI). Some signs of an emerging stability in South Asia appears to be visible. In recent times, for example, Bangladesh has successfully worked out a political arrangement with India on the Tinbigha Corridor, and is currently attempting to reckon with some outstanding issues which need to be solved with Pakistan, such as the question of assets sharing and the repatriation of Pakistanis. All this is in the right direction - but the 'go slow' approach, which is basic to SAARC, may need to be reappraised due to the rapidly changing international economic and political environment and the imperative need to 'strike when the iron is hot'. India's lukewarm attitude towards SAARC may also serve to undermine SAARC, and, to the extent that India is a predominant political and economic entity in South Asia, it is essential that, if required, the political leadership in Delhi is 'wooed'. In the past, Delhi had, on occasions, toed a line in international politics - independent of the SAARC position. This was most noticeable during the Soviet occupation of Afghanistan and also became manifest in the Indian posture on Kampuchea (Halim 1992:118). In more recent times again, India gave the cold shoulder to SAARC when several SAARC states, during the Fifth SAARC Summit, suggested that the SAARC platform could possibly assist in easing India-Pakistan tensions over Kashmir. The Indian response to such overtures was that SAARC was not the proper platform to discuss a strictly bilateral issue such as Kashmir.[8]

A united approach, based on sincerity and a true desire to promote the concept of interdependent development, is essential for the success of SAARC. The ability to generate such a cooperative climate will also make it conducive for ASEAN states to consider joint ventures with SAARC, either collectively or at the bilateral level. Press reports in Bangladesh were indicative of the interest of Indonesia and other ASEAN member states to foster cooperation between

ASEAN and SAARC. In more recent times, the ASEAN states, on account of a reduced American interest (following the demise of the Soviet Union) in providing economic assistance to the region and also due to the linking of future aid by the European Community and Japan to compliance by ASEAN states to democratic and free -market principles, have somewhat intensified their efforts to forge cooperative ties with SAARC states. For example, Malaysia has shown definite willingness to employ Bangladeshi labour to cater for the rapidly increasing manpower needs of a booming Malaysian economy. In addition to this, Malaysia has continued to import shrimps and jute products in good quantities from Bangladesh. On the international front, ASEAN states such as Indonesia, Malaysia, Singapore and Thailand have expressed anxiety over the Myanmar Muslim refugees and publicly appealed to Myanmar to seek a speedy solution to this problem. The climate is clearly conducive for SAARC to initiate dialogues for promoting cooperation and thus interdependent development with ASEAN. The growing emergence of trade blocs around the world makes it imperative that SAARC, akin to ASEAN, progressively explores its economic options in a gradually emerging global village. Cooperation with the technologically- advanced ASEAN states may help to propel the LDC member states of SAARC out of the 'low-wage, low-productivity' category and assist in making them a 'low-wage, high-productivity' category. This would improve the competitive edge of the countries of this region in the world economic market and thereby serve to give their economies a much needed boost.

## Notes

1   According to the World Bank (1992:211-213), low-income economies are those which had a GNP per capita of US$610 or less in 1990; middle-income economies, US$611-US$7,610; and high-income economies, US$7,620 or more.
2   This observation is based on the author's analysis of some empirical findings on this topic.
3   In the case of Bangladesh, the value of exports, as a percentage of GDP, was 7.32 per cent in 1990 (World Bank 1992:244-245).
4   For details, see *ASEAN Experiences of Regional and Inter-Regional Cooperation: Relevance for SAARC* (Dhaka: B.I.I.S.S., 1988), page 64.
5   This comment is based on the experience and observation of the author during the formative phase of SAARC in 1979-80, when the author was affiliated with the Bangladesh Institute of International and Strategic Studies, Dhaka.
6   For details, see *ASEAN Experiences of Regional and Inter-Regional Cooperation: Relevance for SAARC* (1988:55, 64).
7   *Ibid.*, p.55.

8   *Ibid.* India has also dragged its feet on the issue of harnessing the Himalayan water system - which would immensely benefit the populace of the Indus, Ganges, and Brahmaputra basins.  See Ahamed (1986:103).

## References

Ahamed, E. (1986), 'Prospects of SAARC', *Rastrobiggan Somiti Potrika* (June).
*ASEAN Experiences of Regional and Inter-Regional Co-operation: Relevance for SAARC* (1988), Bangladesh Institute of International and Strategic Studies: Dhaka.
*Asiaweek*, 17th May 1992.
*Asia Yearbook* (1992).
*Far Eastern Economic Review* (*FEER*), 8th February 1968.
*Japan and the Pacific Rim* (1991), Dushkin: Guilford, Connecticut.
Md. A. Halim (1992), 'Wither Away the White Elephant Called SAARC?', *Perspectives in Social Science*, Vol. 4, pp. 112-126.
*The Almanac* (1991), Houghton Mifflin: Boston.
*The Daily Star*, 2nd July 1992.
World Bank (1992), *World Development Report 1990*, Washington, D.C.

# 10  Vanishing Borders Within Sub-Saharan African States: Achievements, Counterforces and Prospects

*AGOT Kawango*

## Introduction

Political independence in Africa in the 1960s was immediately followed by a great debate on the strategy for African unity, notably by Kwame Nkrumah (Ghana), Sekou Toure (Guinea), Modibo Keita (Mali), Jomo Kenyatta (Kenya), Kenneth Kaunda (Zambia) and Julius Nyerere (Tanganyika) (Senghor 1990; Mazrui and Tidy 1984; Anyang'-Nyong'o 1990; Rodney 1981; Odiyo 1994). These great African leaders argued that the continent, partitioned into nations, often posed as antagonistic by political and economic entrepreneurs, must be held together if socio-economic progress is to be attained.

The problem of individuality of countries in the continent do not all stem from the events beyond the control of African governments. There is an African, as well as a global dimension to the problem (Diop and Vanderveken 1984; Rodney 1981; Mazrui and Tidy 1984; Odiyo 1994). Historical roots lie in the colonial legacy of exploitation of African surpluses in capital, raw materials and slave labour, on which much has been researched and written (Rodney 1981; Mazrui and Tidy 1985; Odiyo 1994). To this was added the railway network with its two distinct characteristics, namely being parallel to each other and all from interior to coast (Figure 10.1), and with different track gauging systems (Luckam 1987; Hallet 1974). The obvious implications are that the spatial design from the interior to the coast ensured the draining of raw material resources from the farms/plantations and mines to the ports for dispatch to the mother countries, while at the same time the lack of intra-state connectivity reduced the chances of internal trade. Further, the different railway gauging systems effectively ruled out

159

inter-state rail transport. This appears to be a very calculated move to maintain the individuality of the sub-Saharan African countries as separate entities.

The African dimension to the disintegration of the continent began right at the dawn of independence. In 1963, African heads of state met in Addis Ababa, Ethiopia, to set up the Organisation of African Unity (OAU). Without foresight on the implications of the future of the continent, and ironically in a meeting whose framework and agendum was African unity, the OAU Charter actually

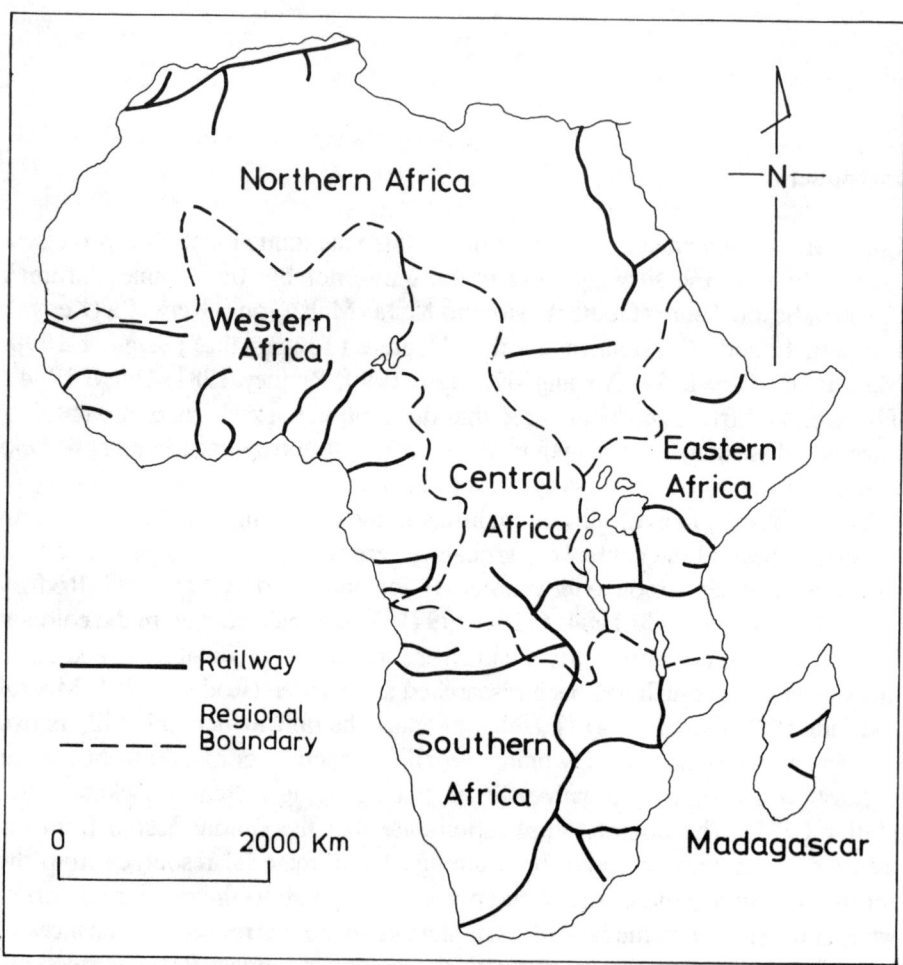

**Figure 10.1   Railway network systems in Africa**
*Source*:          Hallet (1974)

endorsed the 1884-85 Berlin Conference in which colonial powers arbitrarily fragmented the continent among themselves. The meeting passed that:

'... in respect for the sovereignty and territorial integrity of each state for its inalienable right to independent existence.' (Article 3, Section 3, in Odiyo 1994)

This 'oversight' has remained a central retarding force in the continental or regional cooperation and integration (Anyang'-Nyong'o 1990; Odiyo 1994). Individuality of nations have undermined attempts towards regional alliances, and, spiced by the West (particularly the British, French and Portuguese) who thrive on the divide-and-rule strategy, the anticipated progress towards these associations have remained slow (Senghor 1990).

## Case for Regional Cooperation in Sub-Saharan Africa

The promotion of economic cooperation among developing countries is now a well accepted part of international development policy, and regional associations and groupings among geographically contiguous areas are being encouraged. History shows that only large national units have a sufficient resource base, climatic diversity, and population size to afford self-reliance (Asante 1990; Anyang'-Nyong'o 1992).

Africa, like the rest of the world, is suffering under the impact of the most severe world economic recession since the 1970s, being the continent most dependent on imports of food, capital and technology (Diop and Vanderveken 1984; Timberlake 1994; Wagao 1992). The structure of African exports has scarcely changed over the years, leading in the export of primary and semi-finished cash crop and mineral products. The level of transformation has remained very low, with the high value-added processes being carried out in the importing countries. One major reason for the lack of investment in raw material processing is the discriminatory tariffs charged on these products by the industrialised countries (Diop and Venderveken 1984; Odiyo 1994). As world trade in primary products has grown more slowly than the world trade in manufacturing, Africa's share of total world trade has significantly fallen, while the prices of imported goods have risen faster than the prices of exports (Mazrui and Tidy 1984; Odiyo 1994). Reduced export and increased import prices have had a devastating influence on the balance of payments of African countries from the beginning of the 1970s (Diop and Vanderveken 1984).

This vulnerability to the world market prompted the African governments to redefine economic survival strategies, seeing as they did O.A.U. deteriorating into a watered down version of the original plan. Hence, the birth of the Lagos Plan of Action (LPA) in 1980 was aimed at collective self-reliant and self-sustaining development (Diop and Vanderveken 1984; Otieno 1990; Anyang'-Nyong'o 1990; Odiyo 1994). The LPA called for integrated economic and social development with top priority on food production and rural development, as well as the creation of an industrial base which would contribute to the satisfaction of basic needs; the exploitation of natural resources; the creation of jobs; the establishment of bases for developing other economic sectors; and technological progress (Diop and Vanderveken 1984; Ndiaye 1990; Otieno 1990; Odiyo 1994). These strategies were in response to the realisation that regional cooperation is a valuable tool of pooling capital, technology, skills and market based on the principle of economies of scale in the face of persistently scarce resources.

It has been underscored that individual markets in African countries are seriously circumscribed to low income levels and small populations which cannot individually support modern enterprises since unit cost of production are often higher in many cases where economies of scale are not being realised (Ndiaye 1990; Otieno 1990; Odiyo 1994). Apart from fostering modern investment enterprises, creating larger markets through the integration also increases opportunities for specialisation; stimulates technological and infrastructural development; and enhances efficiency arising from competition. Thus, against this backdrop, the LPA set a target to achieve the Economic Community of Africa (ECA) by the year 2000 in which African governments committed themselves to collectively promote (Otieno, 1990; Diop and Venderveken, 1984). Otherwise, as Odiyo (1994) has asked, what chances of survival would a fragmented Africa have in an era dominated by the wealthy countries of the North which have amalgamated themselves into economic and political blocs?

**Achievements**

Although there has been a significant gap between the aspirations and the achievements of regional integration, the gap has not dampened the peoples' spirits and their vision for African unity - they still aspire, more so now than ever before. Behind, yes, but static, no. This vision was seen as early as 1959 with the establishment of Le Conseil de l'Entente in West Africa, and continues to date, with the on-going negotiations for the reestablishment of East African Cooperation (E.A.C.) for Kenya, Uganda and Tanzania incepted on 14th March 1996, and the Inter-Governmental Authority on Development (I.G.A.D) for Kenya, Uganda, Somalia, the Sudan, Eritrea and Djibouti incepted on 22nd March 1996 (Otieno 1990; *Daily Nation*, 15th and 22nd March 1996). Regional alliances have thus been formed based on one or more of the following considerations: economic, political, cultural, environmental, transport and communications, academic and professional, religion and language.


*Economic*

In the African experience, cooperation has been much easier in areas which are functionally diffused and of low political salience, for example, health, communication, and culture (Senghor 1990), yet cooperation in the economic sector is the centre-piece of cooperation. It is through cooperation in this sector that welfare needs are satisfied, which are, in fact, just spillovers from the economic sector. But in Africa, it is in this sector that cooperation is most problematical, mainly because the economic sector is functionally diffused and of high political salience (Senghor 1990; Odiyo 1994). Militating factors notwithstanding, sub-Saharan African states have formed several economic cooperations and integration.

In West Africa, there is a strong will for economic integration, with a large number of such regional schemes existing, for example, the Economic Organisation of West African States (ECOWAS formed in 1977), with its peace-keeping wing, the Economic Community Monitoring Group (ECOMOG). There are also Communauté des Etats de l'Afrique de Ouest (CEAO) of 1973; the Mano River Union (1979); the Liptako Gourma Economic Community (1971); Le Conseil de l'Entente (1959). ECOWAS combines sixteen countries of West African sub-region with a common theme of political and economic decolonisation (Asante 1990; Timberlake 1994). The aim was to overcome the economic fragmentation of the region, with a hope of reducing internal dependency, overcoming existing structures of neo-colonialism and under-development (Asante 1990; Otieno 1990). They follow the market approach by laying emphasis on the integration of markets rather than production, transport, communication and other infrastructure.

Eastern and Southern Africa have also made strides towards economic regional cooperation by instituting Preferential Trade Area (PTA) which provides a framework for inter-state cooperation in trade. Essentially, PTA came as a result of the collapse of the East African Community in 1977, although Southern African countries are now included. It has two major objectives. One, the establishing of a free trade area through gradual reduction and eventual elimination of customs duties and non-tariff barriers to trade conducted among member states. Two, creating a common market known as the Common Market for Eastern and Southern Africa (COMESA) through the free movement of factors of production and commodities within the area (Martin 1990; Odiyo

1994).

Independently, both Southern and Eastern Africa have formed their own sub-regional integration. Southern African Development Conference Coordination (SADCC) was formed with the aim of reducing economic dominance on the then Dutch-ruled South Africa through regional, political and economic integration and liberation. But SADCC has been more a political and cultural alliance than economic (Mandaza 1990). Also, regional cooperations are currently underway in Eastern Africa. Initiated by Kenya, Uganda and Tanzania in 1993 but endorsed on 14th March 1996 is the East African Cooperation (EAC) which is a more direct resurrection of the collapsed East African Community than the PTA. It is hoped that with time it will be enlarged to include Rwanda and Burundi. When it becomes fully operational, it will principally be charged with enhancing regional cooperation in trade including currency convertibility, transport, communications and immigration (*Daily Nation,* 15th March 1990). Again on 22nd March 1996, two of the East African States, Uganda and Kenya, together with Eritrea, Somalia, Djibouti and Ethiopia met to restructure the Inter-Governmental Authority on Drought and Development (IGADD) to stress the importance of regional economic integration under the new name, IGAD (Inter-Government Authority on Development) (*Daily Nation,* 22nd March 1996). In addition to dealing with droughts, desertification and regional development, the restructured body will extend its portfolio to regional economic cooperation among the member countries.

In Central Africa, little headway has been made to establish the proposed Economic Organisation of Central African States (ECOCAS), but some activities are being undertaken within a customs union, Union Douanière des Etats de l'Afrique Centrale (UDEAC); and the Economic Community of the countries of the Great Lakes.

## *Politico-cultural*

Of notable impact under this alliance is SADCC, whose objectives, although including economic integration and liberation, have emphasised more political and cultural alliance. The members are united by Bantu languages and traditions, in addition to all having been colonised by the British, hence having common socio-cultural and political bases. One other factor that has contributed to the alliance is the lateness of the countries in attaining their political independence relative to other African states. The struggle for the liberation of South Africa reinforced a spirit of political and cultural symbiosis - a united African resistance (Mandaza 1990; Otieno 1990). Both scholars observe that although the apparent commonality of historical, political, cultural and economic experiences have inspired the regional integration and economic development of SADCC states, the cooperation is more of political and cultural solidarity than economic, placing more emphasis on national than on sub-regional projects and programmes. Former French colonies have also formed various politico-cultural and economic integrations, notably in West and Central African regions, for example, l'Douanière Union des Etats de l'Afrique Centrale (UDEAC); La Communanté Economique des Etats des Grande Lacs (CEEGL). Although the association may be for economic purposes, the cementing factor is the shared French identity.

*Environmental*

In addition to the various support institutions formed under the umbrella of sub-regional integration schemes, there are also intergovernmental organisations established to promote economic integration through environmental management (Otieno 1990; Diop and Vanderveken 1984). Various river basin authorities have been formed by various states, for example, Organisation pour la Mise en Valeur du Fleuve Sénégal (L'OMUS) formed in 1968 by the governments of Senegal, Mauritania, Mali and Guinea; Organisation de Mise en Valeur du Fleuve Gambie (L'OMVG) formed in 1965 by Sénégal and Gambia. There is also l'Autorité du Bassin Niger (River Niger Basin) established in 1965, and bringing together eight countries; and La Commission du Bassin du la Tchad of 1964 to promote joint irrigation activities among four states. In addition, the Comité Inter-Etats de Lutte Contre la Secheresse dans la Sahel (CILSS) was established in 1972 to coordinate anti-drought activities in seven countries of the Sahel region. As mentioned elsewhere, the six states of Eastern Africa fall under the Inter-Governmental Authority of Drought and Development whose aim includes drought and desertification monitoring and management (*Daily Nation*, 22nd March 1996).

*Transport and Communications*

It has been mentioned that this is one of the 'safe' areas of high functional diffusion, but low political salience, and many governments are not over-sensitive in committing themselves to joint ventures. But transport and communication development becomes a viable project only if it is used to enhance movements of goods and services across borders. Not much has been achieved in this respect, although the movement of people has been enhanced markedly by the improvements in the transport sector. Air Afrique, for example, conglomerates nine countries of Central Africa; while the Regie Abidjan - Niger (RAN) road network has been particularly useful for landlocked Burkina Faso and Niger, as has been TAZARA connecting Tanzania and land locked Zambia. In addition, the Trans-Saharan highway has provided intra- and inter-linkages in the Eastern, Western, Southern and Central sub-regions of the continent. Also, most African countries do not impose travel restrictions to fellow African countries, particularly those within some form of integration.

*Academic and Professional*

Perhaps the most successful cooperation has been achieved in this sector. It is likely that the academicians and professionals have realised that they have common problems that can be tackled better through the pooling of brain-power, and that knowledge is universal and should not be hoarded or guarded. There are many organisations serving regional and continental academic and professional interests, for example, the Organisation of Social Science Research in Eastern and Southern Africa (OSSREA) based in Ethiopia; the Council of the Development of Social Science Research in Africa (CODESRIA) based in Senegal; the Association of African Women in Research and Development (AAWORD) based in Senegal; the Pan-African Anthropological Association (PAAA) based in South Africa; and the African Health Sciences Congress (AHSC) based in Kenya. These organisations are very active, with National Chapters in most countries, and having research, conferences, training and publications as the bases of their existence. The problem is that many of the research findings, conference recommendations, etc., are not effectively translated into the regional policy agenda for implementation.

*Religions and Language*

There have been continental and sub-regional integration of different religious persuasions, for example, All African Conference of Churches (AACC) that pool together most Protestant faiths in the continent; the Arab League for the Muslim faith; and the continental headquaters for the Seventh Day Adventists in Harare, Zimbabwe. One factor that may bring different geographical regions together, but which is not fully being exploited is language. In East Africa, for example, Kiswahili has been a uniting factor, particularly in Tanzania where it is both the national and official language; in Kenya where it is the national language while English remains the official language; and in Uganda where, although it has neither official nor national status, it is passably spoken by many urban dwellers. Rwanda, Burundi and Zaire (now Democratic Republic of Congo) also speak some Kiswahili, albeit rudimentarily. All in all, the language of the colonial powers have brought together different states, and Kiswahili can be used to bring together more countries. Hausa is also relatively widely spoken in West Africa, but its ethnic orientation makes people from other cultures resent it.

## *The African Development Bank (ADB) and Regional Cooperation*

The ADB was established in 1963/64 by the United Nations Economic Community for Africa (ECA) (Versi-Anver 1994; *African Business* 1993). The institute has its roots in Africa's desire for solidarity and it now stands as a good symbol of economic integration and cooperation among African countries. The ADB gives particular emphasis to projects and programmes designed for three objectives: to promote regional integration; to assist in coordinating national plans with a view to promoting a harmonious and complementary growth of African economies; and the expansion of intra-African trade (Ndiaye 1990; Otieno 1990). The ADB defines the concept of regional projects to include multi-national projects, that is, those which jointly concern two or more countries; and the national projects with regional implications, that is, those with physical siting in at least two countries. The latter category would include a project situated in one country but which utilises, as its inputs, the outputs of goods and services from two or more countries; or a project situated in one country but serving other countries (Otieno 1990).

Within the framework of cooperation, financial institutions have been established by the ADB to assist respective regional projects and programmes. A few examples include the East African Development Bank designed to promote trade among PTA members; and the PTA Clearing House which is a mechanism for settling trade accounts among member states. In West Africa, there is the ECOWAS Fund; the West African Clearing House; la Banque Ouest Africaine de Development (BOAD) all of which promote regional development and harmonise the operations of the member states. BOAD governs the UMOA States - a monetary union linking seven Francophone countries: Benin, Cote d'Ivoire, Bukina Faso, Mali, Niger, Senegal and Togo. There is also the Central Bank of West African States (BCEAO), a common Central Bank of the members states of the UMOA which provides a common currency (la Communanté Financière Africaine - CFA); facilitates common credit and payment; and arranges for pooling of foreign exchange reserves. In fact, West Africa has achieved more in the area of monetary integration than any other sub-region. In

Central Africa, a common Bank, la Banque des Etats de l'Afrique Centrale (BEAC), was established to harmonise monetary policies among five Francophone member states: Cameroon, Central African Republic, Congo, Gabon and Tchad which, together with BCEAO, use the CFA as the common currency. The Development Bank of the Countries of the Great Lakes serve the financial interests of the economic community of these countries (Otieno 1990).

In addition to financing projects, the Bank Group (financial institutes set by ADB to finance projects of regional integration) have also taken other initiatives in promoting regional integration. For instance, in creating appropriate inter-state institutions such as Shelter Afrique, a pan-African institution devoted to the promotion of investment in housing in Africa; Africa-Re to coordinate continental reinsurance; the Association of African Development Finance Institutions (AADFI); and the Federation of African Consultants (FECA). ADB has also undertaken private sector promotion, notably Round Tables which provide welfare services across the continent (Otieno 1990). Thus, one can safely state that ADB has been the most invaluable ingredient in the process of regional integration and economic cooperation in the sub-Saharan Africa.

## Counterforces - Operation and Institutional

Numerically, sub-Saharan African states have formed, and continue to form many, perhaps functionally too many, regional organisations and reorganisations. The extent to which they are successful seems to be quite another question. For a number of them, there is some truth in Anyang'-Nyong'o's (1990) statement that 'once created, they simply continue to exist on their past or initial momentum', and that developmental initiatives continued to occur mainly at national and not regional level. In other words, despite the existing diversity in the integration, it does not follow that success has been proportional to the institutional enthusiasm.

Several constraints have beset the numerous attempts towards a politically and economically united continent at this age of internationalism. Topping the list is politics. Political leadership jealously guard their sovereignty and are unwilling to reduce the power and authority of the state; they instead promote national integration and consolidation of national political independence (Senghor 1990; Anyang'-Nyong'o 1992; Mkandawire 1992). Thus, the national sovereignty is still the basis on which negotiations for setting up sub-regional and regional functional organisations are conducted (Senghor 1990; Otieno 1990). This generates strong inclinations to protect national identities and promote national interests. The French-speaking states have thus been keen on maintaining their distinct Francophone identities (Otieno 1990).

Linked to this is economic cooperation. As mentioned earlier, it is in this sector that cooperation is most problematical in Africa. Both individuals and governments look up to the national economy, first and foremost, for the satisfaction of welfare needs, hence the preoccupation with the protection of national economic interests. A paradox then emerges: when the economy is seen to be performing well, there is less initiative to cooperate with others (for example, Kenya and Zimbabwe in PTA); if not, then either cooperation is not viewed as possible means for improvement, or it may be perceived as the cause of poor performance (Senghor 1990). Also connected to the economic factor is the reality that cooperation is likely to produce long-term benefits whereas the short-term costs are usually high. In most countries, economic difficulties, including debt-servicing has seriously constrained the resources, hence reducing the incentives to finance multinational projects (Asante 1990; Otieno 1990; Martin 1990; Mandaza 1990).

Although the benefits of integration are self-evident, integration schemes have, in practice, given rise to problems concerning the equitable distribution of costs and benefits of such schemes among participating countries. The sharing arrangements associated with multi-national projects may not be advantageous to some participating countries, and this inequitability and inequality may dampen the enthusiasm (again, a case in point is Kenya and Zimbabwe versus other relatively poorer members of the PTA, such as Cameroon, Djibouti, Rwanda and Burundi; or between the rich oil producing countries and the poor ones of ECOWAS) (Otieno 1990; Asante 1990; Martin 1990).

Political and economic divergences between different countries and the related development strategies have also played a major role in creating an effective wedge in regional cooperation, especially between Anglophone and Francophone Africa; between countries with different politico-ideological governing systems (from a history of Marxist-Leninist Ethiopia, Mozambique and Zimbabwe, to capitalist Kenya and Zaire or Democratic Republic of Congo, to moderate socialist Tanzania); between the rich and the poor; the large and the small; the landlocked and the ones with access to sea-ports. All this cumulate into differences in capabilities of different countries hence differences in taking advantage of specialisation, economies of scale, augmentation of factors of input and opportunities to improve market structures (Otieno 1990; Katungi 1992; Mkandawire 1992).

The existence of many and diverse sub-regional cooperation has resulted in a high level of overlapping memberships, for instance, SADCC and PTA share most of their Southern African members, while the cooperation between Africa, Caribbean and Pacific countries (ACP) with the European Economic Community

(EEC) has drawn its members from almost all the other Anglophone regional cooperations. This calls for competing interests and commitments (Otieno 1990; Katungi 1992). Furthermore, the North-South cooperation through ACP/EEC has its unique problem. At the inception, enthusiasts saw it as a relationship of interdependence, an 'agreement among equals'. But it really is an enlargement of the colonial links, that is, a neo-colonial tool created to maintain the North-South status quo, another machinery for updating the dependence of the African countries on their former colonial powers. The following views quoted by Odiyo (1994) should make one weary of the wholesale acceptance of the camouflaged Lomé Convention:

- Lomé is neo-colonial in tone, and perpetuates the 'client status' of Africa (Wall 1975)
- Lomé is neo-colonial and representative of the traditional spheres of influence and bloc politics (Donan 1977)
- Lomé preserves the role of the African countries as producers of raw materials and agricultural products ... permitting the emergence of a new international division of labour (Mytelka 1978).

It can therefore be concluded that Lomé constitutes a new and subtle kind of subjugation of the African states, making it difficult for them to industrialise and achieve the much needed diversification of the economies. Hence like the 1884-85 Treaty of Berlin, the first and subsequent Lomé conventions have served to keep Africa as a source of raw material to, and market for Europe. The conventions do not make any fundamental changes in the dependency relationship between industrial and non-industrial countries. One such continued helplessness of African states in negotiating their positions was demonstrated at the General Agreements on Trade and Tariffs (GATT) meeting in December 1993 when a Mauritius Ambassador to GATT expressed:

'We are expected to lay our head on the chopping block. We will do so with dignity, but shall not give a smile to the executioner' (*Daily Nation*, 16th December 1993).

In fact, as one scholar puts it, from both an economic and geopolitical perspectives, Africa is fast becoming irrelevant, often times a nuisance, especially after the former members of the Warsaw pact crossed over the European Union (Odiyo 1994).

## Prospects

A starting point for stimulating economic growth could be the efficient utilisation of the existing resource base - both natural and human, through a pooling strategy. It is widely recognised that one of the main causes of African backwardness is the fragmentation of the continent's markets. Together, the 600 million Africans can provide an inexhaustible market for locally produced goods and services. O.A.U. therefore needs to be revamped to respond to the changing world economic and political order. Africa needs to diversify her external economic relations to include countries outside the European nexus to strengthen their bargaining position to 'play off' one developed economy against another (Odiyo 1994). In this respect, African regional cooperations can be preferential economic and technological links with other developing countries in Asia and Latin America. Local technical capabilities should also be developed so that products and processes can be adapted or designed for domestic production and appropriate technological development for rural areas. Pooling of capital, technology and skills is particularly useful in the development of infrastructure, large scale industries, and transport systems where economies of scale would otherwise be out of reach for individual countries. Kenya, for example, is almost completing an oil pipeline from Mombasa sea-port to the interior of the country. Since Uganda, Rwanda, Burundi and Zaire obtain the bulk of their oil products through Mombasa, with cooperation, this project would easily be extended into these countries.

## Conclusion

Since the Treaty of Rome in 1957, the European states have largely realised their twin objectives of economic and political union by the ratification of the Maastricht on the 29th October 1993, yet the Africans still tend to see themselves in terms of their parochial nationalities. Odiyo (1994) argues that Africans do not yet see themselves as Africans enthusiastically enough to create a sense of a common identity that is necessary to progress meaningfully towards the attainment of a United States of Africa. He asserts that:

'Until the Africans start thinking as Africans, stop fighting one another, forms the African common market, and argue for a United Africa rather than as individual countries, the strides towards the United States of Africa will remain a charade.' (Odiyo 1994:22)

And yet sub-regional integration is the only channel expected to provide the building blocks to African economic solidarity. Granted, the number and extent of existing institutions testify to a widespread awareness of the potential gains which could come from economic cooperations, but serious commitment is still lacking in most projects.

# 172 Vanishing Borders

## References

*African Business* (1993), 'Working Towards African Economic Integration: Special Survey - African Development Bank', No. 178, p. 24(3).

Anyang'-Nyong'o, P. (ed.) (1990), *Regional Integration in Africa, Unfinished Agenda*, African Academy of Science Publications: Nairobi.

_____ (1992), *30 Years of Independence in Africa: The Lost Decade? African Association of Political Science*, Academy of Science Publishers: Nairobi.

Asante, S.K.B. (1990), 'Regional Economic Cooperation and Integration: The experience of ECOWAS', in Anyang-Nyong'o, P. (ed.), pp. 99-138.

*Daily Nation*, 16th December 1993 (Nairobi).

_____, 15th March 1996 (Nairobi).

_____, 22nd March 1996 (Nairobi).

Diop, M. and Vanderveken, J. (eds.) (1984), 'The African Worker and the World Economic Crisis', Paper presented at the Pan-African Conference organised by the International Confederation of Free Trade Unions, Dakar, (7th-9th March).

Hallet, R. (1974), *African Since 1875: A Modern History*, Heinemann Educational Publishers Ltd.: Nairobi.

Katungi, C. (1990), 'Regional Integration in Africa - Regional Cooperation within ACP/EEC Convention' in Anyang-Nyong'o, P. (ed.), pp. 183-203.

Luckam, R. (1987), *Political and Social Problems of Development in Africa South of the Sahara*, Europa Publications Ltd.

Mandaza, I. (1990), 'SADCC: Problems of Regional Political and Economic Cooperation in Southern Africa: An overview', in Anyang'-Nyong'o, P. (ed.), pp. 141-155.

Martin, G. (1990), 'The Preferential Trade Area for Eastern and Southern Africa: Achievements, Problems and Prospects', in Anyang'-Nyong'o, P. (ed.), pp. 157-179.

Mazrui, A.A. and Tidy, M. (1984), *Nationalism and New States in Africa from about 1935 to the Present*, East African Educational Publishers: Nairobi.

Mkandawire, T. (1992), '30 Years of Independence: The Economic Experience' in Anyang'-Nyong'o, P. (ed.), pp. 86-102.

Ndiaye, B (1990), 'Prospects for Economic Integration in Africa', in Anyang-Nyong'o, P. (ed.), pp. 35-41.

Odiyo, E.O. (1994), 'Towards a United States of Africa? The role of Africa in the European Union', Paper presented at the African Regional Conference on *European Economic Integration and Its Implications on Africa*, Gaborone, (20th-24th June).

Otieno, J.W. (1990), 'The Experience of the African Development Bank in Financing Regional Integration Projects in Africa', in Anyang-Nyong'o, P. (ed.), pp. 43-82.

Rodney, W. (1981), *How Europe Underdeveloped Africa*, Howard University Press: Washington, D.C.

Senghor, J.C. (1990), 'Theoretical Foundations for Regional Integration in Africa: An Overview', in Anyang-Nyong'o, P. (ed.), pp. 17-31.

Timberlake, L. (1994), *Africa in Crisis: The Causes, the Cures of Environmental Bankruptcy*, East African Educational Publishers: Nairobi.

Versi-Anver (1994), 'Stoking the Engines of Growth: African Development Bank', *African Business*, No. 192, p. 24(2).

Wagao, J.H. (1992), 'The Economic Aspects of the Crisis in Africa', in Anyang-Nyong'o, P. (ed.), pp. 103-130.

# 11 Transfrontier Cooperation and the Borders in the European Union

*Peter John REID and Andrew CHURCH*

## Introduction

The local political reactions to changing borders are immensely varied. In Europe, many local authorities have been strengthening their cross-border links in response to the restructuring of national frontiers. In a number of locations, this has resulted in the development of transfrontier policy networks and cooperative policy initiatives involving regional, urban and local authorities. This chapter examines three examples of transfrontier cooperation involving UK and French local authorities with very different administrative, political, economic and geographical characteristics, but each has sea borders with its cooperative authority. In each location, cooperation and networking is at a different stage of evolution and funding. The Interreg programme provides European Union (EU) funding, in locations agreed by the European Commission (EC), and for cross-border initiatives (including sea borders since 1987). One of the study areas, the Transmanche Region which includes Kent County Council in Southeast England and the French Region Nord Pas-de-Calais (Figure 11.1) has been in existence for a decade and is already in receipt of funding under the Interreg programme. A second case study is the proposed Transmanche Metropole which is a cooperative grouping of the towns of Southampton, Portsmouth, Bournemouth and Poole in Britain and Caen, Rouen and Le Havre in France (Figure 11.1). This initiative has not received funding from the EU. The final case study of cooperation involves the English County of East Sussex and the Departments of Somme and Seine-Maritime in northern France that will receive funding under Interreg II. The

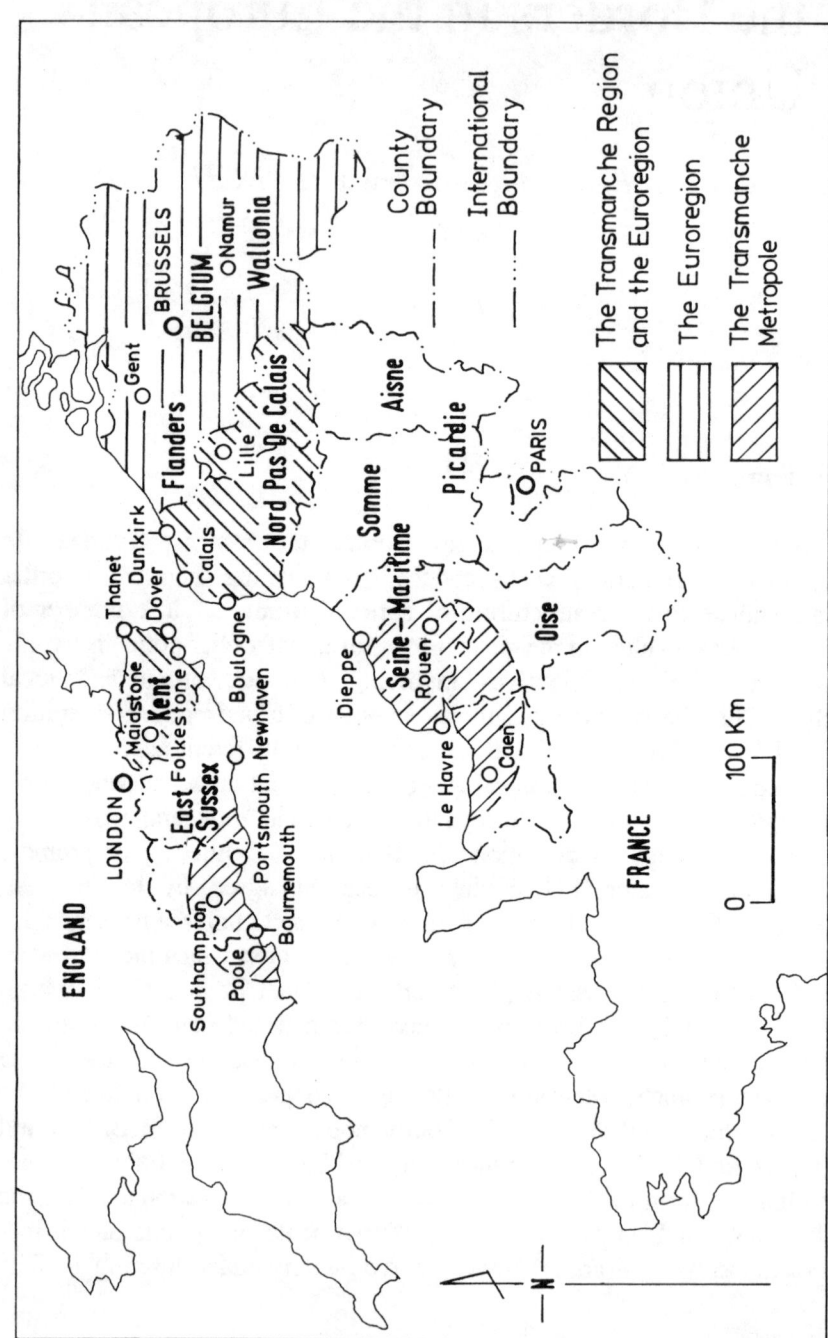

**Figure 11.1   The Euroregion, the Transmanche Region and the Transmanche Metropole**

last two case studies will be examined jointly since their emergence is closely linked. The chapter also considers the political problems and advantages of such cooperation and discusses whether such cooperative activities will affect national borders and regional networking in and adjacent to the European Union.

## The Politics of Networks and Cross-Border Cooperation

In many cases, cross-border cooperative networks were designed mainly for the exchange of knowledge and information, but a growing number were developed either to increase resources mainly *via* EU programmes, or to synchronise policy implementation (Local Government Information Bureau 1992). The emergence of cooperation and networking has led to discussion over the political implications and the effect on policy delivery. At the European scale, such initiatives are now seen as central to the role of the EU as it is transformed from 'a state-centric bargaining system to a transnational policy network' (Dang Nguyen *et al.* 1994). This broad process has seen the rapid growth of horizontal relationships between regional and local authorities to complement the vertical relationships between national member states and the European Commission. This has led to suggestions that conceptions of European government as a series of tiers are not wholly sufficient and must be accompanied by an understanding of the related spheres of policy activity (Baine *et al.* 1992).

Cooperation and networks also have implications for local and urban autonomy. Hesse and Sharpe (1991) identified the changing nature of local autonomy in Europe and the influence of European as well as national government. Cuadrado-Roura *et al.* (1994) are relatively optimistic regarding the beneficial effects of EU-supported networks on local autonomy, whereas Wessels (1990) argues that networks often result in the incorporation of local and urban agencies into EU policies. In addition, regional and local governments may find that national governments strengthen their own position by using transnational cooperation and networks as an argument for limiting domestic dissension (Dang-Nguyen *et al.*1994).

Cooperation and networks may, however, hold out the possibility of increased power for cities and regions as they become more involved in the meso-level of government. This may be perceived as particularly valuable in countries such as the United Kingdom where there are only limited government structures at the regional level (Martin and Pearce 1992; 1993). Whether increased power leads to more effective policy delivery is, of course, a matter of debate. There are, however, some potential problems with the political institutionalisation of regions in Europe since it may lead to simple political opportunism and the strengthening of the power bases of existing regional elites (Hebbert 1993). Nevertheless, EU-supported cross-border initiatives will allow local and urban authorities to become involved in the construction of new regional alliances. Furthermore, in the debate over the benefits of governmental consolidation (Keating 1995) such bottom-up region building is often viewed as a desirable approach to the construction of a meso tier of government and a number of commentators have argued strongly for the development of bottom-up local economic strategies (Martinos 1989; Stohr 1990).

Research into the spatial economic effects of cross-border cooperation has also noted the competitive economic outcomes. Cappellin (1992) argues that transfrontier cooperation may reduce core-periphery disparities by encouraging the integration of peripheral areas into nation states and Europe. The potential economic benefits of cooperation are questioned by Camagni (1992) who suggests that cross-border initiatives are more likely to have a positive affect if they involve regions with differing levels of economic prosperity. Otherwise there is the danger of presenting a negative 'club of the poor' image if less prosperous border regions with similar problems group together to cooperate (Camagni 1992).

Overall, the conclusions of research into the political and economic effects of networks and cooperation show some marked disagreements. Some commentators point to the positive alternative strategies that networks provide for local organisations (Camagni and Salone 1993; Batten 1995). By contrast, Vartianen (1995) argues that networks promote competition that can be harmful to peripheral regions and lead to a policy emphasis on physical infrastructure that may not be environmentally desirable. Vartianen (1995) adopts a pessimistic perspective towards networks and cross-border cooperation claiming that the ensuing competition may threaten the process of urban revitalisation.

Some empirical studies, however, argue that the relative effectiveness of transnational cooperation and networks will result in the continuation of such initiatives even if there is a change in power relations between the EU and national governments (Marin and Mayntz 1991). Obviously some networks and cooperative initiatives may be short-lived whilst others become an established part of urban governance in particular locations. Similarly, cross-border initiatives may be either a passing phase, or part of a wider change which will make cooperation an increasingly important element in the operations of the authorities involved. However, it is becoming clear that at present the trend is towards larger groupings of regions which will create new tensions and competition which could militate against their sustainability. Whatever, the long term effects of cross-border cooperation and networks on urban and local governance currently represent a new and increasingly common form of power distribution.

## Cooperation, Networks and Urban Political Theory

Whilst the reorganisation of border structures and regulations are clearly linked to the emergence of cross-border cooperation, current theoretical perspectives offer a number of possible broader explanations for the growth of such cooperation and networks. The emergence of cross-border initiatives raises important theoretical issues for the study of intergovernmental relations and central-local relations. One response to the development of cooperation has been the use of policy network theory. The value of developing a concept of networks has been debated from both economic and political perspectives. For example, Cooke and Morgan (1993) and Cooke *et al.* (1992) argue that the network is an important concept for examining corporate strategy and uneven spatial development. In political studies, the discussion of networks has emerged as part of the wider conceptual literature on policy coalitions, communities and networks (Dowding 1994; Jordan 1990; Rhodes 1990; Rhodes and Marsh 1992; Sharpe 1985; Van Waarden 1992). Much of this research seeks to identify how a wide range of organisations and actors interact across formalised policy boundaries. For example, Rhodes and Marsh (1992) argue that networks must be viewed theoretically and not as a separate type of initiative, but as a point on a spectrum of policy communities with which local and regional government can become involved.

Conceptual discussions emerging from recent empirical studies of European cooperative networks (Dang-Nguyen *et al.* 1994; Marin and Mayntz 1991) have argued that one of the main motivations for such policy initiatives is the concern of European institutions to operate as corporate actors developing their institutional interests. In addition, Dang-Nguyen *et al.* (1994) claim that intergovernmental relations are a key influence on networks which are partly a response to increased interdependency and the dispersion of power that limits the potential of hierarchical government. Such discussions tend to emphasise the importance of intergovernmental relations and bureaucratic factors in the formation of cooperative initiatives and networks.

Cappellin (1992) argues that economic internationalisation and the increasingly flexible, networked, global economy are the key processes encouraging cross-border cooperation, with further stimulus provided by the European integration. Joint initiatives by the public sector are thus seen as being primarily economic in intent and are designed to generate network economies, lower transaction costs and economies of scale through resource sharing and controls on competition (Cappellin 1992). Such processes encourage not only cross-border cooperation, but a more general internationalisation of local spatial development strategies.

Indeed, the evolution of transnational cooperation and networks is closely linked to the increasing internationalisation of local authority economic policy which has been identified in the UK (Goldsmith 1993), European cities (Harding *et al.* 1994) and major USA cities (Hobbs 1994). Goldsmith (1993) accepts the effect of other tiers of government on the internationalisation and globalisation of local authority activity, but claims that a number of world wide economic processes are primary influences.

The analysis of political cooperation and networks is also a topic of inherent interest to regulation theory due to the increasing role of networking in the organisation of the production of goods and services (Cooke *et al.* 1992; Johannson *et al.* 1994). The emergence of networks, therefore, in both the regime of accumulation and the mode of regulation makes them a potentially interesting focus of analysis. From the perspective of regulation theory the emergence of cross-border cooperation could be interpreted as part of the making and unmaking of regulatory systems at different spatial scales. For Swyngedouw (1992) this is an on-going historical process that creates the mediating structures through which key features of the regime of accumulation, in particular the struggle for the control of space and the global-local interplay, are articulated. Cross-border cooperation and networking generally may be part of a wider process from which new spatial scales in the regulatory system may emerge (Dang-Nguyen *et al.* 1994). Clearly these differing theoretical perspectives identify a number of possible explanations for the emergence of cooperative networks. The case studies presented here provide an analysis of the evolution of cross-border cooperation which is one form of cooperative network and they also highlight some of the key causal processes, besides the restructuring of border operations and legislation, which have led to transfrontier initiatives.

**The Evolution of the Transmanche Region and Euroregion**

For the EU, cross-border cooperation is a precursor to European integration and it has provided funding through the Interreg 1 for 1990-1994 and through

Interreg II from 1995-1999 to support such cooperation. The availability of funds from the EU and a perceived need to be involved with international local economic development are potent joint processes encouraging cross-border cooperative ventures (Cappellin and Batey 1994). In the case of Kent and Nord-Pas de Calais, however, a number of other factors have been important influences in the development of cooperation. In Kent and Nord-Pas de Calais what initially were local and regional policy responses to the Channel Tunnel evolved in 1987 into an internationalised cooperative initiative in the form of the Transmanche Region and the Transfrontier Development Programme (TDP). The Central Governments in both the UK and France are now closely associated with this initiative, but the actions of local and regional governments were responsible for its early development.

The central aim was to maximise the local economic benefits of the Channel Tunnel and the Single European Market (SEM) and to reduce potential disadvantages. This was the first such initiative involving a UK and French region and at the start was characterised by activities involving the exchange of information. A Joint Accord signed in 1986 targeted cooperation on the coastal areas which comprised the five eastern districts of Shepway, Dover, Thanet, Ashford and Canterbury in Kent and in France, the towns of Dunkerque, Calais and Boulogne and their surrounding areas. By September 1990, the Joint Accord had been formalised into a series of potential initiatives grouped together under the Transfrontier Development Programme (TDP). This was submitted for funding under Interreg 1 to the European Commission (EC) and this had been preceded by intense lobbying of both the EC and national government since Interreg 1 was initially only for terrestrial frontiers. Kent and Nord-Pas de Calais argued that the Channel Tunnel link meant they should be viewed as land borders. The EC granted formal approval in May 1992 and until mid-1994, Kent was the only Great Britain area to receive Interreg funding.

Between May 1992 and the end of 1993, the TDP had a total budget of 54 million ECU. Sixty per cent of this came from the local, regional and national government in France and the UK and the remainder from Interreg. The major financial commitment from the local agencies involved indicates the value attached to cooperation and that it was not just a device for obtaining EU funds. Under the TDP, initiatives that receive funding are designed to be simple catalyst projects and certain sub-programmes such as land management and environment, tourism, education and training, economic development, transport and infrastructure have been the focus for expenditure.

Interestingly, the internationalisation of local economic policy has not stopped at neighbouring border regions. Kent County Council are now collaborating with authorities in Hungary, and two local authorities within the Transmanche Region, Dunkerque and Dartford, have signed a Joint Accord to promote economic cooperation. The experience of internationalisation of local authorities through the TDP has encouraged further development of cooperative networks.

The Kent/Nord Pas-de-Calais Interreg II bid was submitted in December 1994. The programme for 1994-99 totals 36.4 million ECU on the match funding basis from EC and National funds. There are now six programme areas as follows: Strategic Planning accounts for 25 per cent of proposed expenditure; Environment 16 per cent, Economic Development 24 per cent; Development of Human Resources 10 per cent; Tourism 23 per cent and Technical Assistance 2 per cent. The key difference between the Interreg I and Interreg II programmes for the Transmanche Region is the increased emphasis on strategic planning. The type of initiatives proposed are more selective and targeted towards a longer term economic strategy. In addition, the Central Government is more closely involved. The Joint Monitoring Committee for the Interreg II programme is chaired by the Director of the Central Government Office for the South East. The bid for Interreg II funding was also led by the Government Office for the South East.

Whilst the TDP bid was with the EC, a larger Euroregion was formed. In June, the five regions of Kent, Nord-Pas de Calais, Wallonia, Brussels Capital and Flanders (Figure 11.1) signed a joint declaration that resulted in the establishment of five working groups promoting cooperation in the Euroregion in the fields of Land Management and Environment, Transport and Telecommunications, Economic Development, Tourism Development, and Education and Training. The Transmanche Region of Kent and Nord-Pas de Calais maintain their separate identities within this larger group and to date there are no major funded initiatives for the Euroregion similar to those in the TDP. Currently, network economies and information exchange are perceived to be the main benefits of the Euroregion (Church and Reid 1994).

Clearly, cross-border cooperation in the case of Nord-Pas de Calais and Kent has developed into a significant initiative despite the marked contrast between the two areas. Until recently, the Kent County Council was controlled by the Conservatives, and the Socialists were the ruling party in the Nord-Pas de Calais region. In addition, the regional council in Nord Pas-de-Calais has broad strategic powers for an area containing a population, in 1991, of 3.9 million compared to 1.5 million in Kent (Eurostat 1993) and the County Council has less strategic but significant responsibilities such as education provision.

The economic contrast between Kent and Nord-Pas de Calais, such as unemployment levels and industrial decline are well known. However, a similarity of the two regions is that the coastal local authorities on both sides of the Channel have certain shared problems, namely, a declining tourist sector and the negative effects of the Channel Tunnel due to restructuring of the port industry (PACEC 1991). A number of these locations have made a revival of the tourism sector the focus of their local economic policy (Church 1995). Sinclair and Page (1993) argue that the Channel Tunnel will have a positive effect on the tourist industry, a view shared by the Kent Impact Study (PACEC 1991). It may be, however, that with rapid transport available to London a corridor effect may be evident with tourists simply passing rapidly through the coastal areas. The restructuring of the port sector has also been a key stimulus to cooperation. The removal of ferry crossings between Boulogne and Dover, apart from the smaller Seacat, has led to considerable job loss in the French town. The recession in both Britain and France has exacerbated the difficulties in both areas . Nevertheless, these key economic influences on the decision of Kent and Nord-Pas de Calais to develop the cooperative ventures of TDP predate the recession (Reid 1993).

Competition from other economic groupings is also quite important in Kent and Nord-Pas de Calais since officials argued that a credible regional grouping is an essential element of any international inward investment strategy. The Transmanche Region was also often portrayed by officials as a counter balance to cooperation between regions in the North East of Spain through Southern France and into Northern Italy (Church and Reid 1994). It is important, however, not to overplay the importance of economic processes.

In addition, the evolution of the TDP was strongly shaped by local political influences and a complex set of relationships between actors and policy organisations. The nature of the link between the cooperating authorities clearly determined the direction of policy, but, as is shown later, relationships with the EU, national governments, other local authorities and the private sector also shaped the form of the TDP. The effect of intergovernmental relations on cross-border cooperation is discussed in detail in a later section of this chapter so as to allow comparisons to be drawn with other case studies.

## The Transmanche Metropole, the Competition for Interreg II Funding and Cooperation Between East Sussex and Northern France

The Transmanche Metropole is an emerging cooperative initiative involving strategy between the city authorities of Caen, Le Havre and Rouen in France and the English local authorities of Southampton, Portsmouth, Bournemouth and Poole (Figure 11.1). Cooperation between the four authorities in the UK started initially with the formation of the South Coast Metropole in May 1993. Each of the UK authorities has differing economic aims: Portsmouth and Southampton are concerned to support existing port and industrial activities, whereas Poole and Bournemouth aim to encourage tourism and specialist activities such as language schools. Despite these economic differences, local economic concerns were a key stimulus to early cooperation. The South Coast Metropole evolved partly as a result of concerns expressed by the four English authorities that they lacked a clear regional economic identity. The area is on the border of the standard regions of South West and South East England but, according to local officials, lacks a strong economic affinity with either region. One of the initial aims of cooperation was to develop a stronger identity for this sub-region that could be used for economic promotion purposes. Furthermore, officials in some of these coastal towns stressed that cooperation was in part motivated by local discontent regarding the policies of Hampshire, the constituent County Council. Certain towns had disputed elements of the County Structure Plan and were keen on initiatives, such as the South Coast Metropole, that allowed them to present an alternative view towards the local economy. On the other side of the Channel the French Towns of Caen, Rouen, and Le Havre had already developed an informal partnership in the early 1990s. These two urban groupings provided the existing networks from which cross-border cooperation was to develop. Of course, potential EU funding was a further stimulus to cooperation between these seven urban areas.

The list of border regions eligible for funding under Interreg II was announced on 1st July 1994 and included certain maritime border areas that were not eligible in the draft regulations for Interreg II issued in February 1993. The Transmanche Metropole, however, was not one of the successful maritime border regions. A complex lobbying of the EU institutions did not result in a favourable outcome for the Transmanche Metropole. In late 1993 and early 1994, a number of coastal regions, including some from both sides of the Channel, lobbied the Assembly of European Regions, the European Parliament, the Regional Policy Committee of the European Parliament, and the Management Committee of the EC with the aim of being included on the Interreg II list. In the UK, eligibility for Interreg funding was strongly dependent on support from central government and central backing was an important factor in determining which coastal areas were included in the revised list. The English county of Essex was seeking Interreg funding based on cooperation with the Picardie Region in Northern France and the constituent authorities of the Transmanche Metropole were also hoping for EU support. Despite close involvement in the lobbying process neither Essex nor the English towns in the Transmanche Metropole were on the Interreg II eligibility list. However, two of the French towns involved in the Transmanche Metropole, Le Havre and Rouen, are now eligible for Interreg II funding since they are in the Department of Seine-Maritime which, along with the Somme Department, has received EU support to cooperate with the English County of East Sussex. Furthermore, the Somme Department was part of the Picardie Region that had initially been seeking Interreg II funding for cooperation with Essex.

The four UK maritime border regions and their partners now eligible for support from Interreg II are Kent and Nord-Pas de Calais, Gibraltar and Morocco, Gwynedd/Clwyd and the Republic of Ireland and East Sussex, and the Department of Somme and Seine-Maritime. Oddly, one of these French departments was not aware of its inclusion on the final Interreg list since most of the applications had been dealt with by its constituent region and the French regional agency DATAR. East Sussex was also somewhat surprised by its success in receiving Interreg II funding and, inclusion on the final list was viewed locally as a considerable achievement. A local economic accord to promote joint initiatives had been signed in late 1993 by the Department of Seine Maritime and East Sussex. At one point in early 1994 East Sussex was very pessimistic about the likelihood of receiving Interreg II funding since it seemed likely that the application for the Channel border areas would be dominated by the Transmanche Region and the Transmanche Metropole. One argument that East Sussex employed in its favour was that the counties' coastal strip was an extension of the depressed coastal areas in Kent and should also receive funding. Furthermore, East Sussex, like Kent, included certain former resort towns that had recently become eligible for UK regional aid. Local officials in East Sussex felt that this was one reason that the central government supported their application and they believed the central government was keen to focus Interreg II aid on areas already deemed eligible for national regional policy rather than extend spatial economic policies to new areas.

In late 1995, the central government in the UK submitted a Single Programme document for Interreg II to the EU that set out the priority themes for the cross-border initiatives involving UK regions. In some locations, the sum of money involved will be small due to the allocation procedure. The total allocation for Interreg II to each member state is set in Brussels and this is divided by national governments. Interreg II funding for the four projects involving UK regions will total approximately 99 million ECU over 4-5 years and this will be match funded. About 75 per cent of the funds go to border regions that are also Objective 1 regions, (those where development is lagging behind). The remaining 25 per cent is allocated in order of priority to Objective 2 regions, (those regions in industrial decline) and   Objective 5b regions (rural problem areas) and unclassified regions. This is indicative of the increasing influence of both EU and the central government on the second phase of Interreg cross-border initiatives compared to the first round. Consequently, East Sussex which falls into the unclassified group, expects to receive only 1 million ECU per annum for five years.

In the longer term the existing cooperative initiatives may develop further and form the basis of an embryonic larger cooperative cross-Channel region. The Arc Manche or Channel Arc has been proposed by the French regions on the northern coast as a group of local authorities stretching from Nord Pas-de-Calais to Brittany in France and Kent to Cornwall in South East England. The justification for such an initiative is that these areas contain a unique type of regional economic problem based on restructuring ports, depressed resort towns and similar coastal pollution problems. This type of cooperative activity overarches the existing agreements and should strengthen them. In the shorter term it is clear that cross-border cooperation has resulted in intense competition for EU funding and the emergence of tensions between neighbouring authorities as they seek to form links across the same border.  In the examples discussed here, local authorities found that the nature of competition required them to switch partners.  City government in Le Havre is keen to maintain its role in the Transmanche Metropole, but may also be required by its constituent Department of Seine Maritime, to cooperate with East Sussex. The other authorities involved in Transmanche Metropole are also seeking to maintain cooperative links despite the failure to gain EU funds. This will be done through initiatives identified in the local economic accord which will mainly involve the exchange of information and joint promotion.

The continuation of the Transmanche Metropole suggests that cooperation in these coastal areas goes beyond simply gaining EU grants and is designed to develop local economic initiatives, which by their cross-border nature, contribute to the general process of local economic policy internationalisation. In the uncertain global economy, the internationalisation of policy based on cross-border cooperation and EU funding is clearly an appealing option for local authorities.  The competition for EU funding under Interreg II indicates, however, the strong and complex political influences on transfrontier networks and cooperation.  Increasingly the EU and the central government have been seeking to shape the nature of cooperation across the English Channel. Equally, however, the approach to cooperation adopted by one authority is determined not only by relations with central government and European bodies but also by links to its cooperating partners to competing neighbouring authorities. Such a range of political influences on policy evolution may also result in complex political outcomes such as the need for French Departments to switch partners to receive Interreg II support. The implications of this analysis is that an understanding of local authority responses to changing frontiers requires a political perspective that takes account of the influence of a wide range of intergovernmental relations and the effects of the pressures on local governments created by economic globalisation.

## Problems and Advantages of Transfrontier Cooperation

The emergence of transfrontier initiatives across the Channel highlights a number of the potential difficulties and potential benefits of cooperation between regions. Within individual authorities the commitment of limited public funds to cross-border cooperation may conflict with the more local concerns of elected councillors. Clearly, local economic development officers are devoting increasing amounts of time to bid for EU funds. Indeed, in Kent concern has emerged recently over the possibility that, in future, the allocation of limited funds may be driving the availability of match-funding from the EU rather than local needs. Currently, this is an expressed worry of a minority of elected councillors rather than an identifiable problem (Church and Reid 1994). At a broader institutional level, cooperation clearly requires the resolution of potential political conflict within a grouping of regions. The former socialist regional council of Nord-Pas de Calais clearly had different ideological commitments to the Conservative controlled County of Kent and yet, in this case, the potential difficulties stemming from differences of political outlook never really emerged. Recent political changes in Kent and Nord-Pas de Calais have shifted both councils towards the centre but the larger Euroregion may contain extra tensions when it comes to agreeing to future programmes. In the Department of the Seine Maritime, which is due to cooperate with East Sussex, there is already a tension with the major towns of Rouen and Le Havre which still have an attachment to the Transmanche Metropole.

Prior to the recent major transfrontier initiatives, these regional and local authorities in France and the UK had often been involved in a number of small scale cooperative schemes, such as town-twinning, and some had contemplated larger scale measures. EU funding, however, provided the catalyst to operationalise the current programme of cooperation. Inevitably, EU expenditure has involved central government appointees in programme administration. In such a situation, regional and local authorities may feel that their sense of ownership of a programme is weakened. Martin and Pearce (1993) have noted how central government seeks to guard its role as 'gatekeeper' in respect to EU funding. In all these cooperative groupings it will also be necessary to keep a balance between strategic initiatives and more localised operational schemes. Maintaining the strategic overview in the more diverse transfrontier cooperative ventures may prove problematic as each participating region seeks to find funding for localised initiatives that benefit their areas. There is a danger that the Euroregion could reflect the same type of squabbles that occur in the EU. The experience of the coastal regions in the Channel suggests that external political factors can create a number of problems for cooperative ventures. The competition for Interreg II funding between East Sussex and the Transmanche Metropole have clearly created problems for the latter. Swyngedouw (1992) argues that the reduction in the scale of regulation intensifies inter-territorial competition. The examples of cross-border cooperation suggest that the same intensification can occur when local and regional agencies seek to expand the regulatory scale and, perhaps, this competition is a general outcome of the process of making new scales of regulation.

Of course, a number of the problems encountered through cooperation can have advantageous outcomes. Time spent by government officers developing international, as opposed to local, initiatives can lead to beneficial information exchange and network economies. Competition within cooperative groupings or with neighbouring authorities could be viewed positively if it were to result in more dynamic local economic policies within each region. The leading role that East Sussex played in lobbying for maritime border areas to be included on the list of eligible regions for Interreg II was in part motivated by the worry of being crowded out of cooperative initiatives by the Transmanche Region and Transmanche Metropole. Also, concerns over the difficulty of maintaining local aims in a cooperative grouping have to be offset against the political benefits of participating at a different scale in the regulatory system. Existing regional elites in Europe will be seeking to gain from the political institutionalisation of regions but cooperative initiatives allow urban and local authorities in nations with a weak or virtually non-existent tier of regional government, to construct alliances and thus develop a role at the regional level. In the case of the Transmanche Region, the County of Kent is able to define a role for itself at a broad regional and international scale. Nord-Pas de Calais views itself as geographically pivotal within the Transmanche Region and aims to reaffirm this position within the larger Euroregion. Alternatively, Kent has acknowledged that it cannot adopt a pivotal role, but seeks to portray itself as having a cross-border role in the Transmanche and Euroregion in order to indicate to investors that the County is influential at the international scale. Indeed, both authorities argue that a key benefit of the Transmanche and Euroregion is that it allows them to maintain international relations and operate more effectively in the global arena (Church and Reid 1995). To what extent cooperative groupings can provide the political basis for constructing spatial development policies that will match those of more established regional agencies and authorities, remains to be seen. Furthermore, the impact of cross-border cooperation on spatial economic variation is also unclear and will be hard to separate from other developments such as the SEM and large frontier infrastructure projects like the Channel Tunnel.

It does seem, however, that a new embryonic scale in the regulatory system is being established based on cross-border cooperation. A new scale of regulation does not, however, necessarily embody a distinct form of regulatory practice. The individual projects that are part of these cross-border programmes are typified by environmental improvements, training provision, tourism promotion and infrastructure projects which are standard elements of current local economic policy in Britain and France. The emerging regulatory scale of cross-border cooperation may simply encourage a conformity of local policy. Furthermore, this new scale of regulation is, of course, part of a broader reconfiguring of the mode of regulation occurring alongside the changes in the regime of accumulation.

## The Effect of Transfrontier Cooperation on National Borders in the European Union

Transfrontier cooperation may also have significant implications for national borders and border activities. The EU considers that cooperation is an important step towards integration in Europe. There has been an increasing interest in cross-border cooperation and in networking both with adjacent and distant authorities. The reasons for such networks are, as shown earlier, complex, although funding is one of the key objectives. The political changes in Eastern Europe and the EU enlargement policy at present being considered in the International Governmental Conference, have also exerted influence on the type, nature and extent of such cross-border activities. This is evident in both local authorities and private sector activities in Europe. Cooperative alliances, networking and competitive groupings are commonplace in Europe and indeed the rest of the world. However, such cooperation does mean that national borders could be eroded over time with the rearrangement of structures of national governments and, subsequently, power could follow. Of course, it could be  that much of this speculation is dependent on the sustainability of the individual cooperative ventures. The rearrangement or renegotiating of such agreements could exert pressure on national governments to impose firm controls on such activities and thus reimposing national boundaries. However, the global nature of economic processes and the increasing competition for mobile capital will result in borders being considerably less important and intrusive in the world of economics and business than hitherto.

## Conclusion

The examples in the chapter suggest that this reconfiguring of cross-border local politics is the complex outcome of the full set of intergovernmental relations. At the European level this has involved the formation, by sub-national government agencies, of new international networks, alliances and partnerships of which transfrontier cooperation is one of the most explicit. For some commentators this is seen as a useful step to strengthening 'meso-government' and establishing a more decentralised, pluralist model of government in highly centralised countries like the UK (Martin and Pearce 1993). From the perspective of regulation theory, a slightly less optimistic conclusion can be drawn. If transfrontier cooperation and international networks serve to focus sub-national governments' attention on the inter-national scale, this may facilitate the activities of large scale corporations who will benefit directly from the global awareness of local and regional governments and also indirectly, if this process serves to distance these state agencies from the demands of local communities for social provision. At a political level, Euro-sceptics might also argue that international initiatives by sub-central agencies could lead to a detachment between the local government and its electorate. By contrast, federalists would claim that local needs and the aim of subsidiarity can only be properly fulfilled by action on a European scale. Nevertheless, the involvement of local and regional authorities in cross-border cooperative programmes is likely to grow as integration continues. Whatever happens this type of international activity will be an increasing phenomenon amongst local and regional authorities, both within and outside the EU and deserves serious consideration politically and theoretically.

## Acknowledgement

Some of the materials used in this chapter has previously appeared in *Urban Studies* 33(8). We are grateful to the publishers for permission to use this material.

## References

Baine, S., Benington, J. and Russell, J. (1992), *Changing Europe - Challenges Facing the Voluntary and Community Sectors in the 1990s*, NCVO: London.

Batten, D. F. (1995), 'Network cities: creative urban agglomerations for the 21st Century', *Urban Studies*, Vol. 32, No. 2, pp. 313-327.

Camagni, R.P. (1992), 'Development Scenarios and Policy Guidelines for the Lagging Regions in the 1990's', *Regional Studies*, Vol. 26, pp. 361-374.

Camagni, R.P and Salone, C. (1993), 'Network Urban Structure in Northern Italy: Elements for a Theoretical Framework', *Urban Studies*, Vol. 30, No. 6, pp. 1053-1064.

Cappellin, R. (1992),'Theories of Local Endogenous Development and International Cooperation' in Tykkylainen, M., (ed.), *Development Issues and Strategies in the New Europe*, Avebury: Aldershot, pp. 1-19.

Cappellin, R., and Batey, P.W. (eds.) (1994), *Regional Networks, Border Regions and European Integration*, Pion: London.

Church, A. (1995), 'Restructuring and Port Cities: The Role of Tourism', in Hoyle, B. (ed.), *Understanding the Contemporary Port City*, Wiley: Chichester.

Church, A. and Reid P. J. (1994), 'Anglo-french Cooperation: The Effect of the Channel Tunnel', Chapter 10 in Gibb, R. (ed.), *The Channel tunnel: a Geographical Perspective*, John Wiley: London, pp. 199-213.

Church, A. and Reid, P.J. (1995), Transfrontier Cooperation, Spatial Development Strategies and the Emergence of a New Scale of Regulation: The Anglo-french Border, *Regional Studies*, Vol. 29, No. 3, pp. 297-306.

Cooke, P., and Morgan, K., (1993), 'The Network Paradigm: New Departures in Corporate and Regional Development', *Society and Space*, Vol. 11, No. 5, pp. 543-564.

Cooke, P., Moulaert, F., Swyngedouw, E., Weinstein, O. and Wells, P., (1992), *Globalisation and Localisation: the Computing and Telecommunications Industries in Britain and France*, UCL: London.

Cuardrado-Roura, J.R., Nijkamp, P. and Salva, P. (eds.) (1994), *Moving Frontiers: Economic Restructuring, Regional Development and Emerging Networks*, Avebury: Aldershot.

Dang-Nguyen, G., Schneider, V. and Werle, R. (1994), 'Networks in European Policy-making: Europeification of Telecommunications Policy' in Andersen, S.S. and Eliassen, K.A. (eds.), *Making Policy in Europe: The Europeification of National Policy-making*, Sage Publications: London.

Dowding, K., (1994), 'Model or Metaphor? A Critical Review of the Policy Network Approach', *Political Studies*, Vol. 43, pp. 136-158.

Eurostat (1993), *Basic Statistics for the European Community*, Eurostat: London.

Goldsmith, M. (1993), 'The Internationalisation of Local Authority Policy', *Urban Studies*, Vol. 30. pp. 683-708.

Goldsmith, M. (1995) 'Autonomy and City Limits', in Judge, D., Stoker, G. and Wolman, H. (eds.), *Theories of Urban Politics*, Sage Publications: London, pp. 228-252.

Harding, A., Dawson, J., Evans, R., and Parkinson, M. (eds.) (1994), *European Cities Towards 2000*, Manchester University Press: Manchester.

Hebbert, M. (1993), '1992 Myth and Aftermath', *Regional Studies*, Vol. 27, pp. 709-718.

Hesse, J.J. and Sharpe, L.J. (1991), 'Conclusions' in Hesse, J.J. (ed.), *Local Government and Urban Affairs in International Perspective*, Nomos Verlagsgesellschaft: Baden-Baden.

Hobbs, H. H. (1994), *City Hall Goes Abroad: The Foreign Policy of Local Politics*, Sage: London.

Johansson, B., Karlsson, C. and Westin, L. (eds.) (1994), *Patterns of a Network Economy*, Springer-Verlag: Heidelberg.

Jordan, G., (1990), 'Sub-governments, Policy Communities and Networks', *Journal of Theoretical Politics*, Vol. 2, No. 3, pp. 319-338.

Keating, M. (1995) 'Size, Efficiency and Democracy. Consolidation, Fragmentation and Public Choice' in Judge, D., Stoker, G. and Wolman, H. (eds.), *Theories of Urban Politics*, Sage Publications: London, pp. 117-134.

Local Government Information Bureau (1992), *International Local Authority Networks Linking to the UK.*, LGIB: London.

Marin, B. and Mayntz, R. (1991), *Policy Networks: Empirical Evidence and Theoretical Considerations*, Campus: Frankfurt A.M..

Martin, S. and Pearce, G. (1992), 'The Europeanisation of Local Authority Economic Development Strategies', *Regional Studies*, Vol. 26, pp. 499-503.

Martin, S. and Pearce, G. (1993), 'European Development Strategies: Strengthening Meso-government in the UK?', *Regional Studies*, Vol. 27, pp. 681-685.

Martinos, H. (1989), *The Management of Local Employment Development Strategies*, LRDP: London.

Pacec (1991), *Kent Impact Study 1991 Review*, PA Cambridge Economic Consultants: Cambridge.

Reid, P.J. (1993) 'Calais, 'the Red City': Its Position in Economic Development in Nord-Pas de Calais', *Modern and Contemporary France*, Vol. 12, pp. 15-34.

Rhodes, R.A.W. (1990), 'Policy Networks: A British Perspective', *Journal of Theoretical Politics*, Vol. 2, No. 3, pp. 293-317.

Rhodes, R.A.W. and Marsh, D. (1992), 'New Directions in the Study of Policy Networks', *European Journal of Political Research*, Vol. 21, pp. 181-205.

Sharpe, L.J. (1985), 'Central Co-ordination and the Policy Network', *Political Studies*, Vol. 33, pp. 361-381.

Sharpe, L.J. (1993), 'The European Meso: An Appraisal', in Sharpe, L.J. (ed.) *The Rise of Meso Government in Europe*, Sage Publications: London.

Sinclair, M., and Page, S. (1993), 'The Euroregion: A New Framework for Tourism and Regional Development', *Regional Studies*, Vol. 27, pp. 475-483.

Stohr, W. (ed.) (1990), *Global Challenge and Local Response*, Mansell: London.

Swyngedouw, E. (1992), 'The Mammon Quest. 'Globalisation', Interspatial Competition and the Monetary Order: The Construction of New Scales' in Dunford, M. and Kafkalas, G. (eds.), *Cities and Regions in the New Europe*, Belhaven: London: pp. 39-67.

Van Waarden, F. (1992), 'Dimensions and Types of Policy Networks', *European Journal of Political Research*, Vol. 2, pp. 92-112.

Vartianen, P. (1995), *Networking Cities - A New Planning Utopia and a Real Challenge to Urban Governance*, Paper Presented at the 10th Urban Change and Conflict Conference, Royal Holloway College, University of London, 5th-7th September 1995.

Wessels, W. (1990), 'Administrative Interaction' in Wallace, W. (ed.), *The Dynamics of European Integration*, pp. 229-241.

# PART IV

# REGIONAL COOPERATION:
# THE ECONOMIC DIMENSIONS

# 12 Ignoring Borders Through Railway: The Proposed Trans-Asia Railway and Regional Development

*Abdul Rahim MOHD NOR*

## Introduction

Compared with motorcycles, personal cars or conventional buses, railway services are highly capitalised, costly to build, less flexible and more difficult to adapt to adverse circumstances. In the event of difficulties arising from declining revenues or financial crisis, reversing investment is much more difficult than other road-based modes of transport. In fact, in many parts of the world, fix-tracked mass transit services are increasingly being threatened by road and motorway-based transport resulting in huge subsidies, nationalisation and closure. Most countries of Western Europe have high levels of state support for railway transport. For example, 10 out of 12 EEC countries have railway systems with a revenue-cost ratio of only between 0.20 to 0.57 while in Britain and Ireland, revenues from rail services covered only about 65 per cent of total cost (Whitelegg 1988). The least subsidised in Europe are Switzerland (0.71) and Sweden (0.79). Even in Scandinavia, where strong pressures from environmental and regional lobbies have reinforced government willingness to support public infrastructure through subsidy, rail services are declining (Fullerton 1988). In Eastern Europe where countries have recently abandoned socialism, there is an extraordinary dependence on railways which are under-capitalised and overloaded (Crouch 1985). In Britain, train services have gone through what was predicted by Patmore (1966) as an historical process of innovation, competition and decline. The country's railway network reached its peak between 1910-1945 but total passengers carried have declined steadily since 1920 when the system was plagued by continuous revenue losses before it was finally nationalised in 1947.

It remained imbued with financial problems with half of the network earning insufficient revenues even to meet essential track maintenance cost, despite efforts such as the 1963 Beeching Report to overcome the rising deficit (Kilvington 1985; Whitelegg 1987). The post-Beeching era saw closures of many railway lines especially in the rural areas. Only after privatisation in 1993, did the rail services manage to break-even although some of the Scottish and London commuter systems are still dependent on subsidies. In the USA where rail services are run by about 30 companies on a private basis, competition from more attractive inter-city passenger services offered by airlines and road services, has led to steeply declining revenues in the post-1950 period while further financial difficulties in the 1970s flung several major rail companies into bankruptcy (Tolley and Turton 1995). Today, the percentage of all freight tonnes-kilometre accounted for by rail in the U.S. is 35 per cent compared with 56 per cent in 1950.

However, several socialist economies such as China, Russia and Poland have shown a different trend in rail network growth. Under centralised development plans which emphasised heavy industries and the restriction of consumer purchasing power, the impetus for the construction and improvement of road systems has been much less than in capitalist countries resulting in a much higher proportion of freight and passengers carried by rail (Leung 1980). In the twentieth century, the levels of railway construction in these economic blocs have been unequaled elsewhere in the world. But most of these countries are recovering from Marxism and are catching up fast with Western-style free-market economy which encourages competition from a wider choice of transportation including passenger transport business.

Despite the gloomy scenario painted for the railway services, ASEAN with the strong support from China, Japan and South Korea, is promoting the idea of upgrading and constructing a 4,700-kilometre railway track linking Singapore, at the southern tip of Peninsular Malaysia, to Kunming in the Yunnan Province of South China. This chapter attempts to provide the geo-political context within which the rail line is to be built, and to analyse the potential development opportunities generated by the project.

## Traversing Borders: The Concept of Trans-Asian Rail Link

The idea of linking Asian countries with a rail track was first mooted by Malaysia in the 5th ASEAN Summit in Bangkok in late 1995. It was proposed that the track should stretch from Singapore to Kunming, passing through the capital cities of Kuala Lumpur, Bangkok, Ho Chi Minh City and Hanoi. The proposal was accepted at the meeting which subsequently appointed Malaysia to prepare a concept paper providing the details of the plan. The proposal was further discussed in the First Asian-Europe Meeting (ASEM) held in Bangkok in January 1996 which was attended by the ten ASEAN nations, China, Japan, South Korea and 15 European countries which had endorsed the plan. It is hoped that the rail link could be planned up to Beijing and later linked with Europe to London through Trans-European track (Figure 12.1).

Although the proposed line stretches for more than four thousand kilometres, a large portion is already in place and may only require some upgrading. Thus, the plan will only have to concentrate on the construction of the missing links from Phnom Phen to Ho Chi Minh City and from Poipet in East Bangkok to Sisophon in Cambodia, which together requires about 498 kilometres of new tracks at an estimated cost of about US$900 million (based on the Asian Development Bank's estimate of US$2 million per kilometre). The recommended route passes through the Mekong Eastern Basin and was preferred over the alternative route which runs *via* Chiengmai, Laos and Myanmar after factors such as terrain and construction costs, were taken into account.

In the first ministerial meeting on the project in Kuala Lumpur in June 1996, the rail track plan was discussed in greater detail by ASEAN member countries with active participation from the Mekong Basin riparian nations of Laos, Cambodia, Myanmar and China. Malaysia has committed herself to finance the first part of the feasibility studies which includes the identification and the evaluation of existing railway lines and facilities and potential improvement to form the link as well as the existing infrastructure. Thailand was appointed as the head of the finance committee to prepare a funding mechanism. Although details on how to finance the project are not available as yet, it is proposed that the active participation from the private sector should be encouraged under the build-operate-transfer (BOT) mechanism, a method of infrastructure development that has been successfully implemented in Malaysia for the past two decades.

## The Supporting Imperative: Resources in the Land-locked Mekong Basin

The proposed rail-link was planned to become the backbone of the Mekong Basin development initiated by ASEAN countries. It was to act as the lifeline for economic activities planned to be carried out in the basin under the Asian-Mekong Development Project (AMDP). The Mekong Basin is divided into two regions: the south which belongs to Thailand, Cambodia and Laos, and the north, which comes under Myanmar and South China. The two combine to form the Greater Mekong Basin in which the borders of the countries lie. The resource-

**Figure 12.1   The proposed Trans-Asian railway track**

endowed basin offers great economic potentials to the riparian nations in mining, forestry, agriculture and tourism while the fast-flowing river and its tributaries can be readily developed into power houses capable of producing the much sought-after hydroelectricity.

The idea to harness Mekong Basin's economic potential was first mooted in 1957 when Vietnam, Thailand, Laos and Cambodia met to form the Mekong Committee with several western countries offering to help and the United Nations giving assurance of involvement. However, the ensuing wars which ravaged the region forced the shelving of the grandiose master plan which included up to 20 major dams along the river, capable of generating an estimated 70,000 MW of hydroelectricity power. Although the basin offers much opportunities to potential investors from neighbouring countries, projects planned were difficult to be realised due to inaccessibility. The land-locked basin is isolated from the outside world by skeletal road and railway network traversing steep mountains cut through by rivers and their tributaries. Today, the basin supports a population of more than 230 million with a combined GDP estimated to be US$184 billion in 1994 (Asian Development Bank 1995). The population is expected to increase to 414 million with a GDP estimated at US$2,157 billion by the year 2010. The latest development to form the Asian-Mekong Development Co-operation (AMDC) is an initiative by ASEAN member countries to revive the basin through a joint effort of member countries with the involvement of China, Japan and South Korea. The AMDC will plan and co-ordinate economic development in the area. China's interest in the Mekong project will strengthen the cause for a trans-Asia rail-link as the track would be very strategically laid and can serve the land-locked region of Yunnan in the south. Kunming, one of the biggest cities in the province, is located in an isolated area separated from the downstream countries of Indochina by the hazardous stretches of the Mekong River. It is expected that the proposed rail will serve as a cheap transport route to send products from this area to markets in the downstream countries as well as to Peninsular Malaysia and other ASEAN countries in the south. The first step in this direction has begun with the opening of the rail link between Beijing and Hanoi in February 1996, after 17 years of wars between the two communist neighbours. This has transformed the once-tense frontiers into a cross-road for peaceful trade. The rail link can act as the infrastructural thrust for the proposed Mekong River Basin Project in which the economic cooperation fostered by it will pave the way for economic integration of all the ten Southeast Asian nations.

## Opening the Economic Borders:  Globalisation of Communist Vietnam

Another supporting factor which enhances the possibility of building rail infrastructure in the proposed track, is the changing political and economic atmosphere of the region through which the rail-link is to be constructed. This can be seen in the fast-transforming politics of Vietnam, Cambodia and Laos.  In recent years, these countries have opened their doors to the outside world by relaxing many of their economic and trade policies previously overridden by egalitarianism and state-ownership to one which is more flexible and freer.  For many years Vietnam's association with Marxism and Communism has pushed it into war, poverty and isolation. Collectivisation of agriculture and the establishment of cooperatives called 'Xa Hop Tac' which was modelled after Communist China, was forcefully implemented in the North in 1955 and later in the south in 1978.  Under this system Vietnam, once hailed as the rice basket of Southeast Asia, saw agriculture production decreased and soon became a net importer of rice.  However, Vietnam started experimenting in economic liberalisation popularly known as the 'doi-moi' in 1989, a year researchers called the 'Big Bang'.  This policy allocated land use rights to individuals by issuing land certificates to individual farmers beginning from 1993. Today, Vietnam stands as the third largest exporter of rice in the world and is expected to rank second soon (Brahm 1995).

The open-door policy was responded to by the lifting of the economic embargo in 1994 by the USA thus increasing contacts between the two countries and providing a fertile ground for economic ventures. The establishment of diplomatic relationships a year later caused the influx of investments from the USA. Foreign-aided economic ventures have remarkably transformed Vietnam's economy which, although still poor, is emerging from years of war and isolation to a 'tigercub' economy.  Economic growth has reached 8 per cent since 1992, while industrial production was growing at close to 15 per cent. Foreign investment grew by about 80 per cent to a record US$7.2 million in 1995.  With the establishment of diplomatic relationships with the USA, the setting up of a framework for relations with the European Union, and joining in 1995, the regional bloc of ASEAN, it is expected that Vietnam's economy will be expanding at vibrant rates in the very near future. Already investments from neighbouring ASEAN countries have reached more than US$2 billion by 1995 with Singapore and Malaysia leading other nations with investments of US$1.2 billion and US$622 million respectively. The opening of Vietnam's economy to the outside world especially to its Southeast Asian neighbours has been facilitated by better understanding and consensus dealing with Vietnam-generated problems, of which the boat-people crisis was one, and which for several decades had soured relationship with these countries. At its height, there were about 1.9 million Vietnamese boat people in Southeast Asia. Eventually, they were slowly repatriated back to Vietnam. Malaysia's last transit camp for Vietnamese illegal migrants was closed in June 1996. It represented the first to be emptied in Southeast Asia, marking the end of the saga of the boat people.

*Political-Economic Reforms in Riparian States: Myanmar and Indochina*

The prospect for a joint development among riparian states in the Mekong and the opportunity to turn the rail-link plan into reality became brighter with several positive political processes taking place in the region. In Myanmar, political reforms began in 1988 when the State Law and Order Restoration Council (SLORC) took control from Ne Win. Efforts were then initiated to improve its international image and speed up economic change after three decades of self-imposed exile. In January 1996, the SLORC announced ambitious plans to sell off many government-owned companies previously nationalised by the Ne Win regime (Vatikiostis 1995). These offers had impacts on local and foreign companies. Consequently, total approved foreign investments reached US$1.3 billion at the end of 1994 from just around US$735 million in early 1992. In February 1996, the national oil company of Myanmar signed an agreement with Total of France and Unocal of USA to pipe natural gas to Thailand. In another show of business confidence, the Bank of Commerce (Malaysia) opened its representative office in Yangon in June 1996 to provide support services to its home-based clients to explore business opportunities in the country. So far, the bank has assisted a Malaysian company to set up a US$9.2 million private hospital in Yangon; provided financial assistance to a listed home-based company to build the proposed Yangon-Mandaly Union Highway; and assisted two companies to set up a glassware factory and a food manufacturing plant.

In Laos, perestroika-inspired economic reforms have been taking place since the early 1990s after about 20 years of rule by Vietnam-influenced Marxist leaders. The country has abandoned Marxist economics and returned to the free market that existed before 1975 and presently it resembles a standard Third World country run by a mildly authoritarian and capitalist regime (Linter 1995). The road to full democracy and *laizes-faire* economy are opening wider with the demise of several old communist leaders who had ruled the country under strong influence from the former Indochina Communist Party of Vietnam. Emerging in their places are younger leaders whose pragmatic economics are more attractive to the present trend of globalisation. Laos's attractiveness to foreign capital lies in its abundant natural resources, especially the large forested areas of teak, mahogany and rosewood, and the deposits of lead, silver, gold, gemstones, tin, limestone and gypsum; its vast and largely untapped hydropower potential, and the fact that it is strategically positioned between three main powers in the region, namely, Thailand, China and Vietnam. A liberal foreign investment law adopted in 1989 has attracted investments in the manufacturing, mining and timber-processing sectors.

In Cambodia, the economic opportunities are less attractive compared with its neighbours although there are signs of political reforms and revival to a free-market economy, and the subsequent opening up to foreign investors. This country was ruled by the Khmer Rouge regime from 1975 to 1978 whose mass killings left the country with few trained people to rebuild it shattered institutions. Later, Cambodia was invaded by Vietnam and for many years the country was run by the Cambodian Communist Party, a regime backed by Vietnam. Political reforms ensued culminating in the 1993 United Nations sponsored general election which raised the royalist Funcinpec Party to victory against Cambodia's People Party.

*Potential Rail Track-based Freight Transportation: Offshore Oil and Gas*

The proposed rail-link can also serve as the transportation line for many untapped resources in the riparian states of the Mekong River of which Vietnam is one. After several relatively dry years of prospecting off the coastal waters of Vietnam, the 1995 oil and gas finds have renewed interest in the country's mostly unexploited offshore oil and gas. Apart from being able to use this potential source of funding for Vietnam's industrialisation drive in the near future (as it did in Malaysia and Indonesia in the 1970s), petroleum and LPG can be transported raw overland for export to neighbouring countries, particularly to the less oil-endowed Thailand, China and, through ports, across to the Philippines. Already, oil exports of US$976 million in 1994 had contributed to 27 per cent of Vietnam's total export revenues (Schwarz 1995).

Locally, Vietnam's hydrocarbon potential sees oil and gas deposits opening the door to new industries by providing the raw materials for refineries and cheap fuel for steel mills, fertiliser plants, petrochemical complexes and petrol-powered electricity power stations. Industries have every reason to be optimistic about this potential because it is estimated that Vietnam has oil reserves to the tune of 3-5 billion barrels, and recoverable gas reserves of some 10 trillion cubic feet. These reserves will have much to contribute to the expansion of industrial-based economic activities throughout the country which, in turn, require an effective means of transportation to deliver the goods produced, to markets in Thailand, Malaysia and China apart from its Laos and Cambodian neighbours.

Equally important is the fact that oil refining is new in Vietnam and this country currently exports much of its oil to Japan and Singapore for refining. While the bulk destined to Japan can be shipped through its ports, the Singapore-bound loads have to be transported overland through Thailand and Malaysia, and the revival of the existing railway track passing through these countries will meet this freight transportation demand. Although there are plans to build its own refineries the proposed locations have been found to be unsuitable. For example, the government's plan to build one near Dung Quat to boost economic development in one of the country's poorest provinces, has been seen by critics as the wrong way to spur development because of its mammoth costs and the highly competitive and well developed international market of Singapore which is only slightly farther from Ho Chi Minh City than Dung Quat. Consequently, the Trans-Asia rail-link is seen as having more advantages.

## *Long-distance Train Passengers: Tourism Potentials*

A well-maintained and internationally-linked railway network providing right-of-way for professionally-managed train services is a concrete platform for domestic and international tourist passengers who can be attracted to natural and historical tourist destinations located not only in the riparian states of the Mekong but also further up in China and India, and possibly even Europe. Cultural sites, especially temples and ancient cities, possess immense economic value linked to foreign tourism. The countries through which the proposed rail link is to be revived have much to offer in this respect (Table 12.1). Top on the list is the Angkor in Cambodia, Southeast Asia's main archaeological site stretching over 200 sq. km. and which contains the splendid remains of the different capitals of the Khmer Empire from the 11th to 15th centuries.

A good Trans-Asian train service will make it possible for foreign tourists landing in Singapore to travel north, visiting the naturally beautiful locations in Malaysia before proceeding to Thailand and Indochina to visit ancient sites and on to China and India, which have equally strong culturally-based tourist attractions. The economic potential of historical sites through tourism in the Mekong Basin has long captured the interest of researchers and leaders in the region. This was clearly seen in a conference organised in January 1995 in Chiengmai to discuss ways of preserving the antiquities of the Mekong region. The significance of the Conference agenda was underlined by the sponsorship of the Asia Society, the Getty Conservation Institute and the Siam Society (Peters

**Table 12.1   Ancient cities and monuments in riparian states of Mekong**

| Tourist cultural sites | Location | Attraction |
|---|---|---|
| Angkor | Cambodia | Southeast Asia's main archaeological site stretches over 200 sq km and contains the splendid remains of the Khmer Empire from 11th to 15th centuries including the famous Angkor Wat. |
| Khai Dinh Tomb | Hue, Vietnam | One of the attractions in the former capital city of Hue, once a city of the Vietnamese feudal empire in early 19th Century. |
| Luang Prabang | Laos | A historical city which served as the capital of the Kingdom of Lau Xang from 1353-1560, of the Kingdom of Luang Prabang (1720-1946) and as the royal capital of Laos (1946-1975). Some 144 buildings have been selected by the government for preservation. |
| Ruins of Wat Phra Ram | Ayuthaya, Thailand | Ayuthaya, a historic city founded in 1350. The second Siamese capital after Sukhotai. Its remains, characterised by *prangs*, or reliquary towers, and gigantic monasteries reflect its past splendour. |
| Temples in Pagan | Burma | Old Pagan was a walled city with more than 1,000 monuments in archaeological sites. The city was severely damaged in a major earthquake in 1975. The 10th Century Nat Hlaung Gyaung is the earliest surviving structure of the ancient city. |

1995) together with the national government and UNESCO initiatives.

Besides the ancient cultural attraction, some recently-announced tourism projects by newly opened economies in the region augur well for international train passengers on the proposed Trans-Asian rail track. In Laos, for example, Syuen Corporation (Malaysia) is developing a RM500 million international resort to be called the Nam Ngum Lake Resort, which is a joint-venture with Laos's Ministry of Defence. Located 70 km from the Laotian capital of Vientiane, the resort which is a flooded valley from the damming of the Laos section of the Mekong, will cover an area of 14,000 hectares by the lakeside as well as more than 700 islets in the lake. The facilities to be developed include, *inter alia*, an island shopping avenue, a safari game park, a commercial area, guest lodging, a wildlife island, and a butterfly and insect museum island. Other than Thailand, which already has an established tourism industry, Vietnam is fast catching up with projects to attract foreign visitors. Saigon tourist officials, for example, predicted an annual tourist growth of 30 per cent over the next few years (Linden 1996). In 1994, over one million people visited Vietnam compared to only 200,000 in 1990. The Master Plan from the National Administration of Tourism estimated that by the year 2000, four million visitors will have come to Vietnam.

## Some Potential Threats Arising From Conflicting Interests in the Mekong Basin

Reviving and building such a mammoth project across international borders of culturally and geo-politically diverse nations is not an easy task. At this stage, it is assumed that the proposed rail link will become a reality if economic development plans in the region including the Mekong Basin initiatives take off. However, threats to these plans, which can delay development, has already surfaced. One of these is the conflicting interests in harnessing the hydroelectricity power resource of the river in which uncoordinated power development projects by individual riparian states could have damaging effects on the river's water flow.

Part of the problem lies in the less than friendly attitude of China to mutually benefit from the river's resources through its plan to utilise upstream water for electricity. Over-exploitation of water in the north could adversely affect the interest of downstream countries. In fact, China has already drafted an ambitious blueprint to build 15 dams with a total generating capacity estimated to be about 20,730 MW, on its stretch of Mekong River through the Yunnan Province. This plan is being implemented with the recent completion of the 1,250 MW Manwan Dam in the middle section of the river in Yunnan which is connected to a grid serving Kunming's fast growing power demand. Yunnan's hydropower potential alone was estimated at over 100,000 MW or 15 per cent of the country's total. China's move was also motivated by its keenness for a niche in international electricity power marketing and development and as a response to demand from neighbouring countries. In mid-1995, China announced a scheme to sell electricity to Thailand which is diversifying its power purchases to avoid heavy reliance on supply from Laos. Prior to this, Thailand's offer to buy electricity from neighbours was taken up by Laos, who agreed to jointly develop along the Mekong, more than 50 electric hydropower projects with Thailand and international investors (Parson 1996). In Laos, it was estimated that at least four power projects are scheduled to be completed before the year 2000, while in Myanmar, the Myanmar's Electricity Power Enterprises (MEPE) has talked to about 30 companies about potential hydropower export projects.

While the China-Thai-Laos plans fit well with Thailand's electricity needs, they have created complications and problems to countries further downstream. One of these, Cambodia, is worried that China's dam construction upstream specifically designed to maintain minimum flow of water to the country's Ton Le Sap Lake runs against the Mekong River Commission (MRC) Agreement, of which China is not a member. Fast developing Vietnam is also concerned about too many dam plans upstream as it could reduce water flow to the southern Mekong Delta on which Vietnam relies for 60 per cent of its farm output. A change in water level will certainly affect these countries in terms of obstruction to navigation in Laos and may cause sea water to push upstream into the Mekong Delta in Vietnam which will be damaging to rice fields. In fact, Laos has already been blamed for causing low water levels along the stretch of the Mekong in Laos which is the lifeline of local fishermen.

## Threats to Regional Integration: Border Conflicts and Boundary Claims

While diplomacy prevailed and talks on regional economic cooperation for the proposed rail-link often end up in consensus, fighting between rebel groups on the borders of some member countries may hamper many agreed plans, for instance, the continuous fighting on the Thai-Myanmar border against the anti-Yangon guerrilla fighters (the Karen National Union). Yangon offensive against rebels pushed them to the border and sometimes forced them to cross over to Thailand. Myanmar's action may have strengthened its control of a 300 km stretch of border but it does not help Myanmar's relation with Bangkok. In

February 1996, for example, following intense Myanmar army shelling, thousands of Karen fighters pulled out of their Kawmoora base on a bend at the Moei River and crossed over the river into Thailand. In the wake of the fighting, Thai Deputy Prime Minister, Supachai Panichpakdi, and the newly appointed Foreign Minister had to postpone an official visit to Yangon to discuss some economic matters, and the postponement was linked to the border fighting.

Economic cooperation also seems to be strained by boundary claims among countries interested in developing the proposed rail track. This is best exemplified by the unresolved claims on the Spratlys, a far-flung cluster of small islands in the South China Sea which is being claimed by China, the Philippines, Malaysia, Brunei and Taiwan. China's interest and relentless efforts in the sea are the strongest as shown by its island-hopping advancement during the last two decades. In 1974, China took control of Parcel Islands from Vietnam. In 1989, it took over six positions in the Spratly archipelago, also from Vietnam. Last year, China occupied Mischief Island, a tiny island in the South China Sea (Chanda 1995). Previously, all the military action in capturing the islands and atolls were directed against Vietnam, an old enemy and ideological rival. The latest island-hopping on a reef 700 kilometres away from its shore but only 200 kilometres from the Philippines, brings China into direct confrontation with not only a non-communist neighbour but more importantly a member of ASEAN. These activities may pose a threat to regional integration and the rail-link project.

### Determining the Right of Way of the Proposed Track

There are also signs of different priorities among the participating countries with regards to which route the proposed rail track should follow. At the first ministerial meeting of the AMDC held in Kuala Lumpur, in which the proposal was discussed at length, Laos suggested that the tracks start from Nongkhai at the Laos-Thai border in the north, run through Vientiane and Luang Prabang (both in Laos) and up to the Laos-China border (Figure 12.2 and Table 12.2). This proposed track which is strongly supported by China, Thailand and Malaysia, will connect with a rail stretch which is under construction from Kunming to the border. This contradicts the initial proposal which envisaged that the major part of the railway should use existing rail tracks running along the coast of the Indochina Peninsula *via* Cambodia and Vietnam, a plan that will give advantages to countries in this region but which will by-pass land-locked Laos and Northern Thailand. Laos has long been a buffer state between neighbours that differ in history, economy and ideology, a place where the interests of China, Thailand and

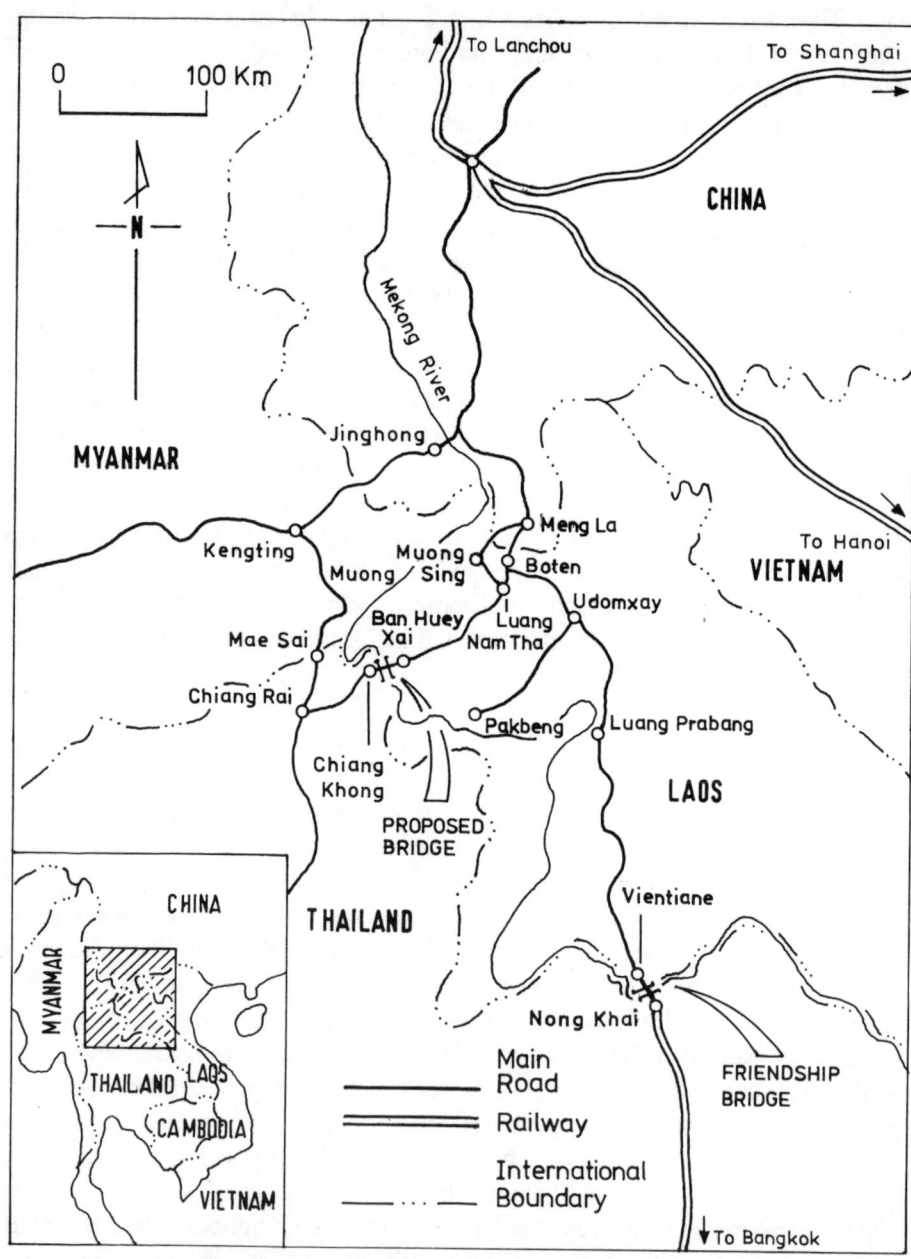

**Figure 12.2   Alternative route passing through Laos**

Vietnam meet or collide. With the opening of China's economy driven by free-market forces, Laos is increasingly becoming a land bridge between China and Thailand, while Vietnam's influences are waning. For China, Laos is attractive both for its natural resources and for its strategic location as a gateway to Southeast Asia where cheap manufactured goods from the fast developing Yunnan Province can supply the growing markets in Thailand, Malaysia and Singapore. Recent reports reveal that Luang Prabang Tha, a small town on the China-Laos border is already full of merchants from Nongkhai, a comparatively poor town on the Laos-Thai border where low-quality but cheap Chinese goods are competing with better but more expensive Thai products (Linter 1995b). Chinese interest in the area is actually bigger than these small-time traders, as shown by an agreement signed by a provincial Chinese carrier, Yunnan Airlines, to buy a 60 per cent stake in Lao Aviation for US$15 million. For Thailand, Laos is a potential market for the products of its rapidly expanding economy, not so much for domestic consumption, because Laos still lacks strong purchasing powers, but as a gateway to the fast growing giant market of China *via* Yunnan.

**Table 12.2    Consideration of alternative routes**

| Item | Alternative I | Alternative II |
|---|---|---|
| Route | Bangkok-Phnom Penh-Ho Chi Minh City-Hanoi-Kunming-Beijing | Bangkok-Nongkhai-Vientiane-Luang Prabang-Kunming-Beijing |
| Missing Link | (a) Poipet (Thai)-Sisophon (Cambodia)<br>(b) Phnom Penh-Ho Chi Minh City | Nongkhai (Thailand)-Kunming |
| Length of missing link (km) | 450 | 540 |
| Supporter | Vietnam, Cambodia | China, Thailand, Malaysia |
| Estimated construction costs (US$ in million) | 900 | 1,000 |
| Disadvantages | (a) Bypassing landlocked Laos<br>(b) Less accessible for Myanmar | (a) Passing through rugged terrain<br>(b) Costlier<br>(c) Time consuming for construction |

Thailand is, by far, the biggest investor in Laos. For Thailand and China, if indeed there is to be a connection between China and Southeast Asia linking it with Vietnam, Thailand, Burma and Cambodia, it makes sense to build it through Laos. Already Nongkhai (Thailand) has been physically connected to Vientiane (Laos's capital) by the Friendship Bridge (completed in 1994) crossing the Mekong River bordering both nations. The Thai government has signed an agreement with Pacific Transportation Company to build a railway track from the railhead at Nongkhai (Thailand) across the Mekong to Vientiane, paralleling the route of the Friendship Bridge which will give Laos its first railway line. From Vientiane the proposed track could be extended north to an area that has rich deposits of iron ore and subsequently be linked to Kunming. In early 1995, the Lao government and a private company from Thailand, the USA Family Company, agreed to build a 250 km toll-highway from Ban Huey Xai on the Thai-Laos Mekong border to Boten, a check-point on the Laos border with Yunnan, at an estimated cost of US$3.1 million.

**Funding Mechanism**

For the proposed rail track to take off, very much depends on the development of the Mekong Basin as mutually envisaged in the 5th ASEAN Summit in Bangkok. But the area for the Mekong development is so large that no one nation alone can hope to fund the necessary projects to provide some of the most basic infrastructure for people in a poor region still just discovering peace. The most urgent concerns revolved around how much each of the 11 nations is expected to contribute and the kind of funding mechanism considered to be appropriate to manage this fund for such a huge project.

The Kuala Lumpur meeting saw several different ideas on this matter, a divergence of opinions that can potentially divide the nations if not properly handled, especially when one considers such sensitive issues as implementing economic projects that will benefit several nations. Already, Malaysia has suggested that each country involved should contribute on a *pro-rata* basis which is against Indonesia's idea that each nation contributes on a voluntary basis. To compound this, there is also concern raised by Indonesia that existing and future aid funds extended by international funding agencies to individual nations may be re-channelled instead to the Mekong Fund. Many countries in the region received aid from international organisations such as the Asia Development Bank, World Bank and the International Monetary Fund of which Indonesia, with its large population size, is one of the major recipients (receiving some US$1 billion annually). Should the aid be re-channelled instead through the Mekong

Fund, a huge chunk could than be directed to the Mekong projects leaving smaller amounts available for existing recipient countries and possibly stalling on-going aid projects in the affected countries. The Kuala Lumpur meeting set up a sub-committee, headed by Thailand, assigned to come up with a viable financing mechanism. At the moment, it is up to the committee to work out a viable financing formula so as to diffuse the concerns, especially among the poorer member countries, on how to finance the projects.

## Conclusion

The proposed Trans-Asia railway is well-received not only by countries through which it will traverse but also by governments outside the region, including the European nations, which see it as a new opportunity for investments. The track is expected to open up the Mekong River basin which is endowed with rich natural resources providing economic opportunities in mining, modern agriculture, industry and tourism. Fast-flowing rivers and their tributaries in rugged terrain will ensure power supply from hydro-electric dams for these economic activities. The abundance of off-shore oil and gas, especially in Vietnam, are ready to be tapped for export, and can serve as fuel for economic development in this country as well as its neighbours. Cultural sites, ancient cities and antiques in Cambodia, Vietnam, Laos and Myanmar offer great potential for tourism involving international visitors. A number of riparian nations in the basin previously bogged down by political instability, wars and power-struggles are now fast opening up and gradually dismantling communist-inspired rules and regulations for freer capital flow especially from foreign sources. It should be emphasised, however, that the road to fully implement and develop the proposed infrastructure is still long and winding. At various summit meetings discussing the project, there were signs of divergent ideas and priorities among the participating countries on the project, especially with regards to the route it should follow. Finally, if the track is to become a reality, participating countries should first settle the issue of who has to finance it and how. Only then can one see the real impact of the proposed railway in facilitating the movement of goods and passengers in the region where international borders will become less important.

# References

Asian Development Bank (1995), *Annual Report*.

Brahm, L.J. (1995), *Vietnam Banking and Finance*, Butterworth Asia: Singapore.

Chanda, N. (1995), 'Territorial Imperative', *Far Eastern Economic Review*, Vol. 158, No. 8, pp. 14-16.

Crouch, M. (1985), 'Road Transport and the Soviet Economy', in Ambler, J; Shaw, D. and Symons, L (eds.), *Soviet and East European Transport Problems*, Croom Helm: London.

Fullerton, B. (1988), 'Scandinavia Adopts the New Realism in Transport Policy', *Research Series* 15, Department of Geography, Newcastle-upon-Tyne University: Newcastle Upon Tyne.

Kilvington, R. (1985), 'Railways in Rural Areas', in Button, K and Pitfield, D. (eds.), *International Railway Economics*, Gower: Aldershot.

Leung, C.K. (1980), 'China: Railway Patterns and National Goals', *Research Paper* 165, Department of Geography, University of Chicago: Chicago.

Linden, J. (1996), 'Investors' Confidence Keeps the Money Rolling', *Asiamoney (Supplement)*, Vol. 6, pp. 5, pp. 37-44.

Linter, B. (1995), 'End of an Era: Vietnam's Influence Wanes as New Leaders Emerge', *Far Eastern Economic Review*, Vol. 158, No. 6, p. 20.

Linter, B. (1995b), 'Ties that bind', *Far Eastern Economic Review*, Vol. 158, No. 6, pp. 18-19.

Parson, N. (1996), 'Race to Sell Power to Thailand', *Asiamoney*, Vol. 6, No. 5, pp. 36-40.

Patmore, J.A. (1966), 'The Contraction of the Network of Railway Passenger Services in England and Wales 1836-1962', *Transaction of the IBG*, Vol. 38, No. 2, pp. 105-118.

Peters, H.A. (1995), 'Culture Vultures: Asian Governments Exploit the Past to Press Their Political Agenda', *Far Eastern Economic Review*, Vol. 158, No. 3, pp. 34-37.

Schwarz, A. (1995), 'When Oil and Water Mix', *Far Eastern Economic Review*, Vol. 158, No. 11, pp. 54-56.

Tolley, R. and Turton, B. (1995), *Transport System, Policy and Planning: A Geographical Approach*, Longman Scientific and Technical: London.

Vatikiostis, M. (1995), 'Catching the Wave', *Far Eastern Economic Review*, Vol. 158, No. 7, pp. 48-51.

Vatikiotis, M. (1995), 'Rude Neighbour: Spill-over of Burmese Fighting Tests Thailand's Patience', *Far Eastern Economic Review*, Vol 185, No. 11, p. 32.

Whitelegg, J. (1987), 'Rural Railways and Disinvestment in Rural Areas', *Regional Studies*, Vol. 21, No. 1, pp. 55-63.

Whitelegg, J. (1988), *Transport Policy in the EEC*, Routeledge: London.

Yusof, R. and Ching, L.H. (1996), 'Estimated Cost of Trans-Asian Rail Project', *New Straits Times*, 22nd April.

# 13  Bothers with Borders?
# Natural Resource Management
# in the Mekong River Basin

*Gerard CHEONG*

## Introduction

International river basins lend themselves well to studies on the nature and effects of borders. Rivers flow according to the dictates of landform and rainfall and often in defiance of political boundaries. Where rivers are used to delimit territories, they can serve as formidable physical barriers to separate people or as a common resource to unite them. Rivers are not static - they carry impacts far from the point of disturbance, whether upstream or downstream. Banks erode and sediments are deposited to change their courses. There is unpredictability in floods or droughts. This chapter describes the Mekong River Basin and its natural resources and offers a structural approach to natural resource management (NRM). It attempts to highlight the role of borders by examining existing or potential conflicts over natural resources and discusses the way ahead for sustainable development of the Basin.

## Geography of the Basin

The Basin lies in a northwest-southeast arc, stretching from the Tibetan Plateau to the South China Sea. Apart from being the largest in Southeast Asia, the Basin is the tenth largest in the world, discharging 475,000 cubic metres of water per annum. The Mekong River is 4,200 kilometres long, spanning a wide range of altitudes, latitudes, climates and vegetation zones. The total drainage or catchment area of the Basin is 795,000 square kilometres, encompassing territories in six countries: China, Burma, Lao PDR, Thailand, Cambodia and Vietnam (Table 13.1). Almost all of Lao PDR and Cambodia are located within the Basin. The Thai portion of the Basin is comprised of two portions, one in the northern tip and the other in the north east or the Korat Plateau. Vietnam also has two separate portions, the Delta and part of its central highlands. The Burmese portion is limited to a small part of the eastern Shan State while in China, the Basin area comprises just over a third of Yunnan Province.

Snow melt in the Tibetan Plateau first feeds the river which runs for about half its length in Yunnan Province. In this, the Upper Basin, the steep topography and narrow gorges form an elongated catchment with short and fast flowing tributaries. The Lower Basin commences where the Mekong River meets Lao PDR and comprises about 77 per cent or 609,000 square kilometres of the total Basin area. The Mekong River is the third most biologically diverse in the world after the Amazon and Zambezi Rivers (Sluiter 1992). Its basin area is also highly biodiverse and is home to some of the last remaining wild populations of large mammals in mainland Southeast Asia. As recently as 1992, a new species, the Vu Quang Ox or *Sao la*, was discovered in the mountainous region between Lao PDR and Vietnam. Most of the Basin's discharge comes from rainfall and the dominance of the monsoons results in a wide variation between high (September) and low flows (May) in the order of about 15 times.

*Key Socio-Economic Features*

About 60 million people of diverse ethnicity inhabit the Basin. The most heavily populated regions are in the Korat Plateau in Thailand and the Mekong Delta in Vietnam. Table 13.2 shows some basic socio-economic indicators in the Basin. Lao PDR has one of the lowest population densities in the world and the lowest in the Basin area. However, it has the highest population growth rate leading to increasing pressures on natural resources and government services in common with the other riparian nations. In the rapidly growing economies, rising affluence is another strong causal factor in the degradation of natural resource endowments. The GDP per capita figures need to be qualified by the regional disparities that operate within each country, in particular, Thailand and Vietnam. The Korat Plateau in Thailand is the poorest part of that country with income per capita figures about ten times less than that for Bangkok. On the other hand, the Mekong Delta in Vietnam is relatively well off compared to the rest of the country (though pockets of extreme poverty exist, for example, the ethnic Khmer). In contrast, the Central Highlands of Vietnam which also lie in the Basin is one of the poorest parts of the country. Most of the economic activities in the

## Table 13.1 Biophysical features of the Mekong River Basin

|  | Burma | Cambodia | Lao PDR | Thailand | Vietnam | Yunnan | Total |
|---|---|---|---|---|---|---|---|
| Contribution to runoff (%) | 2 | 18 | 35 | 18 | 11 | 16 | 100 |
| Drainage area ('000 sq km) | 24 | 155 | 202 | 184 | 65 | 165 | 795 |
| Drainage area (%) | 2 | 20 | 25 | 23 | 8 | 21 | 100 |
| Hydropower potential (MW) | 300 | 2,200 | 13,000 | 1,000 | 2,000 | 13,000 | 31,500 |
| Hydropower potential | 1 | 7 | 41.5 | 3 | 6 | 41.5 | 100 |

*Sources*: Choung Phanrajsavong (1994); Mekong Secretariat (1994a)

## Table 13.2 Basic socio-economic indicators in the Mekong River Basin

|  | Burma | Cambodia | Lao PDR | Thailand | Vietnam | Yunnan |
|---|---|---|---|---|---|---|
| Total population (million) | 44 | 9.9 | 4.4 | 59 | 72.5 | 37 |
| Population in Basin area (million) | - | 9.9 | 4.4 | 20.9 | 15.9 | 9.7 |
| Population growth rate (%) | 2.0 | 2.1 | 2.6 | 1.3 | 1.9 | 1.6 |
| GDP per capita (US$) | 250 | 206 | 335[a] | 640 (2377)[b] | (240)[b] | 465 |
| GDP annual growth rate (%) | 6.4 | 4.9 | 8.0 | 8.5 | 8.8 | 11.8 |

[a]US$335 GDP per capita figure for Lao PDR is unlikely to be correct and is calculated at US$229 in Government of Lao PDR (1994)
[b]number in brackets is the average GDP per capita figure for the whole country
*Sources*: DFAT (1994; 1995); TDRI (1996); TDRI (1996); General Statistical Office (1994); Mekong Development Research Network (1993); World Bank (1994); Bangkok Bank Monthly Review (1995)

Basin are based on agriculture, forestry and fisheries, mostly at the subsistence level. Intensive cash cropping and commercial capture fisheries or aquaculture are carried out in various parts of the Basin.

The delta in Vietnam supplies half that country's rice, making it the third largest rice exporter in the world. The Basin is relatively lightly developed and major industrial projects include hydropower schemes in China, Thailand, Lao PDR and Vietnam. Industrial development in the Vietnam Mekong Delta is growing, for example, in cement, steel and agrochemical production while in Thailand, light industries such as food processing are fairly well developed.

*Borders Operating in the Basin*

Two main borders overlay each other in the Basin: the political and the biogeographical. The biogeographical boundaries divide the Basin into seven main zones (based on the Mekong Committee 1988) (Table 13.3). The borders of district, province and state are not necessarily consistent with the natural biogeographic boundaries. In addition, another series of overlays comprise informal jurisdictional boundaries which reflect quasi-political, cultural, economic and various other influences. These include the widely known Golden Triangle which straddles the common borders of Burma, Thailand and Lao PDR, and the proposed economic polygons supported by multilateral agencies such as the Asian Development Bank and ASEAN.

## Some Natural Resources of the Basin

*Land*

The Basin shows wide variation in land capability for agriculture. Over 90 per cent of the Basin population is agrarian-based and the land is therefore not significantly urbanised. However, there are regions where agricultural development has greatly altered the land. The Korat Plateau has been extensively logged and together with the Delta, has experienced the most irrigation development. Diminished tree cover in the Plateau has, however, brought naturally occurring salts closer to the surface of the land, resulting in severe land degradation. This, combined with soil fertility problems, has serious repercussions for agriculture. The draining of swamps and flood protection measures while increasing the availability of land, can have drawbacks due to the destruction of the fish habitat. Land reclamation activities in the Delta have contributed much to rice production but the increasing problems of soil acidity from acid sulphate soils threaten many of the rice fields.

*Water*

Table 13.1 shows the relative flow contributions of each riparian country. Of the 475,000 cubic metres discharged per annum, Lao PDR provides the highest volume or 35 per cent of all runoff. Yunnan, Thailand and Cambodia contribute from 16-18 per cent while Vietnam provides 11 per cent. Burma, with only a small amount of its territory within the Basin, contributes only 2 per cent. Caution needs to be exercised when considering the volume and quality of Basin water. It is often quoted that Lao PDR has the highest freshwater per capita ratio in the world and that water in the Mekong River and its tributaries is relatively unpolluted. Yet, there is local scarcity of water in Lao PDR and Basin-wide, periodic droughts and flooding occur. Saline water is a major problem in the Delta due to sea water intrusions. The Delta is also severely affected by acid sulphate soils which cause highly acid water especially early in the rainy season. Sediment loads in the Tonle Sap system in Cambodia are increasing due to deforestation in the watersheds and leading to a shallowing of that important water body.

The heaviest rainfalls occur in the Eastern Highlands in Lao PDR (up to 4,000 milimetres) while rainfall is lowest in the Korat Plateau (about 1,000 milimetres). The annual floods coincide with the south-west monsoon and the inundation of the surrounding countryside deposits fertile sediment, while also forming ephemeral fish habitats. The steep topography and the abundant rainfall in Lao

**Table 13.3 Biogeographical zones and locations in the Mekong Basin**

| Biogeographical Zone | Location |
|---|---|
| Upper Mekong | Yunnan Province |
| Northern Highlands | Burma, Thailand, Lao PDR |
| Eastern Highlands | Lao PDR, Vietnam, Cambodia |
| Korat Plateau | Thailand, Lao PDR |
| Lowlands | Cambodia, Lao PDR, Thailand |
| Southern Uplands | Cambodia |
| Delta | Cambodia, Vietnam |

PDR offers great potential for hydropower developments in the numerous tributaries and over 50 possible sites have been identified, with a number under construction or at the feasibility study stage. The Tonle Sap or Great Lake in Cambodia swells to three times its size (from 2,600 to 10,500 square kilometres) as flood waters reverse the flow along the Tonle Sap River which connects the lake to the Mekong River. At least 20 per cent of the Mekong River flood waters is taken in by the Great Lake and gradually released as the floods recede.

*Forests*

Deforestation has resulted in a large decline in forest cover in Thailand and Vietnam. Lao PDR, Burma and Cambodia hold some of the last remaining large tracts of undisturbed forests in the region (Table 13.4). The Central Highlands region of Vietnam is the most heavily forested part of that country, with about 60 per cent forest cover and holding about half the country's timber reserves (EIU 1994). The remaining tracts of forest are important repositories of biodiversity of regional and global significance. Rare and endangered animal species supported by these forests include the Javan Rhinoceros, Vu Quang Ox, tiger, elephant and numerous others including those that live in the vast wetlands of the Lower Basin. Forest cover is rapidly depleting and may even accelerate in particular areas, for example, Cambodia, where a number of very large logging concessions have recently been announced.

*Fish*

Knowledge of fish biology and ecology in the Mekong Basin is characterised by its paucity, in contrast to the fact that fish is the predominant source of animal protein for the Basin's population. Surveys have identified over 200 species of fish from the 1,800 kilometre length of the mainstream and in numerous tributaries in Lao PDR alone (Taki 1974). This high degree of biodiversity supports a yield of 620,000 to 890,000 tonnes, mostly from capture fisheries. These production figures underestimate the contribution of subsistence and small scale fisheries, especially in Cambodia and Vietnam (Mekong Committee 1992). Many fish species in the Mekong migrate in search of food or breeding grounds. The giant catfish, *pla beuk*, is thought to migrate from Cambodia to Lake Tali in China to spawn (Sluiter 1992:73-74). Aquaculture is most developed in the Delta in Vietnam but shows signs of following the boom and bust cycle of shrimp farming in Thailand. This is due to the destruction of mangroves which form the natural habitat for shrimp breeding stock and the over-intensification of shrimp farming leading to severe disease outbreaks such as in the bacterial contamination of about 85,000 hectares of ponds in Ca Mau peninsula in 1994. Nevertheless, aquaculture is expected to make up the increasing deficit between fish yields and consumption due to the deterioration of capture fisheries from overexploitation.

## A Multi-Perspective Approach to Natural Resource Management

Taking into consideration the multiplicity of jurisdictional and natural boundaries and the diversity of people and their activities in the Basin, the process of NRM will necessarily take a multi-perspective approach.

*   Most obviously, the perspectives of individual riparian states are important. For example, the role of Thailand as an electricity consumer *vis a vis* Lao PDR as a supplier underlies a programme of hydropower development in the latter country. The perspective of China, the furthest upstream nation, in river basin management can be a decisive factor in the programmes run by downstream nations.
*   There is also a need to take a sectoral perspective of, for example, the forestry sector in Basin NRM. Other important sectors which can drive basin development are hydropower, tourism, aquaculture and farming/irrigation. Sectoral demands and influence can supersede the jurisdictional reach of individual countries, as illustrated by the extensive illegal trade in timber within the Basin. In the case of Lao PDR, this approaches about one-third of total yields or 100,000 to 150,000 cubic metres per annum (GOL 1994).

**Table 13.4    Forest cover and deforestation rates in the Mekong Basin**

|  | Burma | Cambodia | Lao PDR | Thailand | Vietnam |
|---|---|---|---|---|---|
| Forest cover (% of total land area) | 47 | 49-62 | 47 | 26 | 27 |
| Deforestation rate (%) | 6 | 3 | 2 | 1.5 | 3.2 (Central Highlands) |

*Sources*:   Miller and Thinh (1996); Pednekar *et al.* (1996); Hirsch and Cheong (1996a) and World Bank (1994)

- The perspectives of key actors such as multilateral development banks, non-government organisations and local communities are also crucial to form a complete picture of the NRM jigsaw. Individual actors, such as the World Bank, can be instrumental in deciding whether projects such as the Nam Theun 2 Hydropower Scheme in Lao PDR will go ahead.

## Country Perspectives

The different political and socio-economic backgrounds of the Mekong riparian nations result in a wide range of perspectives to NRM. These national perspectives often lead the agenda for resource use within each country, depending on the level of dominance of ruling political groupings and their policies. Significant shifts within the Basin are tagged by the geopolitical continuum of Cold War divisions and superpower rivalry to communist victories in Indochina in 1975 and their contemporary economic liberalisation policies. The Mekong River has moved from being a divide formed by ideology to becoming a focus for collaborative resource development.

Thailand is, by far, the most industrialised country in the Basin and the Chatichai government's call to convert battlefields to marketplaces reflects its self-perceived role in the region, that is, as a leader in economic growth. The resource frontiers, represented especially by Burma, Cambodia and Lao PDR, are important in feeding Thailand's continued industrial growth and maintaining its position as a key economic player in the region. Economic integration in the Basin is particularly beneficial to Thailand as illustrated by the acceptance of the baht as a common currency in many transactions.

China is an upstream country with strong interests in harnessing the Mekong River resources for hydropower. The only mainstream dam, the 1,500 MW Manwan, has recently been completed without consultation and about five more are under construction or planned, despite the trepidation of downstream nations. On the other hand, China has entered into dialogues with other Basin countries on the development of road, rail and river routes which will open up important links with the burgeoning markets down south.

Cambodia is largely preoccupied with internal issues and the need to rebuild a war ravaged economy. Political divisions within this, a country with two prime ministers and lack of central control, strongly influence the process of decision making on resource management. A major concern for Cambodia is in maintaining the productivity of the Tonle Sap Basin which supplies most of the country's food. Flood control measures in Vietnam and upstream development, threaten Cambodia's food security by negatively affecting the Tonle Sap Basin.

Lao PDR straddles a central position in the future of the Basin's water resources by virtue of its large share of those resources (Table 13.1). The more than fifty potential hydropower sites in Mekong tributaries in Lao PDR are a windfall for that country's prospects for economic development. Like Cambodia, Lao PDR is an extremely poor country with strong pressures to quickly exploit its natural resources to earn much needed foreign exchange.

## Sectoral Perspectives

This section will focus on two sectors, hydropower and forestry, in discussing the importance of the sectoral perspectives for NRM.

*Hydropower:* Lao PDR has signed a Memorandum of Understanding (MOU) with Thailand to supply it with 1,500 MW of electricity by the year 2,000, reflecting its large hydropower potential. So far, MOUs have been signed for 23 individual hydropower schemes throughout Lao PDR (Ounthoung 1995). This large scale proposed hydropower development in Lao PDR underlies the projected 1,000 MW increase per annum of power demand in Thailand which eclipses that of the other riparian countries. A strong link therefore exists between Thailand's energy needs and Lao PDR's optimistic hydropower building plans. The hydropower sector has dominated plans for the Mekong River development. The then Mekong Committee in 1970, planned for a cascade of dams on the Mekong River which would have completely regulated the flow of the river and created a generating capacity of over 24,000 MW. Recent plans have scaled down these developments to about 13,000 MW of installed capacity (Mekong Secretariat 1994b). China's mainstream dams will have over 10,000 MW of installed capacity when completed and their effects on the Basin are unknown. The hydropower projects that have been built, or are under construction or are planned either in the mainstream or the tributaries, pose the most critical issues concerning sustainable development of the Basin's natural resources. They have the potential to convert the river to one that is highly regulated, making it a totally different habitat and also to displace many thousands of people as reservoirs fill up.

*Forestry:* As described earlier, forestry is occurring at unsustainable rates in the Basin. In Lao PDR, Cambodia and Burma, timber is a significant component of foreign exchange earnings, much of it exported either legally or illegally to China, Thailand and Vietnam. Earnings from the timber trade are often siphoned off by the local authorities and traders who resist intervention by central governments.

On the other hand, central government authorities, such as in Cambodia, are also implicated in the excessive extraction of timber. Thailand announced a logging ban in 1989 in response to devastating landslides caused by the deforestation in highland areas. This has resulted in Thai timber companies looking to its timber rich neighbours for supplies of logs. Lao PDR announced a logging ban in 1991 which was lifted shortly after. Vietnam announced a ban on the export of logs and sawn wood in 1991 while Cambodia imposed a ban in 1995. These bans have largely been ineffectual in controlling the rapid depletion of forests. The Cambodian government recently announced 17 deals with Thai companies for the supply of over a million cubic metres of timber. This is on top of large concessions to companies, some of which are based in Malaysia and Indonesia including Samling and Macro-Pannin (Grainger 1996). These deals effectively tie up all the timber reserves in Cambodia, making no sense of the logging ban of 1995. Deforestation is also due to the practices of subsistence shifting cultivators in many highland parts of the Basin. However, the extent to which they contribute to forest depletion is a subject of intense debate. In this debate, it is also important to consider the effects of encroaching lowland farmers who are not familiar with hillslope farming and increased pressure from commercial logging activities which reduce fallow periods.

**Perspectives of Key Actors**

There is a wide range of perspectives held by the various key actors within the Basin, among them are the government, business, community and international perspectives.

*Mekong River Commission (MRC):* The Mekong Committee formed in 1957 was a precursor to the MRC which came about with the signing of *the Agreement on the Cooperation for the Sustainable Development of the Mekong River Basin* in April 1995 by Thailand, Lao PDR, Cambodia and Vietnam. The MRC and its predecessors are characterised by a leaning towards large scale water resource development projects and it is unlikely this will change in the short to medium term. The new Mekong Agreement, for example, now reduces the need for consensus by member countries in various water resource development projects. Any intra-Basin uses and inter-Basin diversions in tributaries and intra-Basin uses in the mainstream need only to notify the Joint Committee comprised of bureaucratic representatives from each member country. One serious drawback to the MRC is that it does not include China and Burma and although the MRC has an open invitation to both to join, there has yet been no positive response.

*Royal Forest Department (RFD), Thailand:* The RFD is responsible for the management of national parks in Thailand and is probably the most effective body of its type in the Basin. Park management is a complex issue and the rights of local communities are affected by the declaration of national park boundaries. While there are good examples where parks and local communities coexist, there have also been cases where RFD rangers have forcibly evicted local villagers who have used the forest resources for generations. The RFD has also embarked on reforestation programmes and has reforested over 1,000 square kilometres from 1988 to 1992. In tandem with this, the Department of Land Development (DLD) is planting large areas with eucalypts. These reforestation programmes are controversial due to the type of trees being planted (eucalypts) and also when it involves farmed land being taken over.

*Asian Development Bank (ADB):* The ADB has an ambitious list of about 70 projects worth over US$40 billion in the Greater Mekong Subregion. A series of annual consultations by riparian nations (including China and Burma) have been brokered by the ADB in its technical assistance programme since 1992. They clearly illustrate the importance of this region to the ADB and set the scene for long term and increased involvement in the development of the Basin's resources. The ADB also contributes to the MRC and supports a large number of projects in the region (US$800 million in 1993).

*Non-Government Organisations (NGOs):* There are numerous NGOs operating in the Basin and they include both overseas and locally-based groups. The most experienced local NGOs are Thai and they have built up vast expertise as a result of numerous campaigns for equity and environmental protection. They are often rural based and have been effective in negotiating through tough issues with the government. The status of NGOs in the other countries is mixed but generally positive. In Lao PDR, for example, local NGOs are not permitted but many foreign NGOs now operate there. A Thai-based NGO, Towards Ecological Recovery and Regional Alliances, is working closely with the Lao Department of Forestry in watershed management. This is a good example of successful collaboration between governments and NGOs.

## Borders and Potential Natural Resource Management Disputes

Borders are delimiting lines which may exist not only in the political context but also as somewhat more ambiguous cultural, social or economic boundaries. These various contexts for borders form a strong basis for NRM decision-making. The different perspectives outlined above are representative of these different contexts and need to be understood and respected in order to achieve sustainability and to avoid or manage disputes. Disputes are situations which clarify the operation of borders to participants and observers. The list below is not exhaustive by any means but represents a cross section of some of these potential areas of disputes.

*Fisheries at Khone Falls, Southern Lao PDR (Lao PDR/Cambodia):* The use of explosives by the Cambodian fisherfolk who then sell the fish to Lao traders has been a serious problem until recently. Fishing with explosives and chemicals still continues and the Lao authorities have reacted by banning the sale of fish between provinces in southern Lao PDR. The use of highly efficient fishing methods, for example, gill netting is slowly being regulated by district authorities in southern Lao PDR to try to stop the decline in fish stock and to allow fish to migrate along the river. Such a process will not be effective unless there is cooperation by fisherfolk in the various districts and even between villages.

*River banks at Vientiane (Thailand/Lao PDR):* Bank stabilisation on the Thai side of the Mekong River is of concern to Lao PDR authorities as it is claimed to contribute to bank erosion on the Lao PDR side. This has implications for national boundary demarcation.

*Flood control in the Vietnamese Delta (Cambodia/Vietnam):* Under the Mekong Delta Master Plan (NEDECO 1993) wide ranging flood control measures are proposed to stabilise agricultural land which is subject to annual flooding during the rainy season. However, dykes reducing the flow of water into Vietnam have the potential to cause increased flooding in Cambodia.

*Hydropower developments in the mainstream and tributaries (Entire Basin):* Chinese dams in Yunnan and dams in Thailand such as the Pak Mun completed in 1995 have unknown effects on river flow, fisheries and agricultural land. The Yali Falls Dam in the Central Highlands of Vietnam has the potential to affect Cambodian fisheries. Various dams in Lao PDR also have similar problems. Further dam construction is proceeding and there is no region-based environmental assessment of cumulative effects. The potential impacts are wide ranging and mitigation may be an impossible goal due to the scale of development. The effects are also within the country as there is strong opposition to the Pak Mun Dam by the local Thai farmers and fisherfolk who would be displaced or lose their fishing grounds. The hydropower schemes in Lao PDR are intimately linked to Thai demand and most of the electricity will be sold to Thailand. This exposes the Lao PDR government to inordinate pressure due to the dependence on Thailand for foreign exchange.

*Deforestation (Entire Basin):* Excessive logging in neighbouring countries promoted by Thai firms has caused serious human and environmental problems. China and Vietnam also obtain logs from Lao PDR, Burma and Cambodia. The nature of the logging industry does not result in adequate returns to source countries and the potential for future conflicts within those countries is large.

*Khong-Chi-Mun intrabasin water diversion (Entire Basin but particularly downstream of Thailand):* This large-scale water diversion is planned by Thailand to provide water to its dry Korat Plateau. However, the water is likely to become saline and will reduce in volume as a result of agricultural use, seepage and evaporation. This will reduce flow volumes and water quality in the Mekong River.

## Conclusion

Undoubtably, the Mekong Basin is currently subject to intense development interest. It is clear also that this unprecedented pressure is largely due to the relaxation of hostilities in the region. Seemingly impenetrable borders reinforced by political and military opposition during the Cold War era are now becoming porous to, not only, the flow of refugees but to money, raw materials and technology. It is, however, far from the borderless marketplace where political jurisdictions play host to business imperatives (Ohmae 1994). It was only in 1988 that Lao PDR and Thailand engaged in a short but bloody interprovincial border conflict. More recently, Cambodia has warned of military action against border incursions by Vietnamese (Barber 1996). These are the exceptions but are reminders that national sovereignty is still a powerful and asssertive force in the Basin. At the same time, however, environmental changes often do not recognise national borders and therefore challenge the effectiveness of nation state delineations. The trend in international environmental relations may posit regional and local actors rather than the nation state in the centre (Dyer 1996) underlining the importance of the multi-perspective approach to NRM discussed above. Such an approach is also supported by the various theories on borderland cultures and their role in intra- and inter-state conflict (Grundy-Warr 1993).

Regional groupings such as the MRC and the ADB economic cooperation dialogue have had some successes in facilitating development collaboration in the

Basin. Proposals for various economic polygons or development zones are much discussed and options for regional economic integration highlighted. Vietnam's recent admission to ASEAN, followed by Lao PDR and Burma in 1997 and later, Cambodia, will boost Basin-wide cooperation and increase pressure for development. The recent ASEAN inspired foreign and economic ministerial and senior officials meeting in Kuala Lumpur in June 1996 to discuss Basin development, included the non-ASEAN riparian countries, China, Lao PDR, Cambodia and Burma (*Bernama* 18th June 1996). This has advanced the scope for economic cooperation in the Basin but it is too early to tell to what extent cooperation will occur. The various models of economic cooperation currently being played out, take a top-down approach with little or no input from the affected communities. Claims of taking a sustainable development approach are therefore dubious on this point alone.

The Basin may well move on to become a model of regional collaboration and integration in the future. But, in essence, the future is now. The scope of what the future will operate as, is dependent on how the natural resources of the Basin are managed now. A rush to develop, to dam the rivers and deforest the land, will reduce options and will set the seed for future conflicts. Such future conflicts will not be based just on the borders of past decades, as natural resources are not necessarily aligned according to the notions of national sovereignty. The examples above attest to the potential for intra- as much as inter-state disputes. The existence and operation of borders is a conundrum in NRM in the Basin. At one level, divisions of the past reduced the prospects for large-scale developments with large negative impacts such as the mainstream dams. On another, they reduced prospects for collaboration on, for example, sustainable management of fisheries. The multi-perspective approach discussed above adds more complexity by enlarging on the concept of borders. However, this is a necessary complexity as the full range of political and economic forces act on the Basin to rapidly unlock its natural wealth. The key to managing this wealth wisely, lies in first understanding the various perspectives to NRM.

## References

Bangkok Bank (1995), *Monthly Review*, Vol. 36, No. 4-6, (April-June).

Barber, Jason (1996), 'Talks Aimed to Defuse Border Tensions with Hanoi', *Phnom Penh Post*, 22nd March-4th April 1996.

*Bernama* (18th June 1996), 'Other Nations Welcome to Join Effort to Develop Mekong'.

Choung Phanrajsavong (1995), *Integrated Water Resources Management in the Lower Mekong Basin: Progress and Prospects*, Mekong Secretarial, Bangkok: Thailand.

Department of Foreign Affairs and Trade (DFAT) (1994), *Country Economic Brief, Cambodia*, Canberra, Australia.

Department of Foreign Affairs and Trade (1995), *Country Economic Brief, Myanmar*, Canberra, Australia.

Dyer, Hugh C. (1996), Environmental Security as a Universal Value, Implications for International Theory, in Vogler, J. and Imber, M. (eds.), *The environment and international relations*, Routledge: London.

Economist Intelligence Unit. Country report (1994), *Indochina: Vietnam, Laos, Cambodia* (1st quarter).

General Statistical Office (1994), *Statistical Yearbook*, Socialist Republic of Vietnam: Hanoi.

Government of Lao PDR (1990), *Lao People's Democratic Republic. Tropical Forestry Action Plan (First Phase)*, Main Report, Ministry of Agriculture and Forestry (August).

_____ (1994), *Socio-economic Development Strategies*, Paper prepared for the 5th Round Table Meeting, Geneva, 21st June 1994.

Grainger, Matthew (1996), 'PMs Sign 'Million Metre' Timber Deals with Thais', *Phnom Penh Post*, (5th-18th April 1996).

Grundy-Warr, Carl (1993), 'Coexistent Borderlands and Intra-state Conflicts in Mainland Southeast Asia', *Singapore Journal of Tropical Geography*, Vol. 14 No.1, pp. 42-57.

Hirsch, P. and Cheong G. (1996a), *Natural Resource Management in the Mekong basin: Lao PDR*, Unpublished working paper.

Mekong Committee (1988), *Perspectives for Mekong Development, Revised Indicative Plan for the development of land, water and related resources of the lower Mekong Basin*, (Commitee Report), Interim Commitee for Coordination of Investigations of the Lower Mekong Basin, Bangkok.

_____ (1992), *Fisheries in the Lower Mekong Basin* (Main Report), Interim Committee for Coordination of Investigations of the Lower Mekong Basin, Bangkok.

Mekong Development Research Network (1993), *Investigation and study of the current status of the Lancang River - Mekong River Basin in Yunnan, PRC*.

Mekong Secretariat (1994a), *Annual Report*, Bangkok, Thailand.

_____ (1994b), *Mekong Mainstream Run-of-river Hydropower* (Main report), Bangkok.

Miller, F. and Thinh, N.V. (1996), *Natural Resource Management in the Mekong basin: Vietnam*, Unpublished working paper.

NEDECO (1993, October), *Master Plan for the Mekong Delta in Vietnam. A Perspective for Sustainable Development of Land and Water Resources* (Summary Report), Ho Chi Minh City.

Ohmae, Kenichi (1994), *The Borderless World. Power and Strategy in the Global Marketplace*, Harper Collins: GB.

Outhoung, Thanousay (1995), 'Integrated Water Resources Management in the Lao PDR', Paper presented for AusAID workshop on *Integrated Water Resources Management*, Vientiane, 10th-13th October 1995.

Pednekar, Sunit *et al.* (1996), *Natural Resource Management in the Mekong Basin: Thailand,* Unpublished working paper, Thailand Development Research Institute, Bangkok, Thailand.

Sluiter, Lisbeth (1992),'The Mekong Currency', TERRA/Project for Ecological Recovery, Bangkok.

Taki, Y. (1974), *Fisheries of the Lao Mekong Basin,* US Agency for International Development mission to Laos, quoted in Mekong Commitee (1992), Fisheries in the Lower Mekong Basin, Annexes, pg A6-3, Interim Committee for Coordination of Investigations of the Lower Mekong Basin, Bangkok.

World Bank (1994), *World Development Report,* Oxford University Press: New York.

# 14 Integrating West Africa Through the Economic Community of West African States (ECOWAS)

*Daniel BUOR*

## Introduction

A modern paradigm in the geographic discipline is the analysis of inter-relationships between spatial phenomena using appropriate statistical techniques buttressed on the systems theory. Such analysis could be based on an identified theme and organised into regional patterns. A regional analysis using the systems approach will eventually lead to greater integration, hence weakening the political boundaries of regions and sub-regions. The Economic Community of West African States (ECOWAS) is an interesting case study to analyse the integration-and-political-boundary-demise syndrome. The bases of spatial interaction are identified by Ullman as complementarity, intervening opportunity and trans-ferability (Abler, Adams and Gould 1977:133). The diversity of resources in the West African sub-region, which is the function of colonialism, and the not-too-many physical barriers among the countries, coupled with salient economic considerations like local winning and processing of resources to reap in the surplus value, and other multiplier effects, reinforce the argument for economic integration.

Colonialism had introduced monocultural economies into the various countries of the West African sub-region. Each country was made to cultivate crops over which it had the comparative advantage. Therefore, whereas Ghana emphasised the production of cocoa, Nigeria concentrated on palm-fruit and groundnuts, Sierra Leone and Gambia on groundnuts, Ivory Coast (La Cote d'Ivoire) on cocoa and coffee, Liberia on rubber, etc. Apart from the cash crops, there are also diversities of renewable and non-renewable resources that necessarily establish the basis for intra-regional trade. Whereas Ghana can boast of metallic ores like gold, manganese, bauxite and timber, Nigeria abounds in crude oil, natural gas, tin, coal and timber resources, whilst Guinea, Sierra Leone and Liberia are rich in iron ore. These, coupled with the hydro-electric power resource, constitute the bedrock for an industrial take-off in the sub-region. A joint exploitation and processing of the resources, it is hoped, would ameliorate the scarcities in the various countries in the sub-region, due to the disparities in resource endowments and skilled personnel, and create employment opportunities. Joint efforts will also relax the over-reliance on foreign imports and capital which has adverse effects on the economies of member countries. Another argument for an economic integration which will eventually promote the free movement of people in the sub-region is that, member countries trace their origins from the ancient kingdoms of Western Sudan, namely the successive kingdoms of Ghana, Mali and Songhai. So, they have a common socio-cultural origin. After independence, the black government of Gold Coast felt so impelled by the strong ties of its people with the ancient kingdom of Ghana that the new nation was named Ghana.

The attempt to integrate the sub-region, buttressed upon common economic policies with trade as an isolated factor, is riddled with teething problems. Links with past colonial authorities with different perspectives on development planning, unstable political regimes, border disputes among member nations, restrictions on movements of people and goods among member states, and internal political, economic and social crises that divert attention from the community's preoccupations, have imperilled efforts at integration. Yet, the socio-economic gains to the individual states of the Community would be superfluous in the 21st Century, when the whole world would shrink into a small village through uniform economic policies, improved inter-and intra-continental communication network, and a better understanding of a common universal brotherhood.

This chapter discusses the objectives of ECOWAS and trade links within the sub-region during the pre-colonial and colonial times. The pattern and volume of trade within the sub-region and the ease of movement during the early years after independence, are contrasted with the post-ECOWAS times, in order to assess the impact on the Community of such patterns. The limitations on free trade and movement within the sub-region and other hindrances to integration are also analysed. Finally, recommendations are made as to how to achieve a consensus in aggressive efforts to stabilise the community and to achieve its aims and objectives.

## The Concept of Economic Integration

Economic integration occurs whenever a group of nations in the same region join together to form an economic union, by raising a common tariff wall against the products of non-member countries while freeing internal trade among members (Todaro 1992:384-385). The concept of economic integration involves the dual concept of customs union and a common market. Nations that levy common external tariffs while freeing internal trade are said to have formed a customs union, whilst a common market possesses all the attributes of a customs union plus the free movement of labour and capital among the partner states (Todaro 1992). Integration is a mechanism to encourage a rational division of labour among a group of countries, each of which is too small to benefit from such a division itself. The absence of integration will weaken the market potential of each component state. This will not help local industries to lower production costs through the economies of scale. The absence of integration will also duplicate industries in various countries in a region or sub-region, hence, the tendency of each to operate below the optimal capacity. Thus, for coordinated industrial planning, there is the need for the removal of barriers to trade among countries in a region or sub-region, to create the foundation for multiplier effects in the joint winning and processing of resources. Such concepts and models bring into sharp focus the urgent need for the West African sub-region which has fragmented material resource endowments and a diversity of human resources to form an economic union in order to ensure a steady progress towards a take-off.

## The Pre-ECOWAS Trade Patterns

Trade in West Africa antedates the medieval times before the advent of colonialism when bartering was the main feature. There were examples of exchange of commodities during the medieval times between the states of the Western Sudan and the southern forest zone on one hand, and Western Sudan and the Arabs in North Africa, in what was popularly termed the 'trans-Saharan trade' on the other. The states of the Western Sudan depended on their control of the north-south trade in gold and slaves from the forests, salt from the Sahara, and European metal manufacturers from the Mediterranean (Grove 1989:90). The earliest states which arose in the open savannah zone of West Africa were Ghana, Mali and Songhai. Old Ghana controlled the trans-Saharan trade in Guinea gold. The Negroes of the south gave their gold in exchange for salt excavated by slave labour from ancient lake beds in the Sahara, and the gold paid for European goods brought south by desert Arabs and Berbers from Morocco

(Grove 1989). The successive empires of Mali, Songhai, Kanen-Bornu, etc. also had strong trade links with the states of the southern forest zone. There has, thus, been strong trade links between the savanna and forest states of West Africa in pre-colonial and colonial times. There was free movement of goods and people across the weakly-defined political boundaries of the sub-region. Boundaries did not constitute impediments to free movement. Though minimum tolls were paid for the use of markets in the sub-region, such tolls constituted the least hindrance to free movement.

With the partition of Africa by the European powers for economic advantages in the nineteenth century, clearly defined political boundaries were mapped out. Minor principalities were united into larger political entities. Money economy saturated the sub-region, and the zone which was almost like a single village, in view of the free movement and trade, became widely separated fragmented entities due to immigration restrictions and exchange controls. These forces became more stringent a few decades after independence, when the economies of the various countries began to face a downward trend. Ghana, which was the centre of attraction of skilled and unskilled labour in view of her booming economy instituted the Aliens' Compliance Order in 1971 which forced out of the country, aliens without the requisite resident permits. The order was intertwined with strict immigration controls. Before the formation of ECOWAS, trade within the sub-region (intra-West African trade) had not been encouraging, even though there was the critical need for it within the sub-region.

A survey of the resource potentials of the various countries which show disparities and spatial scarcities, called for the need for strong intra-regional trade links. Each ecological zone, namely forest, savanna and semi-arid zones which span West Africa, has the potential for the production of certain commodities. For instance, whereas forest products like timber thrive in the forest zone, cattle are suitable for production in the savanna and semi-arid zones; and whereas Nigeria is naturally endowed with crude oil, Guinea has an abundant stock of bauxite. Such national endowments and the suitable environment for the production of others at comparatively cheaper costs, should necessarily establish the basis for intra-regional trade to ensure the supply of commodities at relatively cheaper costs. The export trade of some selected West African countries from some years before the formation of ECOWAS as seen in Table 14.1 emphasises the differential resource potential of the various countries. The pattern of some West African countries clearly showed the need for trade within the sub-region. For instance, the imports of Ghana in 1975 clearly indicate the scarcities of certain commodities which could be derived from within the sub-region (Table 14.2).

Ghana could, for instance, derive her meat and live animals from the semi-arid nations of Mali, Niger and Burkina Faso, whilst importing crude oil and petroleum products from Nigeria. Indeed, Nigeria could be a source of import of crude oil for the ECOWAS countries. Contrary to expectation, in 1975, Nigeria supplied only 6.8 per cent of all Ghana's imports, which even fell short of her crude oil and petroleum product imports. Apart from Nigeria, no other country in West Africa was a major supplier of Ghana's imports. In 1975, no country in West Africa was Ghana's leading trading partner. Trade with the United Kingdom constituted 15.3 per cent of total imports and exports, the United States, 12.8 per cent; The Netherlands, 11.4 per cent and all other minor partners (including a few in West Africa) totalled 20.0 per cent. The low level of trade among West African states before ECOWAS was primarily due to the critical need for Western capital for the development of their economies. Other supporting factors were poor intra-regional transport network, immigration restrictions, association with the economies of former colonial masters, a low-level of industrial development, and political instability. Such forces kept the subregion apart, other than bringing the component states together as existed in the pre-colonial and early colonial times.

**Table 14.1   Export trade of selected countries in West Africa**

| Country | Year | Exported commodities | % of total exports |
|---------|------|----------------------|--------------------|
| Nigeria | 1974-1976 | Petroleum | 93.0 |
|  |  | Oil-palm products/cocoa/wood/tin/others | 7.0 |
| Liberia | 1974-1975 | Iron-ore | 70.0 |
|  |  | Rubber | 14.0 |
|  |  | Others | 16.0 |
| Mali | 1974-1976 | Cotton | 43.0 |
|  |  | Live animals | 15.0 |
|  |  | Groundnuts/Groundnut products | 14.0 |
|  |  | Others | 28.0 |
| Ghana | 1974 | Cocoa | 64.0 |
|  |  | Wood | 12.0 |
|  |  | Gold | 11.0 |
|  |  | Aluminium | 4.0 |
|  |  | Others | 9.0 |

*Source*:    Senior and Okunrotifa (1991:87)

There was, thus, the need for an economic union to fuse together the otherwise fragmented economies and spatial entities towards the close of the 1970s. It therefore came as a welcome relief when in May 1975, through the instrumentality of President Gnassingbe Eyadema of Togo, and General Yakubu Gowon, then Head of State of Nigeria, the Treaty of Lagos which established ECOWAS,was signed.

**Table 14.2  Ghana's leading imports in 1975**

| | Commodity | | Percentage |
|---|---|---|---|
| 1. | Food and Live Animals | | 11.5 |
| | Cereals | 3.3 | |
| | Fish | 3.3 | |
| | Sugar | 2.3 | |
| | Meat and Live Animals | 1.0 | |
| | Dairy Products | 0.9 | |
| | Other Foods | 0.7 | |
| 1. | Manufactured Products | | 65.2 |
| | Machinery | 15.6 | |
| | Transport Equipment | 9.5 | |
| | Chemicals | 14.0 | |
| | Textiles | 5.5 | |
| | Iron and Steel | 5.1 | |
| | Paper and Paper Products | 2.6 | |
| | Other Manufactured Goods | 12.9 | |
| 1. | Mineral Fuels | | 16.6 |
| | Crude Oil | 13.5 | |
| | Petroleum Products | 3.1 | |
| 4. | Others | | 6.7 |
| **Total** | | 100.00 | 100.00 |

*Source*:    Senior and Okunrotifa (1991:88)

## The Establishment of ECOWAS

ECOWAS was established with the signing of the Treaty of Lagos by 15 states. Cape Verde joined in 1977 to bring the membership to 16. The constituting states are Benin, Cape Verde, Gambia, Ghana, Guinea, Guinea-Bissau, La Cote d'Ivoire, Liberia, Mali, Mauritania, Niger, Nigeria, Senegal, Sierra Leone, Togo and Burkina Faso. The organisation aims at a customs union, free trade among the partners and a common external tariff (Sodersten 1988:239, 496). It seeks to promote cooperation and development in economic, social and cultural activities, particularly in the field of trade, customs, immigration, industry, agriculture and natural resources, transport and communications, and fiscal policies. ECOWAS operates through the Summit of Heads of State and Government which is the highest decision-making body of the organisation; a Council of Ministers; an Executive Secretariat based at Lagos; Specialised Commissions; and a Fund for Cooperation, Compensation and Development based at Lome, Togo. There are plans to establish a Tribunal to deal with interstate disputes and issues of infringements on agreed principles and protocols. The realisation of the high-sounding aims of the organisation, especially with regard to free movement and trade, would diminish the hindrances of the political boundaries, and ensure the full integration of the sub-region. Member states have 'agreed on several policies and protocols aimed at ventilating the noble aims and objectives of the organisation. There have been agreements signed in areas of customs union, common policies on trade, free movement and development planning.

*Customs Union*

The treaty spelt out the elimination of tariffs and other obstructions of trade among member states, and the establishment of a common external tariff over a transitional period of fifteen years (Owosekun 1985:91). At the Third Conference of Heads of State and Government in Lagos in April, 1978, a protocol was signed that no member state may increase its customs tariff on goods from another member. The 1978 protocol was the first step at the abolition of customs duties within the Community. During the first two years, import duties on intra-community trade were maintained, and then eliminated in phases over the following eight years. Quotas and other restrictions of equivalent effect were abolished within the first ten years. All differences between external customs tariffs were eventually abolished. The 1980 Conference of Heads of State decided to establish a free trade area for unprocessed agricultural products and handicrafts from May 1981. Tariffs on industrial products made by specified Community enterprises were abolished from that date.


*Common Policies*

The Treaty also contains a commitment to abolish all obstacles to the free movement of people, services and capital, the harmonisation of agricultural policies, the promotion of common projects in marketing, research and the agricultural-based industries. At the 1979 Conference of Heads of State, a protocol was signed relating to free circulation of the region's citizens, and to rights of residence and establishment. The right of entry without a visa and the right of stay for a period of 90 days came into force in July 1980, following a ratification by eight members. The 1979 Conference also adopted a programme for the improvement and extension of the internal and inter-state telecom-munications network, estimated to cost US$35 million scheduled for completion by 1985. The 1980 Conference adopted a programme for the development of regional transport. It included the harmonisation of road signs and laws and the construction of new road and rail links between member states. There is also the ECOWAS Brown Card, established by the Conference of Heads of State and Government on 29th May 1982, at the Cotonou Summit. In this, a holder of a Brown Card whose vehicle is involved in an accident in any member country of the sub-region is assured of a prompt and equitable compensation in the country in which the accident occurred. This scheme, it was hoped, would enhance the free movement of persons and goods within the sub-region (*Daily Graphic*, 25th July 1995). The protocols, programmes and policies, if implemented, should ensure successful trade links among member states, an industrial take-off, and indeed, the overall development of the sub-region without too much reliance on foreign aid. The sub-region would come closer together, and be like a large village.


**Post-ECOWAS Trade Patterns**

There has not been any significant change in the patterns of trade within the West African sub-region since the establishment of ECOWAS. Since tariff and non-tariff barriers have not been reduced, trade among its partners is at the level of the early 1970s, at about 3 per cent of the group's international trade (World Bank 1993:149). With a dearth of data on the imports and exports situation within the sub-region, Ghana is used as a case study. The share of Africa in total imports of Ghana fell to less than 18.2 per cent between 1983 and 1987. Africa's position as the number two trading partner of Ghana in 1983 (18 per cent) dropped to the last position in 1987 (3.5 per cent) (ISSER 1992: 65). This is a reflection of the whole of the West African situation.

In 1990, the major African countries which traded with Ghana, in terms of exports were Togo, Niger, La Cote d'Ivoire and Burkina Faso with export shares of 0.95 per cent, 0.67 per cent, 0.60 per cent and 0.53 per cent respectively (ISSER 1993:68). The extremely low export shares for these ECOWAS countries illustrate the low-level of trade among ECOWAS nations. On the contrary, the volume of trade with the industrialised nations had increased. It is clear from the foregoing that trade within the ECOWAS sub-region had not been encouraging. Since trade was identified as the key factor in the economic integration of the sub-region, its paralysis means a steady retrogression in efforts to increase the closeness of member states. Clearly, it is important to look at these obstacles towards sub-regional integration.

## Obstacles to Integration

It has been made clear in the foregoing analysis that trade could be a major tool in 'diminishing' the political boundaries, by ensuring free movements across the national borders. Free trade would mean free movement, breakdown of tariff barriers, the development of roads, rail and telecommunications networks within the sub-region, and a common customs union. Protocols have been signed though, with the view to realising such objectives, yet certain serious bottlenecks make their realisation a near-impossibility.

First, there is lack of political will on the part of some West African states to push for integration. Such leaders are not fully committed to protocols on free trade and movement within the sub-region, and the demolition of tariff walls. This has been acknowledged by some leaders. For instance, in a final communiqué at the Training Seminar on the integration of West Africa as a step towards globalisation of the world economy held at Marseilles in November 1986, Sey Adama of the Finance Ministry of Banjul commented seriously about the lack of political will of the West African leaders towards integration (Maxwell 1995:1953-1954). At the seminar, the consensus was that the three regional groupings in West Africa, namely ECOWAS, UEMOA (a union of Francophone States) and the Mano River Union comprising Liberia, Sierra Leone and Guinea, must integrate or converge if the sub-region were to remain relevant in a globalising economy. Although members of UEMOA and Mano River Union are also members of ECOWAS, their strong attachments to their minor unions could weaken full commitment to ECOWAS.

Tariff barriers rank high in the impediments to free trade and economic integration. Tariff barriers have not been removed and the concept of free trade zones not metamorphosed. To qualify for the organisation's tariff preferences, products must be made by firms which are at least 51 per cent domestically-owned. This rule promotes indigenous manufacturers but restricts exports from La Cote d'Ivoire and Senegal (since their industrial plants are considered foreign investments) and discourages foreign investment (World Bank 1993:149). With regard to labour mobility, there have been serious set-backs. Nigeria expelled more than 1 million Ghanaian guest workers in 1981 and 1983. There is also the consideration of the welfare of indigenous labour force rather than alien workers from sister countries.

Moreover, colonialism has divided West Africa into two blocs - the Anglophone and Francophone - each having strong attachment to their former colonial masters. Of stronger link is the Francophone bloc, which until recently, had their currency (CFA francs) linked with the French currency. The policies of these capitalist giants affect those of their satellite states. The strong links within each of these blocs jeopardise the unity of ECOWAS and the realisation of its objectives. At the first ECOWAS Fair held in Dakar in June 1995, goods sold by Francophone nations attracted only 0.05 per cent duty, whilst English-speaking West African countries paid between 30 and 40 per cent (Ashirifie 1995:7). Some observers saw this as crystal discrimination which could seriously affect the prospects for the economic integration of the sub-region.

The relief barriers and numerous rivers and streams also pose a hindrance to putting in place any trans-regional transport network. The Guinea Highlands, Futa Jallon Plateau, Togo-Atacora Highlands, Jos Plateau and Mandara Mountains, some of which exceed 1,000 metres, impose constraints on road and rail networks (Figure 14.1). Coupled with a low technology and a weak capital base, road and railway development hardly cut across several political boundaries. The river transport system is also poorly developed in view of the several waterfalls and rapids along the waterways; and the seasonality of some of the rivers and streams (Pritchard 1985:219).

Besides, for there to be prosperous trade, the movement of capital across the borders of ECOWAS calls for the establishment of capital markets which are least developed in the region. There is also the problem of inter-state disputes based on border irregularities. The Ghana-Togo border, for instance, has been an age-long dispute which disrupts unity in the sub-region and weakens efforts towards economic integration. The incessant closure of national borders for security reasons, especially during military take-overs, cannot be underestimated as a factor inhibiting the free movement of goods and labour, hence, acting as a

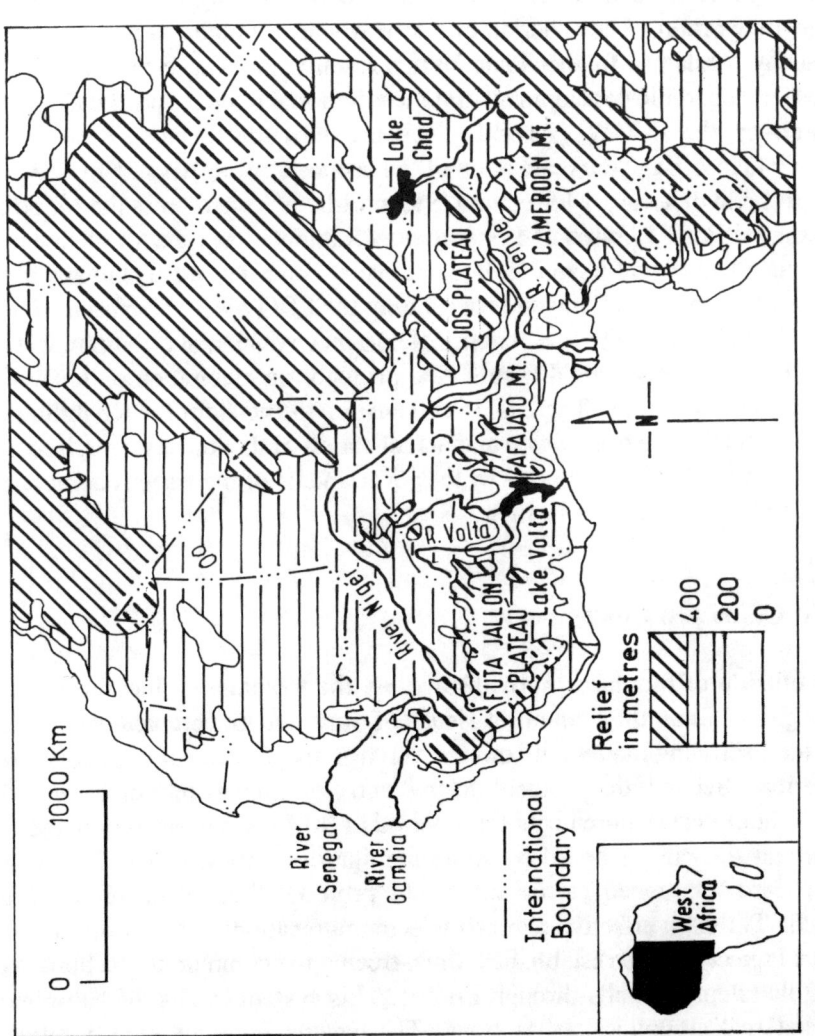

**Figure 14.1   Relief and drainage of West Africa**
*Source:*      Senior and Okumrotifa (1991:59)

stumbling block to integration. Borders are closed for several weeks during coup d'etats, and even longer when there are threats to internal security from external forces. Togo closed her borders for several weeks before and after her parliamentary and presidential elections, and on 29th March 1996, Nigeria closed her border with Benin for security reasons. This was shortly after Benin had decided to close its own frontier (*Daily Graphic,* 30th March 1996:2). The profusion of civil wars in the ECOWAS sub-region has had serious effects on free movement and the development of trade links within the Community. There have been civil strifes in Togo, Liberia, Sierra Leone, La Cote d'Ivoire and Ghana. These have, in no small way, distorted economic programmes and efforts towards integration. The Liberian civil war which still rages on has caused the Community substantial financial and human resources and have set the wheel of progress in economic development and intra-regional trade decades back.

Moreover, the ECOWAS Fund which provides the financial base for an economic take-off and the realisation of the economic objectives of ECOWAS, is said to be in disarray. More than US$3 million is locked up in the Meridian International Bank Limited of London, now liquidated as a result of financial mismanagement (Ben Ephson 1995:8). Several countries are also in arrears in their contribution to the Fund and for running the ECOWAS Secretariat. There are also linguistic barriers and diversities of currency which make communication and economic transactions difficult. The protocol on a common currency lies putrefied in the archives. There is, in conclusion, the need for the rehabilitation of the Community, the reactivation and actualisation of its objectives, indeed, the need for a renewal of commitments by the governments of the various component states, or else, its demise is in sight.

**Modest Gains and Challenges**

The profusion of hidrances notwithstanding, the Community has made some modest gains. First, the Summit of Heads of State and Government serves as a forum for discussing matters of common interest and as a ray of hope for future integration. Second, the protocol on free entry of citizens into other member states without visa requirements for a period of 90 days is in operation, though not without difficulties posed by some immigration officials. The ECOWAS Brown Card mentioned earlier on, could promote free movement, if fully executed. Third, an effective regional telecommunications network through the Intelcom Project has been established, thus, freeing the community the burden of routing its telephone calls through Europe. This system brings the sub-region closer and weakens political delineations. These gains, however are insignificant when weighted against the lofty aims of the organisation especially with regard to free trade and movement.

ECOWAS seems to be at the crossroad and needs the capacity to plan and realise its objectives. The Minimum Agenda For Action (MAFA), a review of the original Treaty, which was adopted at the Dakar Summit of July 1992, must be given serious thought. It calls for a renewal of commitments to the various Protocols which sought to enhance the achievements of the community. Leaders of the community need a strong political will if integration were to be a reality. National aspirations must converge with the attainment of the objectives of the Community. There must be aggressive efforts at a customs union, the demolition of the high tariff walls, and the creation of a free trade area. This calls for sacrifice on the part of countries in the sub-region which are endowed with minimum resources and are gradually developing their manufacturing and export capacities. To strengthen trade ties also calls for the joint processing of raw materials into manufactured products. This would place a limitation on the importation of manufactured products, thus, conserving the scarce foreign exchange. In entrenching the foundation for economic survival and free trade, the ECOWAS Fund must be well administered. Member states should endeavour to contribute to the Fund, based upon individual's financial strengths. The sub-grouping within the sub-region, namely UEMOA and Mano River Union, must place their Africanness above their colonial heritage, and labour tenaciously to realise the objectives of the Community. The Anglophone-Francophone colonial links must not supersede the links within the community. The peoples of the sub-region must see themselves as one people with a common destiny and heritage. Finally, intra-regional highways and rail network must be developed to establish the basis for greater spatial interaction and exchange of commodities.

## Conclusion

The West African sub-region has wallowed in underdevelopment for far too long. The diversity of resources, both human and material, calls for the harmonisation of economic policies, joint winning and processing of resources, and strong trade links among member countries. These superstructures of integration and the phenomenal 'vanishing of the national borders' constitute the dynamic means for the sub-region to emerge from poverty, ignorance and disease, political irredentism, and the over-reliance on foreign aid and loans. It must be emphasised that, there is no recipe for integration, although the cluster of geopolitical determinants and domestic interests provides a strong motivation for its promotion. The fundamental problems faced by ECOWAS are, therefore, not unnatural. Unity of purpose, sacrifice, political will and commitment, can create a holistic economic union which will result in the imaginary eradication of the political boundaries.

## References

Abler, R., Adams, J. and Gould, P. (eds.) (1977), *Spatial Organisation: The Geographer's View of the World*, Printice Hall International Editions.

*Daily Graphic*, 'The Accra ECOWAS Summit - Challenges Ahead', 25th June 1995, Graphic Corporation: Accra.

_____, 30th March 1996, Graphic Corporation: Accra.

Ephson, Ben (ed.) (1995), *Business in Ghana (Magazine)*, July/August, Wabis Ltd.: Accra.

Faustina, A., 'The First ECOWAS Fair - An Overview', *Daily Graphic*, 20th June 1995.

Grove, A.T. (1989), *The Changing Geography of Africa*, Oxford University Press: London.

Institute Of Statistical Social and Economic Research (ISSER) (1992), University of Ghana: Accra-Ghana.

_____ (1993), University of Ghana: Accra-Ghana.

Maxwell, N. (1995), 'Is West African Union Possible?' in Whiteman, Kaye (ed.), *West Africa*, pp.1953-1954.

Owosekun, A. (1985), 'Some Thorny Issues In The Economic Community of West African States', in Ndongkun, W.A. (ed.), *Economic Cooperation and Integration in Africa*, CODESRIA: Accra-Ghana, pp. 90-91.

Pritchard, J.M. (1985), *A Study Geography for Advanced Students*, Longman Group Limited: Essex.

Sodersten, Bo (1988), *International Economics*, Macmillan: London.

Senior, M. and Okunrotifa, P.O. (1991), *A Regional Geography of Africa*, Longman Group Limited: Essex.

The World Bank (1993), *Sub-Saharan Africa - From Crisis to Sustainable Growth*, New York.

Todaro, P.M. (1992), *Economics for a Developing World - An Introduction to Principles, Problems and Policies for Development*, Longman: London and New York.

# PART V

# CONCLUSION

# 15 Globalisation and the Paradox of Enduring National Boundaries

*Gerald H. BLAKE*

## Introduction

The death of the nation state has been predicted by a number of academic writers, and on the face of it, their arguments are quite convincing (Anderson, Brook and Cochrane 1995; Demko and Wood 1994). The aim of this chapter, however, is to sound a note of caution against the uncritical acceptance of some of the more exaggerated predictions about the world in the 21st Century where borders vanish and the first global civilisation is created. It is common ground that the present system of nation states will change in form and function largely in response to the powerful impulses collectively known as globalisation. On the other hand, current trends hardly seem to justify the view that the state is on the way out, to be replaced by alternative regional and global political structures. Of course, it might be a very good thing if the end of the state was in sight because of the widespread misery created by the promotion of state nationalism, but that is a rather different issue.

## The Diminishing Power of the State

The debate about the future of the state intensified during the 1980s as the trend towards globalisation accelerated, not least because capitalism extended its influence dramatically throughout the world with the demise of the Marxist alternative. In many ways, the power of the state had been declining for several decades with advances in technology and the proliferation of international agencies and organisations. The past decade has seen more spectacular technological and political developments which have markedly diminished state power and authority. These can be summarised briefly as follows:

- *The globalisation of economic activities:* The rapidity with which capital, technology, and ideas can transfer between states has transformed international economic relationships. Although state capitalism still has a role to play, capital investment, job creation, and economic development are largely in the hands of international banks and multinational corporations. Governments have only limited ability to attract and retain investments, much of which are concentrated where labour is cheap. Kennedy (1996) has drawn attention to the serious implications of this process for western economies over the next generation as many millions of workers in Asia and South America move to market production, forcing wages down in the west in certain sectors by 50 per cent or more.
- *The communications revolution:* All kinds of advances in communications have clearly assisted in the globalisation of capital mentioned above. Together, the new technologies have brought about the time-space compression of the globe, although it has to be remembered that many poorer parts of the world do not yet enjoy the telecommunication services regarded as commonplace in advanced capitalist societies. The whole elaborate system is highly regulated at the international level by regional organisations governed by the International Telecommunication Union (ITU). The implications for state sovereignty are obvious, since no government can effectively control the international flow of information by broadcast, electronic mail, fax, or on the Internet which connects millions of computer users worldwide. Some fear that the ultimate result of the exchange of information and ideas by these means, together with the all- pervading influence of television and cinema will mean the emergence of a mediocre 'global culture'. It is a depressing prospect, in the face of which national cultures may feel obliged to reassert themselves.
- *International agencies:* A vast array of international agencies and organisations now assist the state in the pursuit of worthwhile objectives, and which require international cooperation to make them work. These range from large regional organisations such as the European Union and ASEAN to numerous international agreements in connection with pollution or crime or outer space, or human rights or control of terrorism. In other words, states can no longer provide all the apparatus necessary to govern without international help. They are not (if they ever were) closed territorially bounded systems. As these international agencies proliferate, state

governments clearly lose a measure of sovereignty. This is seen most acutely in respect of human rights. There is an international human rights regime expressed in the International Bill of Human Rights incorporating not only the U.N. Convention of 1948 but a number of subsequent conventions. Governments are, therefore, subject to external scrutiny in respect of human rights, and a number of regimes resent the intrusion. Ironically, some groups in certain states are more likely to be protected by the international agencies than by their own governments.

- *Security:* National security is increasingly interconnected with the dynamics of regional and global security regimes. Few states can sustain their own arms industry, and no state has a monopoly of strategic materials. States can no longer defend themselves exclusively from their own territorial base. Moreover, state security considerations are commonly being extended to include other concerns such as terrorism and environmental pollution.
- *Transboundary environmental management:* The oldest and most obvious example of transboundary management concerns divided river basins. International agreements for collaboration over river basin management go back nearly a century, but they have multiplied in recent years as demand for water and river exploitation for hydro-electric power (HEP), fisheries etc. has escalated. Similarly there is now a recognition that states must collaborate to protect the environment and there are an increasing number of agreements for that purpose (Blake *et al.* 1995). There is growing interest in the potential for 'parks for peace' jointly managed along international boundaries (Thorsell 1990; Westing 1993). Thus, states no longer see themselves as being able to deliver effective environmental management, or to exploit borderland resources peacefully without acting in collaboration with their neighbours. There is a long way to go, however, before effective agreements are in place to bring about real cooperation.

Inexorably, it seems, the nation state is losing many of its former functions and a growing degree of sovereignty is being lost to international and supranational organisations and agencies. The end of this process, according to some commentators, is that states will no longer have any useful functions to perform.

## The Resilience of the Nation State

These powerful forces are, undoubtedly, bringing about changes in the nature of the nation state, but it is difficult to conclude that they will bring about the death of the state, at least not for a very long time.  There is no evidence of this even though some of these factors have been operating for some time.  On the contrary, the evidence suggests that the nation state is likely to remain the basic building-block for political associations in the future.  The durability of the nation state is proven by two major sets of evidence - the emergence of new states, and the behaviour of existing states.

## *The Emergence of New States*

Paradoxically, the same communications revolution which is said to be undermining the state system is also one reason why a considerable number of new states are likely to emerge in the next half century or so.  Most of these will be rather small states depending on regional groupings for their military security, and on international flows of capital, labour, and technology to sustain their economies.  Size of territory and population is no longer deemed to be crucial for the survival of the state.  There could be anything from 25 to 100 new states by the middle of the 21st Century.  Some states might also disappear by amalgamation, but in general this would seem to be against the trend.

How will the new states be created?  Four broad categories can be suggested. First, there are still some 50 dependent territories in the world (Glassner 1996:273).  Many are small territories, mostly island states, but a number can be expected to achieve independence following the example of several micro-states which successfully achieved sovereignty in the 1980s.  Secondly, more independent states will be created from the breakup of large states.  There could be more desertions from the Russian Federation, notably perhaps some territories with a Muslim majority, although the war with Chechenia is proof that breakaway states will be stoutly resisted.  Several other states are sometimes cited as possible candidates for disintegration including the United Kingdom, Canada, Belgium and India.  Thirdly, it seems likely that in various parts of the world there will be a resurgence of claims for autonomy by peoples who regard themselves as suppressed.  Surprisingly, perhaps, such movements are evident in western Europe as graphically shown by Griggs and Hocknell (1996a; 1996b). Worldwide, there may be as many as 5,000 indigenous peoples with their own language and territory although only a fraction of these will be able to make a credible bid for independence.  The emergence of  several such 'fourth world' people demanding autonomy in recent years is, in part, a reaction to the globalisation process which threatens regional and national cultures.  Fourthly, Cohen (1990) foresees the emergence of 40 or more 'gateway states' during the next century.  Such states he argues, will achieve independence at locations which are geopolitically and economically favourable. They will survive on specialised manufacturing, trade, tourism, and financial services. Their sovereignty may be 'qualified' and they will not represent a military threat to their neighbours. Hong Kong, Singapore, and Gibraltar are perhaps current models of what Cohen (1990) had in mind. Among his examples are Western Australia, British Columbia, California, Catalonia, and Gaza.

The idea that there will be a number of new micro-states in the 21st Century fits well with predictions that the nation state will survive, but generally within strong regional economic and security arrangements. The functions of governments will thus be divided between the state and international organisations.

## *The Behaviour of Existing States*

There is very little evidence today from the behaviour of governments or people that they foresee the end of the nation state. In certain respects, at least the nation state idea is becoming more entrenched, not less, and international boundaries still clearly delimit the transition from one jurisdiction to another. The boundary is clearly thriving as the following paragraphs suggest.

*Boundary delimitation:* States are as eager as ever to define and protect their territories, including their offshore areas. Land boundary agreements continue to be made, while existing land boundaries are being more accurately mapped and demarcated with the help of Global Positioning Systems (GPS) (Adler 1995) Offshore, approximately one third of the world's potential maritime boundaries have been formally agreed. The remaining 270 or so maritime boundaries will, no doubt, be negotiated with the same painstaking care that went into the existing agreements. Far from becoming a borderless world, the oceans are being progressively partitioned between coastal states. Where serious disagreements over the location of offshore boundaries persist, states sometimes adopt joint development zones, but there is nothing vague about these. They are precisely delimited as with agreed boundaries.

*Territoriality:* The territorial instinct is still very strong among the world's states. Wars are fought and people die in defence of state territory even if the land in question is desert sand or mountain glacier. Nationalism is also alive and few matters can ignite nationalistic fervour more readily than threats to territory. The aftermath of the breakup of Yugoslavia has been a frightening example of violent conflict over the extent of ethnic territories. Nor is the territorial instinct confined to a few xenophobic governments and extremist groups; states are still willing to pay for very costly litigation to prove title to small tracts of territory or tiny islands. Traditional attitudes towards national territory are not easily eradicated. In some states the territorial instinct is promoted by overt propaganda, but in many more the state image becomes ingrained through the powerful effect of school texts, national atlases, and even the maps used daily by national weather forecasters.

*Boundaries as barriers:* While it is true that boundaries in general are becoming more open to the flow of people, goods, and ideas, there are a considerable number of land boundaries which remain largely closed. There are also calls from right wing politicians all over the world for more effective barriers both to protect industries and to control the flow of international labour, especially illegal migrants. Even in the European Union, which in so many ways exemplifies the benefits of open borders, concerns have been expressed that there are now insufficient checks on the movement of illegal drugs, criminals and so on. Such movements have to be checked along the outer margins of trade blocs and regional organisations. The journey towards more open borders is likely to be marked by barriers going up as well as coming down.

One reason why states continue to behave as though not very much has changed since the emergence of the nation state in the nineteenth century, may be that politicians and statesmen have not given the matter very profound thought. For those whose states belong to one of the world's great trading blocs such as ASEAN, NAFTA, or the European Union there is perhaps a belief that it is possible to enjoy the best of both worlds. Indeed, this may be a good working description of the 21st Century. While the former functions of the nation state have clearly diminished, and in several areas of national life authority is being exercised from outside, the territorial functions of the state remain sufficient to give credibility to the old idea of the state. In every state there are people only too happy to support the traditional view of the nation state as offering continuity and security, and who fear the onset of internationalism.

## International Boundaries of the 21st Century

It seems probable, therefore, on present evidence that the state will survive as the basic building block for political arrangements far into the next century. It would of course be foolish to suggest that the state will endure for ever, since it is a relatively recent phenomenon, created primarily from the experience of Europe. The nature, shape, and functions of the state will, however, evolve in future more radically than in the past. In most parts of the world state economies will be dominated by their membership of a major trading bloc, and a wide range of tasks and duties formerly undertaken by state governments, will have been taken over by international organisations. At the same time, states will retain a variety of functions of importance to the everyday lives of their citizens. What then might be some of the characteristics of the boundaries of such states?

- *There will be more of them.* If more states exist, as seems probable, there will inevitably be more international land boundaries than the 308 or so existing in 1996. The number could increase by two or three for every new state which might mean 100-150 more boundaries in the next century. At sea it can be assumed that many more maritime boundaries will be delimited. In 1996, approximately 150 out of a potential 420 offshore boundaries had been agreed upon. As states proliferate, more potential maritime boundaries will be added to this number.
- *Their functions will change.* Boundaries will become more permeable in many respects, particularly within the major trading blocs. In some parts of the world, however, borders will continue to act as real barriers. Concerns over illegal migrants will grow as the poor seek work in more favoured countries with ever greater persistence. The borders most at risk in this respect are those which divide rich and poor economies most sharply as between Mozambique and South Africa, Mexico and the United States. In addition, there will always be national governments which wish to exclude certain types of visitors, such as some Islamic countries which do not wish to receive mass tourism.
- *They will retain important functions.* Even in a world where the globalisation of economic activities is far advanced, state boundaries will continue to mark the limits of important state functions. Different legal systems, property rights, tax laws, local government jurisdictions, overflight rights, concession areas for mineral exploration, internal security, etc. will be territorially defined by state boundaries. Certain activities might overlap; for example, police might patrol into the territory of a neighbour (as occurs in parts of the European Union already) but it is difficult to imagine all state functions being harmonised to the extent that boundaries wither away. Boundaries of states which coincide with regional groupings will have particular responsibility for filtering out unwanted movements of people and goods, thus reinforcing their barrier function.
- *Alignments will alter.* It is not always appreciated how much international boundaries have changed their locations through time. The historic map of Europe is specially remarkable in this respect. Occasionally, spectacular

upheavals occur as a result of war, or the collapse of a power such as the Soviet Union. More often the process of boundary change is slow and peaceful, and an agreement is reached to rectify an anomaly, perhaps even to exchange territory as Jordan and Saudi Arabia did in 1973. The world political map has always changed, and will continue to change through a wide variety of processes (Goerts and Diehl 1992). While this is true, it is also worth noting that there are powerful forces at work to discourage change. The United Nations Charter, for example, upholds the territorial integrity of states, while African and South American countries have agreed in principle to accept their inherited colonial boundaries for better or worse.

- *Alternatives to state territory will emerge.* Alternatives to absolute state sovereignty have been surprisingly successful; for example, neutral zones, international zones, demilitarised zones, protected zones and buffer zones. Most have been relatively short-lived, but in future more durable agreements may be reached particularly in areas of former conflict and territorial dispute. The increasing role of peacekeeping forces will encourage such non-state territorial areas. There are already 15 formal agreements between states to establish common zones offshore associated with joint development of hydrocarbons or living resources. Many more such offshore zones are likely to be agreed in future. Once it is recognised that the entire land surface of the globe does not have to be divided between independent sovereign states, what might emerge is limited only by the imagination. The Antarctic Treaty and the little-known Svalbard Treaty of 1925 provide potential trend-setters in this context.

## Conclusion

It seems clear that the world political mosaic of the next century will be far more complex than the world today. The precise nature of political relationships is difficult to foresee because the transition from a world dominated by nation states to one in which authority is shared between the state and international/regional agencies is only now gaining momentum. There will be a greater number of states although they may not conform precisely to the current state model. Many will probably have little political power but considerable economic power. The oceans will be progressively partitioned between coastal states so that eventually one third of the surface area of the oceans will fall within some kind of state control. The exclusive economic zone to a distance of 200 nautical miles will be the most important, spatially. These offshore areas will be jealously protected and carefully managed by governments, while on land, territorial attitudes will die hard. The concept of absolute state sovereignty up to the international boundary will be vigorously defended particularly in the poorer parts of the world where economic cooperation is at a low level.

The world political map in the 21st Century will superficially appear much as it is today, with boundaries and state territories the dominant features. Regional groupings will, however, be extremely important although it would be a mistake to assume that the European Union model or the ASEAN success story are prototypes for similar unions all over the world. There will no doubt always be states which do not fit into any international groupings, and some states which are not welcome to join such groupings. Today, for example, Libya, Iran and Iraq are regarded as outcasts from the international community in some sense, and it is likely other political entities will be similarly boycotted in the next century. It must not be assumed that the new pattern of inter-state relations is exclusively about trade or defence. Religion may prove to be the basis for important state cooperation, the most likely candidate being the Islamic world. An Islamic confederation would be immensely powerful, controlling a high proportion of the world's oil reserves, and being guardians of several of the world's most crucial international waterways.

Relations between states during the next century are likely to be conducted at a number of levels with functions divided between national governments and international agencies and organisations. The process has already begun, especially in Europe, Southeast Asia and North America. The experience of these regions illustrates the problem, as much as the potential for international cooperation. The United Kingdom is a prime example, torn between a desire to be part of a greater Europe and a desire not to forfeit too much authority to the European parliament in Brussels. At the same time, the constituent parts of the United Kingdom are looking for a greater degree of local autonomy over their own affairs. The political implications of such radical change are difficult to understand and describe. It is necessary to see the emerging political arena as one in which 'nation states are conceived as the sites of flows and connections rather than primarily as containers of political power and action' (McGrew 1995). The contemporary world has been aptly described by Camilleri (1990) as 'bifurcated', in which the nation state survives, but against a background of overlapping loyalties and authorities. It remains to be seen whether this model persists into the next century, or whether there is a marked shift towards reinvesting the state with some of its lost power (which is unlikely) or towards international government. In weighing up these possibilities, not enough thought is given to a number of African states such as Liberia and Somalia whose economy and government have effectively collapsed. Such states may be held together by their borders until a new authority emerges, or they are absorbed by their neighbours.

They are certainly in no condition to join the global network of interacting states which some foresee.

Whatever happens in future, international boundaries will lose some of their former significance, but they seem destined to remain in place. Unfortunately, they are likely to retain their capacity to cause conflict and impede peaceful interaction between peoples.

## References

Adler, R. (1995), 'Positioning and Mapping International Land Boundaries', *Boundary and Territory Briefing*, Vol. 2, No. 1.

Anderson, J., Brook, C. and Cochrane, A. (eds.) (1995), *A Global World?* Oxford University Press: London.

Blake, G.H., Hildesley, W.J., Pratt, M.A., Ridley, R.J. and Schofield, C.H. (eds.) (1995), *The Peaceful Management of Transboundary Resources*, Graham and Trotman: London.

Camilleri, J.A. (1990), 'Rethinking Sovereignty in a Shrinking, Fragmented World', in Walker, R.B.J. and Mendlovitz, S.H. (eds.), *Contending Sovereignties: Redefining Political Community*, Lynne Rienner Publishers: Boulder and London.

Cohen, S.B. (1990), 'The World Geopolitical System in Retrospect and Prospect', *Journal of Geography*, Vol. 59, No. 1, pp. 2-12.

Demko, G.J. and Wood, W.B. (eds.) (1994), *Reordering the World: Geopolitical Perspectives on the 21st Century*, Westview Press: Boulder.

Glassner, M.I. (1996), *Political Geography*, John Wiley: New York.

Goertz, G. and Diehl, P.F. (1992) *Territorial Changes and International Conflict*. Routledge: London.

Griggs, R. and Hocknell, P. (1996a), 'Fourth World Faultlines and the Remaking of 'Inter-National' Boundaries', *Boundary and Security Bulletin*, Vol. 3, No. 3, pp. 49-58.

_____(1996b), 'The Geography and Geopolitics of Europe's Fourth World', *Boundary and Security Bulletin*, Vol. 3, No. 4, pp. 59-67.

Kennedy, Paul (1996), 'Globalisation and its Discontent', BBC Radio 4 Analysis Lecture, 28th May.

McGrew, A. (1995), 'World Order and Political Space' in Anderson, J. *et al.*, *A Global World?*, OUP: London.

Thorsell, J. (ed.) (1990), *Parks on the Borderline : Experience in Transfrontier Conservation*, World Conservation Union (IUCN): Gland.

Westing, A.H. (ed.) (1993), *Transfrontier Reserves for Peace and Nature: A Contribution to Human Security*, UNEP: Nairobi.